Copyright © 2022 Brad Cousino

ISBN: 979-8-8691-9221-9

Unwanted, Unworthy, UNSHACKLED

Rejected, Reviled, and traumatically abused...

From cleaning putrid sewers, to playing in the NFL...

A Spiritual battle rages to destroy a man's heart, life, & family!

A MEMOIR

Author
Brad Cousino

Co-Author
Mitch Neu

Contents

Acknowledgments

<u>Unwanted, Unworthy, UNSHACKLED</u> has benefited from contributions and the wisdom of many others -- some directly and others indirectly. I'm grateful for all those who have helped in making this memoir a reality.

- My board of advisors: **Joe Callahan, Keith Lawrence,** and **Danise DiStasi**; thank you for your wisdom, encouragement, and recommendations. I needed each of your valuable feedback, to get me started on this journey.

- **Mitch Neu:** Thank you for your writing expertise and background research. Your writing skills enhanced <u>Unwanted, Unworthy, UNSHACKLED</u>. May this book catapult you into a career using your awesome talent to write more books and future screenplays.

- **Nita Ritze:** Thank you for your vital advice, research, input, and introducing me to Mitch (& Brian); even as you faced difficult times in your own family.

- **Wendel Deyo:** Thank you for being a significant part of my life and that of my family since 1975. I learned how to be a better dad & husband by watching you raise your family. You are a testimony to loving Cindy the way God intended... in sickness & health, in good times and not so good. You inspire me to be a better man because of you & your family.

- **Gary Lessis**: Thank you for your invaluable help in digitizing photos that were scanned into high resolution 'tifs' so it could be used in my memoir.

- To my many **Manuscript Readers** who provided invaluable feedback. Thank you for taking your valuable time to read my evolving UNSHACKLED manuscript. Each of you provided great insight and made our memoir far better. It is with great appreciation I extend my sincere thanks to: *Ellie Mallory, Wendel Deyo, Steve Cesler, Coach Ron Corradini, Karen Corradini, Coach Dick Crum, Colin Flynn, Peter Bronson, Kathy Stallard, Shelly Meuer, Jay Fry, John McVay, Joe Callahan, Doug Howe, Paul Apyan, Larry Larson, Danise DiStasi, Steve Kramer, Keith Lawrence, John Bishop, Fritz Geer, Randy Gunlock, Doug Krause, Lindsay Merten, Rita Caruso, Gary Baz, Tom Ember, Jerome Addis, Bernie Hoyt, Dylan Lowry, Sandy Leary, Sherman Smith, Mel Edwards, Ronnie Grandison, Tom Pappas, Michael Perry, Debby Schaefer, RJ Lowry, Dan Tarkington, Christel Skorup, Shaedyn Bogle, Cole Cousino, Brooke Cousino, Case Cousino, Cortt Cousino, and Tami Cousino.*

Introduction

"Often, it's the deepest pain which empowers you to grow into your highest self. -- **Karen Salmansohn**

Do you like books or movies that depict tremendous pain, suffering, and people not being treated fairly who against all odds finds a way to overcome and turn tragedy into ultimate life success? Movies and books like - *Rudy, Facing the Giants, Braveheart, The Shack, Gladiator, The Matrix, The Lord of the Rings, Seabiscuit, Field of Dreams, Shawshank Redemption, The Legend of Bagger Vance, Mr. Holland's Opus, The Chronicles of Narnia, The Passion of the Christ, & American Underdog.* If so, you will resonate with my captivating, true life-story.

Unshackled from What?

Great question! I was on a personal quest, searching for answers of my trauma inflicted life, when I stumbled on the word 'Unshackled' (also the book's main title) which means to be *liberated, released, rescued & set free.* For me, it was to be set free from the depraved lies that bound me for decades. In the depths of despair, a key word or two can impart vital clarity that changes everything.

Armed with the knowledge of a few transformational words, I embarked on my life's most critical mission, to find a way to make it become my new reality. My goal was to discover the underlying reasons why I believed the hundreds of lies and deceptions so I could become unshackled from them. Once I was unshackled, then I could replace those lies with ultimate truth that the ancient Greek word *SOZO* promises; *to be transformed, redeemed, restored, salvaged, saved, and rescued.*

Why did I write my story?

I've been blessed to speak to thousands of people in hundreds of audiences since 1975. Invariably, after telling my "story", one of the most asked questions was... *"Do you have a book about your story. My _____ (fill in the blank) son, daughter, husband, father, mother, son-in-law, neighbor, co-worker, relative, etc., needs to hear / read your story."*

After a few years of that same request, I came up with a "work-around" where I created a handout that encapsulated my story, along with pictures when I played with the Bengals and/or Steelers. I let the audience know if they wanted an '8½ x11' two-sided handout they could come up after my talk ended and pick one up for FREE and I'd autograph it for them if requested. It turned out those handouts were in high demand. I was shocked at how many people would stand in line for up to 30 minutes just to have my autograph on those free card-stock handouts... that was surreal to me! (See Appendix #1D of the sample two-page autographed handout I freely gave away for over 25+ years)

****

While I was strongly encouraged by my audiences to write a book, I never felt a strong desire, nor did I feel I had the skill set, to seriously consider it. However, I had this recurring thought that wouldn't quit. *"Brad, do you think you went through all the physical & emotional abuse and all that has happened to you for yourself. There are hundreds of thousands more people that need to hear or read about your story that will never hear you speak."* I subtly kept ignoring it. But over the last few years, I became increasingly convinced (convicted is a better word) that I needed to write my early life story as a memoir.

There are many people who will benefit from my true story. I promise to be authentic, vulnerable, and transparent; it's the only way I know to be. All those who attended grade school, high school, or college with me and / or those that know me as a high school, college, or pro teammate; or that I've known in the workplace, neighborhood, church, etc., and all my close & distant relatives and childhood friends that think they know me well -- ALL will be SHOCKED and ASTOUNDED about what I share in this book!

I've been told by those who know far better than me, that **Unwanted, Unworthy, UNSHACKLED** has ALL the necessary ingredients to be made into an inspirational movie. It may or may not come to fruition. Regardless, I will share my story via speaking engagements, podcasts, and through people reading this book and/or listening to my soon to be published audiobook of my memoir.

Family Friendly Disclaimer

I made a strategic choice to **<u>NOT</u>** use the actual cursing, swearing, and blasphemous language that I was raised under daily. Based on wise counsel from my advisory team and those who read the earlier manuscripts, it was recommended that I needed to "tone" down the language and the physical abuse inflicted on me because it was just too brutal and severe.

My goal is to be transparent without being crude or insensitive. It is my hope and intent that you will feel compelled to want your kids, grandkids, spouses, friends, relatives, co-workers, etc., to read or listen to **Unwanted, Unworthy, UNSHACKLED**. As such, I've purposely made my memoir family friendly, for your friends and family, **_and_** MINE!

My desire is for you, your family & friends to be blessed by my life story!

Brad Cousino, April 5, 2023

Chapter 1
Life Sentence

*"How do you let go of shame - when shame won't
let go of you?"*   *-- Unknown*

"I'm pregnant."

Gene's parents looked at the two kids in stunned silence. The words sank in like a cancer diagnosis. "No!" Gene's mother cried out, as she sank to her chair and folded her face into her hands. Gene hung his head low. He knew what was coming, so he might as well get it out of the way.

"It's mine."

His horrified parents immediately tore him apart. "Are you sure it's yours?" his mother asked.

"What will our friends and neighbors say... what about our church community?" his father cut in. *"Our grandchild will be a ba***rd. Lord help us; you have gotten yourself in a big mess!"* he barked. Gene instantly recoiled. Gene's mother crossed her arms, deep in thought. She seemed to concur with her husband's statement. She looked at Annette in disgust. "How could you, Gene? You're only sixteen!" she cried. "How old are you, child!?" she asked of Annette.

"Fifteen, ma'am," Annette said.

She turned back to Gene. "Do you realize what you have done? Now you must get married! Oh my God..." She sat down and folded her face into her hands again as if she had just learned of a loved one's death.

Chester, Gene's father, glared at Gene. It seemed as if he was staring into his soul.

"You two will have to get married, and you need to do it as soon as possible. But" here, he held up his index finger. "You are not getting any help from me or your mother. You are going to have to deal with the consequences yourselves."

All Annette could do was nod and feel ashamed.

Annette's parents responded similarly once they heard the news. Though reluctant, they were at least a little more forgiving. They just resigned themselves to the situation at hand. Annette's mother cried, barely able to speak through the tears.

"We'll help you plan the wedding, but it'll have to be soon." Annette's father confirmed. "You can't be an unmarried pregnant couple. I won't have you wearing a white dress with a big pregnant belly. You can't bring that kind of shame and embarrassment upon yourself, upon all of us."

"You'll live with us until you can afford to rent an apartment or house of your own." He placed his hand on Gene's shoulder. "You, Gene, are going to have to get a full-time job to support Annette and the baby. I might be able to help you with that. I bowl on Friday nights with one of the foremen at Libby Owens Ford (LOF) Glass Factory. I'll call and see if they have any openings. It's hot, tough work. The pay starts out low but raises after 90 days on the job because they have a strong labor union."

Gene and Annette had known each other for a relatively short period of time – about six months - and this lapse in judgment had sealed their fates. Gene lived in Erie, MI, about five miles over the Ohio/Michigan State line. Meanwhile, Annette lived in Point Place, OH, less than half a mile from Ohio/Michigan state line boundaries.

Being fifteen and sixteen years old in 1952, they were now forced to give up their lives to raise an unwanted child, while being children themselves. Like it or not, in 1952, there were no viable or acceptable alternatives; their only course of action was a hasty (shotgun) wedding. While Gene's parents pushed them to get married, they really wanted nothing to do with the wedding, believing it to be a huge mistake in their young lives. They were not involved in any of the planning, nor did they (or the entire side of their family) even attend the wedding.

Although Gene's parents were his legal guardians until he was eighteen, there was not a dime of financial support given. Annette's parents accepted it, although very reluctantly, as something that had to be dealt with. It was more about saving face and minimizing the shame brought about by the lustful impulses of two naive teenagers.

Annette and Gene ultimately had to drop out of high school, sacrificing everything they ever wanted for themselves. Annette would often see her friends in the small border town of Point Place at the drug store, grocery store, post office, etc., living their lives like normal teenage girls, when she was out and about, with her baby in tow. She was now 16. The unwanted child was her "*Scarlet Letter*" that branded her to the friends and family of the only world she knew. She was ashamed to be seen with her baby as she knew that her friends and classmates continued to judge her for her "mistake".

Every day, she would watch the life she longed for pass her by as she coped with the shame and embarrassment that her family and society had placed upon her for the life she now had. Annette, or Toni, as she was known, often thought to herself: I wish I could have those days with my friends back. Living in constant shame was crushing her. Her innocence as a young teenager had been shattered. *She was an immature child herself, who grew up in a highly dysfunctional home – now forced to raise a child she never wanted... and could never love.*

Meanwhile, Gene got that job at the LOF glass factory and went to work full time in the afternoon & midnight shifts. He chose to escape his life of misery by drowning his sorrows at the many bars situated near the glass factory after getting off from his stifling hot, dead-end job. The long-term ramifications of that one simple "mistake" were bigger than either of them could have imagined.

Who were these two teenage kids?

My parents. I was their "mistake".

And they were the source of my living hell!

Chapter 2
Spilled Milk

"One believes things because one has been conditioned to believe them." -Aldous Huxley

Rrrrrrrring! Rrrrrrrring!

I reached for the alarm - 7:00 am. Time to get up for school. School started at 8:00 am for fifth graders, and since I lived just one block away, I didn't have to get up early for the bus. I was so tired, and my back, butt, arms, and legs hurt. I had a rough night and did not get much sleep. I was getting ready for school and having a typical school morning, where *mom was yelling, cursing, screaming, hitting, pinching, slapping, and bullying me for any number of reasons.* It was just another day growing up in the Cousino household.

On this morning, mom was enraged at dad for not coming home for more than three days and nights due to his continued drinking. That always led to a huge physical fight when dad finally came home – after the bars closed at 2:30 am! As usual, dad wanted to crash, but mom was itching for another fight. Often, they were yelling and cursing so loud that the neighbors on both sides of our house would be looking out their windows.

My brothers and I witnessed our parents physically and verbally fighting at least three to four times per month. Mom would get in dad's face, cussing and cursing him out, sometimes even hitting him with her fists. It was scary, because there were times when my brothers and I would be watching as they screamed curses at each other while wrestling on the basement concrete. Dad wasn't a "mean" drunk. He didn't come home looking for a fight; he just wanted to crash. It was mom who was always the aggressor.

As the oldest, I tried to stop their physical fighting, but then mom would start crying and demand that dad should whip me because of something she claimed I did three days earlier -- and mom had already whipped me for the incident! Based on history, dad knew that if he whipped me, that would appease mom, and then he would be able to finally crash and get some sleep. I believe, deep down, dad knew I wasn't deserving of a beating; so, what did he do? With tears in his eyes, he whipped me hard until mom was satisfied, and then he crashed. It wasn't the type of whipping you'd expect a parent to give his kid. That was never satisfactory for mom.

***

About five hours later, I was rushing to get to school on time and needed to finish my bowl of Cheerios, when I spilled some milk and cereal onto the kitchen table.

Mom went BERSERK! She grabbed me by my neck and began choking me. At the same time, she was slamming my head against the wall. Even though I was in pain and couldn't breathe, I would not cry. I could see the pain in mom's eyes. With tears running down her cheeks, teeth clenched, she yelled out a guttural cry filled with agony, rage, and hatred as spit spewed from her mouth with every word directly into my face.

*"It's your fault…you son of a b**ch… it's your g*d d**n fault…you are to blame for all of this-- if it wasn't for YOU – you ba***rd…your dad would come home after work, and I wouldn't be in this god-awful mess of a life".*

I wish I could say that the above was an anomaly – but it wasn't. In my younger years, I was physically and emotionally abused repeatedly -- some days two or more times a day-- and there were hundreds of similar traumatic encounters – most often involving my mom physically, verbally, and/or emotionally abusing me (never sexually). Being only eleven (11) years old, I did not understand why she had such rage and anger toward me. I was brought up believing I was "born bad" and somehow, I "deserved this".

I'm sure when I was a newborn, mom and dad must have held me, but from my earliest memories, I can never, ever remember being held, cuddled, loved, or wanted by either of my parents. Based on my mom's own words, I assumed my parents messed-up lives was my fault.

*****

The Teachers' Lounge

I cried most of way as I ran the half mile to school. I couldn't stop thinking of what my mom screamed at me. My fifth-grade teacher, Mr. Meyers (we called him Mr. M), recognized that something was bothering me. Mr. M was one of those teachers that all the boys wanted to hang with. He would take certain members of his class to football or basketball games, go to movies, the zoo or out for pizza, etc. He was the most popular teacher in the school, and all the "cool" boys wanted to be in his class and be one of the "chosen" ones that would be asked to special events. I'd been asked a few times to one of his extra-curricular events, but mom didn't have a car, so I did not have a ride to the pickup point.

I was emotionally distraught as I remembered what mom screamed at me as she cursed me while slamming my head on the kitchen wall -- an endless repeat of her screaming "it's all your fault" echoed in my head! Mr. M wanted to know if I was ok? I didn't know how to reply – as tears flooded my eyes. What was I supposed to say: *"my mom was choking me while slamming my head into a wall and cursing and screaming at me that dad and her life were a 'mess' all because of me – it was my fault?"* I couldn't go there because everyone at our school believed the *Cousino Lie – that mom was the perfect mom, and we were the perfect family.*

He walked me out to the hallway and pointed to the private teachers' lounge which was two doors down from his classroom. He told me that if there were any teachers in the lounge, I was to return to the classroom. If no one was there, I was to wait in the lounge, and he would be there in a few minutes. No teachers were present, but I was quite nervous because the teachers' lounge was off limits to all students. A few minutes later, Mr. M entered the teacher's lounge.

"What's the matter, Brad?" I teared up but couldn't answer.

"Did something happen at home?" The tears just flooded my eyes, streaming down my cheeks. Mr. M was leaning up against the table where the teachers would sit. He put his hands on my shoulders and then wrapped his arms around me as he hugged me. He brought me even closer to him. Tears streamed down my face. He then kissed my neck and ran his hands down the back of my shirt and outside my pants over my butt. I froze! Immediately I struggled to get out of his arms, so I could bolt for the door. Fortunately, two teachers started talking just outside the teachers' lounge door as they were getting ready to enter. He quickly let me go. It was my chance to escape, and I took full advantage of it, almost knocking down one of the teachers as I walked briskly out the door.

This turned out to be the worst day of my miserable, young life!

My "worst day" happened in mid-May. Fortunately, in two weeks, I'd "graduate" from Mr. M's fifth grade class. I wanted nothing to do with him ever again. A week after the school year ended, Mr. M suddenly resigned and took a job as a teacher in one of the Cleveland area parochial grade schools.

About a year later, rumors floated among the school kids & staff that Mr. M was caught molesting a sixth-grade boy at the Cleveland school. Based on my teachers' lounge incident with Mr. M, I knew it could have been possible – but that only added to my pain.

Why?

Because I was a coward – afraid to tell my parents, the principal, or any nuns, priests or teachers at my school or church.

I never told anyone what happened...

Until *NOW!*

Chapter 3
Panic Attack

"Life is ten percent what happens to you, and ninety percent how you respond to it."

- Charles Swindoll

January 1971. My Senior year. Five months until high school graduation. No money to pay for college application fees, let alone a college tuition. I had good grades and decent S.A.T. scores, but not enough to earn an academic scholarship.

How was I going to get out of this hellish prison? Our small, two-bedroom, one bathroom, 750 square foot bungalow was not my prison, nor was the glass factory. My prison was much bigger. The northern-most suburb in Toledo, OH -- Point Place, was not my prison either. They may have been components of my prison, but it was much bigger than any physical location...and infinitely more painful. And it was the only life I had ever known.

My only escape route seemed to be through my athletic abilities. I was hoping to earn a football scholarship, but that appeared to be a remote possibility based on all the rejection letters I received. Student loans and grants were not yet readily available to the public. Panic, fear, hatred, anger, resentment, set in. No one to trust. No kind words of wisdom. My eighteen-year horror story may never have an ending.

I was desperate, afraid, and alone.

***

Even though I was a dominant high school athlete, I was undersized. I was less than 6 feet tall (actually 5' 11") and weighing 185 lbs., I was a relentless offensive fullback and defensive linebacker for Toledo's Central Catholic high school. I made first-team All-League, All-City, All-District, and All-Regional on offense _and_ defense. Despite my many achievements and awards in high school, I was rejected for a football scholarship by over two dozen colleges: from big schools (Ohio State and Michigan) to mid-sized colleges (Toledo U, Bowling Green, Miami U, and Ohio U), to even small Division III colleges (Ashland College, Findley College, Tiffin College, etc.)

Time was of the essence. High School Football season ended Thanksgiving weekend. I had no contact from any college coaches that initially had shown interest in me. Christmas and New Year celebrations were a distant memory. I was desperate. I felt as if I was being buried alive by my life circumstances. I feared that unless something happened soon, I'd end up working at the Libbey Owens Ford Glass Factory (LOF), where many from my hometown, including my father, worked. In the 50's, 60's & 70's Toledo was known as the "Glass City" and often referred to as the "Glass capital of the world."

As a fifth (5th) grader, I participated in 'bring your kid to work' day, where dad brought me to the LOF glass factory for five (5) hours during the month of July. In those five hours, I saw dozens of dad's fellow workers almost like they were zombies moving slowly, without purpose or passion. After that 'visit', nightmares plagued me regularly. A recurring nightmare was seeing myself as an older man, mechanically laboring under the intense 145-degree heat right next to the huge blast furnaces, while choking down handfuls of abhorrent salt tablets. I often awoke panicking, drenched in sweat, realizing that time was passing me by, and I had yet to escape my intolerable existence.

During one of these episodes, a radical idea began to form in my mind. This would be a real long shot, but what did I have to lose? At least I would be doing something about getting out of here and going to college instead of wallowing in self-pity. No! I had to somehow, someway, earn a scholarship, and the way my life was going, if I didn't try, then I would certainly have zero chance...and no one to blame but myself. I decided to devote every fiber of my being towards the cause of going to college. I would do whatever it took.

In desperation, I picked up a pen…

An hour later, I stared at my handwritten letter; a plea begging for a football scholarship. This one-page letter would become the model. I decided that I would not send out just one or two letters, but instead, I'd send out two dozen packets, some to the same schools that already rejected me. I would include my handwritten letter, and a copy of my football highlight film of my junior and senior years. So, in mid-January 1971, I sat up in our cold, dimly lit, unfinished attic and hand-wrote twenty-five letters to college football coaches within a 250-mile radius of Toledo, Ohio.

I didn't care what anyone thought of my leap of faith; I was dead set on my goal: to not only be the first member of the Cousino family to graduate from an accredited high school – but then be accepted and graduate from a quality four-year university. I would be the very first member of my "Cousino" lineage to accomplish that goal. But my goal was much more than that. It was driven by a need to escape the living hell I had lived from my earliest memories, waking most every morning in fear. Waking up in the same place with desperation and a gloomy future sneering back at me. I was determined to break the cycle.

Virtually none of the twenty-five college coaches even acknowledged my letter. I then followed up with phone calls to each coach. All I got in return for my efforts was a receptionist asking, "Can I take a message?" A week goes by. Two weeks. Three. Heavy shadows of defeat were taking over. All the panic, fear, anger, and frustration came to a head. All the hope I was bursting with while writing the letters was nowhere to be found. Then, a ray of hope. The phone rang.

"Hello, may I speak with Brad... *Casino?*" **

*** It was common for people to mis-pronounce our last name, usually as 'Casino'. I'm of French descent and our family name was originally spelled COUSIN<u>EAU</u>, but my ancestors decided to change the spelling to COUSIN<u>O</u> – (pronounced Cooz-eh-NO) upon moving from Quebec, Canada to southeast Michigan in the late 1800's.*

Chapter 4
Sewer Spelunking

"The road to Easy Street goes through the sewer."   **- John Madden**

In mid-to-late February 1971, I received a call from Coach Bob Reublin of Miami University (OH). He was the assistant coach, who was responsible for recruiting in the Northwest Ohio area. I knew who he was immediately; one of the many coaches who already rejected me due to my size. However, he now shared that he and the entire staff of Miami coaches took some time to watch the highlight film I sent.

He also played the film for four of the current Miami Varsity players without disclosing who they were to review. Instead, he asked them to select the jersey number of who they thought was the best player on either of the teams in the film. It was unanimous... #32 (my high school number). They saw raw potential, despite not having the necessary height, weight, and speed for my position as either a fullback or linebacker. Ultimately, he asked, "Brad, that was one bold move you made sending us your personalized hand-written letter and highlight film, knowing we had already turned you down. Are you still interested in coming to Miami?"

"Absolutely, sir," I said. "Are there any scholarships available?" I asked enthusiastically.

"No," he responded to my dismay.

I was crushed.

"But" he continued, "we have an alumnus (Mr. Pres Bliss) who lives in the Toledo area with contacts in the construction industry. He thinks he can get you a decent-paying job. However, it's not going to be an easy job, nor will it be one you're going to like."

Coach Reublin went on to say he would commit to helping me get accepted into Miami if my grades and SAT scores were good enough. He also promised that I would be invited to try out as a non-scholarship "walk-on" at the upcoming 1971 football summer camp. There were no scholarship offers or promises made other than the chance to try out. It wasn't much, but at this point, with no other options, how could I refuse? Beggars don't get to be choosers. It was my "get out of jail free" card that came with the standard "Do not pass Go. Do not collect $200" as there were no scholarships to be had. Without hesitation, I agreed. "Coach, I'll do whatever it takes."

I had many reasons as to why I should consider giving up. Every college coach told me I did not have the necessary ingredients to make it at the college level – this included my own high school coach, who resigned after accepting a coaching position in Cleveland, so he didn't help my cause in any way.

However, one overriding thought stood above the rest. At the end of this dark tunnel, my dreams lay as bright as the early morning sun calling out to me. I was determined. I vowed to do whatever it took.

Sewer Rat

The job that Pres Bliss, the Miami alumnus, arranged for me was one of the most challenging jobs I could have ever imagined, both physically and psychologically. I was hired to clean out the sewer system about twelve to twenty feet below the Toledo interstate highways. Really? I didn't know much about Coach Reublin, and I started to wonder if he really considered me as a viable candidate for Miami's football program. Or was he just using me to help Press Bliss, a very generous Miami Alumni, who loved Miami Athletics? Was it possible that he couldn't find an able-bodied person to take on the job of cleaning out sewers for a few dollars over minimum wage? After some research, I found out that the job was indeed legit.

It seems that every five to seven years, the State Highway Department contracts with a construction company to clean out the sewers. This job is considered a temporary seasonal job, and by the first day of work, I was pretty sure I knew why. There was no way a construction company could pull one of their full-time construction workers out of the fresh air to go underground into this putrid, rancid, cesspit environment eight to ten hours a day to shovel out the rancid sludge in the sewers. No way! They had to hire a temporary employee… and pay him a few dollars more than minimum wage. Yep, I was that guy! I was paid $4.50 an hour. The minimum wage in 1971 was $1.60 an hour.

It was truly like something out of your worst nightmares; the worst kinds of filth and stench possibly invented; just imagine a deep, dank, totally underground, pitch-black cave-like environment that was hundreds of miles long. It could be an excellent horror movie scene.

Each morning, I'd put on my "uniform", which comprised of a miner's helmet with a headlamp, gloves, boots, coveralls, and goggles, and climb down into the manhole with a lantern to provide some ambient light in the depths. I was also given "tools" for the repugnant tasks ahead, but they might as well have been kid's toys: a big scoop-shovel and a four-wheel Red Ryder wagon that served to transport the rancid material back to the manhole opening. At the manhole, I emptied the Red Ryder Wagon into a large bucket and sent its contents up as needed until the massive dump truck was full.

I worked in that dark, dank underworld non-stop from early morning till lunch, when I came up for some sweet fresh air, chowed down, and rehydrated for 45 minutes. Then I got into my gear again and took the plunge back down into the filth, sludge, and various forms of fecal matter until the end of the day. Depending on the day, there could be 24 to 48 inches deep of repulsive, nauseous substances backed up for miles. One day, I might be in a 60" to 72" pipe, another I'd be in a 42" to 48" pipe, literally shoveling sludge on all fours because the pipe would not be tall enough for me to stand. I spent the bulk of my 1971 spring and summer cleaning out those putrid, rat invested sewers.

Miami Bound

Once I was officially accepted into Miami, I followed up with Coach Reublin and let him know that I wanted to try out for the football team as a non-scholarship "walk-on". I couldn't believe that I was going to be a "college student" at such a great school. Miami University has been recognized for decades as a top-tier public college. Robert Frost described Miami as, "The most beautiful campus that ever there was." Even if it was just going to be for a little while, it was going to be "my school." The image of me as a Miami student, on that beautiful campus, was what kept me going down in those sewers. After visiting many college campuses in my recruiting phase, Miami was my clear number one choice. To this day, it has an excellent reputation for academics, athletics, and quality of student life. In my opinion, Miami was the perfect college atmosphere.

At the end of my time in the sewers, when it was time to show up for football, I managed to save enough for almost two quarters at Miami. I didn't know how I was going to pay for the balance of the year, but I just had to go, even if I only had the money to be there for a short time.

Summer football training camp started in early August. In 1971, the freshmen football players were not allowed to play at the varsity level per the NCAA, only upperclassmen. That changed in 1972. So, all freshmen were assigned to be the de facto "scout" team or practice squad - against the varsity offense and defense. In high school I played fullback and linebacker. Miami coaches projected me to be a linebacker, so I was assigned to the second team inside linebacker position on the freshmen squad.

*****

From Cleaning Sewers to Wrestling Giants

Even though we were much younger and smaller than the older, stronger, varsity guys, no mercy was given. We were put through the wringer. Not even the varsity coaches cared if we got injured. The cruelty only grew harsher for those players without any football scholarships, like me. A non-scholarship "walk-on" was the lowest man on the pecking order. We received the oldest equipment and had additional duties such as holding "dummies" for the varsity to fire out on. Or we would stand around and wait until we could get a few plays in, so the starting scout team could get some water and rest.

Due to my short stature of 5'11" and weight of about 192 lbs., I was virtually written off by anyone who had a say in my future as a collegiate football player. It became even more obvious of my lack of size compared with the huge giants when they were dressed in full football equipment, helmets, shoulder pads, neck braces, padded forearms, football pants, etc.

I was treated as a piece of practice fodder and received zero encouragement to have a chance of ever being anything more than a temporary scout team player at the college football ranks. I found that most non-scholarship "walk-ons" would quit within a few days, weeks, or maybe a month – and a very few die-hards would "gut it out" and then quit at the end of the season.

As a lowly, non-scholarship *walk-on*, the coaches, trainers, and even the student managers made sure that I knew my place in the pecking order...last! Even so, I was mentally prepared, and knew coming in, that would be the case. I was able to dismiss the naysayers by telling myself over and over: "Just watch me show you otherwise!"

Kong is M.I.A.

I vividly remember the day I got my first chance because destiny handed me a shot that I never imagined. The second practice of the day began as routine. Seven-on-seven team drill, freshmen scout team defense vs first team varsity offense. When the players huddled in, our highly recruited freshmen middle guard, whom I call Kong, (as in King Kong) was missing.

We were about two weeks into our two-a-day hot summer practices, and Kong had a very bad day at the morning practice. Several coaches tore into him for his numerous blunders. Maybe it was just one of those days for him where everything that could go wrong, did. When the team was dismissed from morning practice, Kong was so upset, that something inside must have snapped. He stormed out of the locker room, went to his dorm, packed all his belongings, jumped in his fancy sports car, left the team, and drove four hours home – without informing any coach, trainer, or manager.

It was common knowledge that the coaching staff had recruited Kong to be next year's heir apparent to replace the graduating Miami's Senior All-MAC star middle guard #58 Doug Krause. Kong was the top recruit on the freshmen team. Even though he was only 18 years old, he was already a goliath of a man at 6'3", 240 lbs. (who would grow significantly bigger and stronger in the next few years) who could give Paul Bunyan insecurity issues... The coaches asked around for Kong's location. "Go check with the trainers to see if he's injured, but we don't have all day! In the meantime, I need a middle guard, NOW!" the varsity coach bellowed, scanning the field for a logical replacement candidate.

My heart practically leaped out of my chest. It was at least a chance - one I had been hoping for. Without hesitation, I bolted from the sidelines and into the huddle. Now was my time to shine, to show the coaches, the varsity offensive players, and my freshmen teammates what I could really do when given an opportunity. As I stood in the huddle, I remembered the quote I placed on my mirror as I moved into the dorm two weeks ago with the freshmen players:

*"**Your big opportunity may be right where you are <u>now!</u>**"*

- Napoleon Hill

As I expected, I was immediately called out by the varsity offensive line coach, Coach Reublin.

"Cousino, get the hell out of there! You're too small; you'll get killed."

"No, Coach, I can do this," I said, defiantly. No matter what, I was not going to leave that defensive huddle. This was my first real chance to show the coaches and my teammates what I was made of. I was not backing down for anything, even if I was going up against much larger players – averaging 6'4", 250+ lb. offensive linemen.

The coaches were stunned to silence, thinking I was joking. When they realized I wouldn't budge, their brows quivered with curiosity. They wanted to see what I could do, the guinea pig in their little experiment. "Fine, but don't expect any mercy!" came the response.

"None given, either!" I retorted, which elicited hearty chuckles from both the coaches and my freshmen teammates. I was staring down one of the huge senior offensive guards (Freddie Brisker) glaring at me when I said this. He rolled his eyes, gave me a menacing look, and whispered with malice:

"OK *walk-on rookie* -- strap it up and get ready for the PAIN!"

From that point on the entire offensive unit declared war on me. Every day brought the ultimate challenge - my 5'11", 192 lb. frame against these behemoths!

No one knew how hard I fought to get here...

The life of misery I lived daily for the past 18 years...

how determined I was to break free of the traumatic abuse...

and they had no idea how much harder I would fight to stay!

Chapter 5
David vs. Goliath

"Most of the important things in the world have been accomplished by people who have kept on trying when there seemed to be no hope at all."

Dale Carnegie

The live team drill began. The first play was about to happen. I had to prove that I could fill Kong's shoes. Adrenaline pumped through my veins. I knew I was going to have to work harder and exert much more energy than anyone else to make up for my reduced stature and that bold statement that I had just made. Otherwise, I'd be laughed off the field, bringing an end to my entire college career before it had even begun. Really, I'm going to show them NO mercy? Why'd I have to go shoot my mouth off? Remaining at Miami all depended on earning a future scholarship. I realized that I had no other way to pay for it. My future seemed to hang in the balance.

This was my make-or-break moment. Time to put up... or shut up!

On the very first play, I broke through the offensive line and made the tackle. The team, the coaches, everyone, was shocked to the core. The junior and senior offensive linemen were most displeased to be shown up by a lowly freshman, particularly a "walk-on" nobody. Perhaps they considered that pure luck because their next play was aimed directly at me. Nonetheless, I made another unassisted tackle on the starting senior fullback, Chris Brockmeyer. As I picked myself up off his legs, he turned around.

"Cool it, Cousino! This is practice, not a game!" Brockmeyer barked.

Coach Reublin yelled out, "Keep going, Cousino, this is just what the offensive line needs!" Then he directed his attention to the fullback.

"Hey, prima donna! If you want to remain in the starting lineup, you better play every play like it's a game! Your problem isn't Cousino, is it? Who is your problem?"

"My offensive line?" The fullback responded.

"That's right, your offensive line! If we want to be a great team, we need every player to practice with the intensity and heart of Cousino!" Then the coach yelled at the offensive line. "Are you going to let a walk-on freshmen break through your line and make the tackle every time? You guys are supposed to be the #1 offensive line. You better get with it before we find someone to take your place!" The linemen were embarrassed, and I could see the contempt in their eyes for me. The kid-gloves were off! I'd never back down, despite the odds against me.

As the drill continued, I played like a man possessed. I blew up many of the offensive plays the coaches could throw at me. By the end of practice that day, the offensive coaches were so upset at their offensive line that they made both the first and second team offensive lines run extra sprints after practice. You can just imagine how popular I was with those older, massive giant men who had to run an additional eight (8) 50-yard sprints – after the hot afternoon practice - because of me! While the offensive varsity coaches were ticked off; the defensive coaches were delighted. I got my first taste of serious competition, and I came out the winner; at least for that one afternoon's practice. David had slain Goliath!

***

When I came to camp, I knew I needed to make a big enough impression to get the coaches' attention at each practice session. However, my first real chance to do so only happened because of finally getting my "break" when Kong was M.I.A. At the college & professional levels, virtually every practice is filmed 15 to 20 feet above the offensive and defensive practice fields, so nothing was ever missed by the "eye in the sky". Each night, the offensive and defensive position coaches would gather to watch all the footage of that day's practices. They ran back every play repeatedly so they could grade out each player. Every play that was made was thoroughly analyzed and charted to check the team's progress to determine what was needed to improve.

It just made sense, that if I was ultra-competitive against the older, bigger upperclassmen of the first and second-team varsity lines, then I would have to be noticed by the freshmen head coach (Ron Corradini), our defensive line coach (Jerry Angelo), and the two most important coaches of all – Defensive coordinator Dick Crum and Head Coach Bill Mallory.

The plan worked! After that one practice, the coaches saw enough potential in me (despite my size disadvantage) that I was moved from inside linebacker to the middle guard position (also called nose guard) on the freshmen team depth chart. I made up for my diminutive stature with quickness, never-give-up attitude, and relentless tenacity. This didn't stop me from being picked on, though. When I was initially moved to the middle guard position, as a member of the freshmen scout team, I was forced to fight to protect myself daily against offensive linemen who were at least forty pounds heavier, and three to four inches taller.

The giants on the offensive line had me listed as their public enemy #1. Why? Because I would not ratchet down my aggressive play. I stopped worrying about whether I was aggravating the giants by how hard I was trying. I was on a mission, and this might be my only chance. I had to get a scholarship, and I would do whatever was necessary to earn one. It was an anomaly to have the starting varsity offensive line upstaged by an undersized, non-scholarship *walk-on* nobody. I was picked on, belittled, teased, and scorned by the upper-class giants -- but even that ceased after three to four weeks as I earned their respect.

Don't get me wrong, I love the game of football, but it was primarily a means to an end. I had to play well enough to get a football scholarship to stay at Miami. Although I was making great progress on the team, every day had a bittersweet ending.

I had ongoing financial problems that plagued me day and night. With summer football underway, I wasn't sure how I was going to afford the balance of winter quarter's tuition and spring quarter's tuition and living expenses. I was able to come up with enough to pay for the first quarter and about 75% of the second quarter, but had no way to pay for the balance of the Winter (2nd) quarter or all the Spring (3rd) quarter. The remaining savings, as well as my leftover funds from my work in the sewers, was all spoken for with school bills. I was broke! And Miami's winter tuition bill would be due in early January.

Sometimes I'd wake up in the middle of the night with the same panic and fear that I had my senior year in high school when I had no way of paying for college, nor any college football teams interested in me. Now that I'd journeyed from my life of hell and had tasted a little piece of Heaven with Miami college life, the thought of returning to my parents' house in Point Place was even more painful.

Living away from my house was the first time in my life I had ever woken up without fear gripping me of what I might have to face that day from mom. I was out of sorts, but I loved it, and hated it at the same time because I was hanging on by a thread. I vowed that I would never spend more than a weekend in my childhood house. I have never and will never refer to that place as my "home".

I looked up the true meaning of "home". *"Home means an enjoyable happy place where you can live, laugh, and learn. It is somewhere where you are loved, respected, and cared for."* (Quoted by Wynn, grade 5)

This had <u>NOT</u> been my experience of "home." Not even close!

Every day that week, I woke up wondering if Kong would show back up at Miami again. But he didn't show. Each day he was gone was another day to prove myself. But could I repeat what I did yesterday or the day before? Could I do it again tomorrow if I had another chance? Or the next day? Or the next? What if Kong came back? Would the coaches put him back on the field and shuffle me to the sidelines?

My body ached from getting hit. But that was only fair. I'm sure my opponents were aching too. I was used to going to bed aching all over from getting hit from my earliest memories. But there were no pads back then. In fact, I wasn't playing football either, nor could I hit back. Maybe those past experiences gave me an unfair advantage?

It taught me how to tolerate pain!

****

Between my many job experiences, plus the money I saved from the sewer job, I had stashed away enough in savings to pay for my first quarter's tuition, room & board, books, etc. I did not have enough to cover approximately 1/4 of Miami's second quarter tuition, room and board and related school expenses - and that bill would be due in about three months. I knew my parents had no money. There was no available time for any kind of job due to the time constraints of football & school. I finally asked my grandpa (Cleo Gamble) for a loan to help cover the amount I was short. He agreed, and disaster was averted at least for a few more months. But I had no money for anything else.

I couldn't fathom giving up a full scholarship. Who gives up a full four-year scholarship like Kong did – unless money was not an issue? His parents must be loaded. Thoughts of envy and jealousy plagued me; to have money, a scholarship, decent clothes, and a nice late-model car were so foreign to me. In fact, I had never been exposed to such wealth. Now it was everywhere. Rich kids seemed to be everywhere at Miami. It seemed like most of the families of the students who went to Miami were wealthy. Did they all go home to their ivory towers, country clubs, and high-net-worth communities, far away from people like me?

Envy is one of the Seven Deadly Sins, and I lived every day consumed by it. The money, the expensive toys, the fancy cars, the beautiful homes, the extravagant wardrobes, unlimited partying budgets. Why couldn't I have been born a "have" instead of a "have-not"? I wondered if any of the kids at Miami ever worried about tuition expenses.

Do they even know when the payments are due, or do their parents just get the bill and pay it?

Even though I tried to fake it, I reeked of a poverty mindset, and felt inferior because of it. I was fighting not just for my chance to earn a football scholarship, but for the future I had dreamed of for most of my eighteen years of misery. A week went by, still, Kong was MIA.

We were off on Sunday, but early Monday morning, I was summoned to Coach Mallory's office. Something was up. *Oh no, Kong must be back!*

Chapter 6
Walk-On Warrior

"The future has not been written. There is no fate but what we make for ourselves."   - Unknown

"You have earned yourself quite the reputation, Cousino," Head Coach Bill Mallory told me when he called me to his office. "I admire your determination."

His words of appreciation meant a great deal to me, but he wasn't done yet. What he said next was the best news I could have received at the time.

"Son…I'm sure you have questions about Kong."

"Yeah, he's a great player, and I appreciate the opportunity to take his place in his absence. Is he coming back?"

Coach Mallory smiled, yet with a hint of sadness in his eyes. *"He's gone. He left a note, and I spoke to his father last evening -- he isn't coming back."* And just like that, Kong threw away a four-year, full-ride football scholarship.

"That being said," Coach Mallory continued, *"You, Cousino, have played so well that I would have replaced him with you had he come back."*

"Thanks, Coach, are you saying that—"

"Yes…You have earned the spot on the freshmen team as 1st Team Middle Guard. Congratulations."

"Thank you, Coach! I will keep at it; I won't let you down!"

Though this was great news, thoughts of my ever-present reality crept back in.

"How was I going to afford to stay in Miami? I would be out of money by the middle of the second quarter."

"Seeing the potential in you," Coach Mallory continued, "*I am prepared to give you a one-third scholarship for the entire school year. You can use it to pay for spring quarter.*"

I was shocked. "How did you know?"

"Coach Reublin clued me in that you probably didn't make enough in the sewers to cover the expenses for the entire year. We don't want to give you any reason to leave, so keep it up, and you'll be just fine this year, with no financial worries. We want you concentrating on football, not on tuition bills!" He then added, *"If you keep this up, there's a strong probability of a full scholarship after spring football as you move up to the varsity team. There are no guarantees, so you're going to have to work to prove that you deserve it.*

Congratulations, Cousino. I applaud your tenacity and never-give-up attitude. Just think of where you'd be if you hadn't sent us that letter and your highlight film – even after we had turned you down. You are charting your own path to a better future. Good job! I wish everyone on this team had as much heart as you."

I couldn't believe what I was hearing. A partial scholarship before the first quarter of school had even begun. It was more than I thought possible...so soon. I was ecstatic. I learned that it was rare for a *walk-on freshman* to receive any money in his first year, let alone before school even started. I told Coach Mallory I was grateful for this gesture, and that I was ready to go above and beyond to earn the rest of that scholarship. And I meant every word.

Now that Kong was officially gone, I had to continue to prove that I could take his place. But could I? The offensive varsity linemen were going to do anything they could to stop me. They loathed me and my relentless, never-quit mentality. It made them look bad. I became embroiled in daily scuffles with the offensive linemen over the next three to four weeks.

They would initiate fights by holding me, leg-whipping me, tackling me if I got by them or in desperation, grabbing my face mask and trying to rip my head off. I wouldn't initiate the fights-- but I'd never back down. I was a threat to them. For me to survive meant I could not allow these acts to go on without responding accordingly. Otherwise, they would never stop until I was injured, or I quit because it was just too difficult. There were simply too many giants who were committed to gang-up on me until I either quit or was injured.

To survive, I used my skills as a good high school wrestler. I was quick on my feet and understood the value of leverage against a bigger opponent. This became my game plan; I would never allow the giants to win if they tried to cheap-shot me. Yep, I reverted to using my high school wrestling moves to bring my much larger opponent to the ground. Then I'd just go wild on him before the offensive coaches would intervene and drag me off them.

But I vowed to never, ever quit, not even to occasionally "just coast". I had a fire inside of me. I didn't look for trouble, but they knew I didn't care who I was up against, or how big they were, or how many years they had on me, I was going to play every play with the intention of beating them. In my mind, I MUST get a football scholarship, if not, I would have to drop out of Miami!

It was a difficult period for me. Despite my wrestling skills, I was vulnerable, helpless, alone. It was me against the far bigger giant players. No one to trust or count on but myself. The only thing I could do was just get back in the huddle and get ready for the next play.

Within-three to four weeks, however, I was no longer their target. I earned their respect as one of the freshmen team's top defensive players on the scout team. Coach Reublin told me that our freshmen defense was better when I was on the field than when I was not. We held our ground far more effectively against the much larger varsity offensive line, pushing them harder. This, in turn, helped them improve to be an even better offensive unit...which is ideally what the "scout" team's mission is supposed to be!

What encouraged me the most was my defensive coaches' reactions to my performance on the field. They supported and emphasized specific aggressive actions I did and encouraged me to continue playing as hard as I could. One of my freshmen coaches, Jerry Angelo, *(who would become the future General Manager of the Chicago Bears),* encouraged me to never give up and believe in myself. He told me that if I kept up my ferocious mentality and work ethic on and off the field, then I could be one of the greats. I promised not to let him or any of the other coaches down. And I meant it. He was one of the first Miami coaches to encourage and believe in me. Because of coach Jerry Angelo, I began to be a difference-maker on the defensive scout team.

Many nights I'd lay awake wondering why everything was so hard. Even though I had earned a 1/3 partial scholarship for this year, I wondered why I was not happier or more content. What was I going to do for the next 3+ years? I had come so far already, but there was still a very long way to go. Why am I always so worried and so unhappy?

Because I'm desperate, broke, & unwanted...

And I've got NO place to go!

Chapter 7
The Good, the Bad, & the Ugly

"Endurance is not just the ability to bear a hard thing but to turn it into glory."   - William Barclay

"We don't develop courage by being happy every day. We develop it by surviving difficult times and challenging adversity."   - Barbara De Angelis

When I was a child, I was under the impression that everything was my fault. My mom reminded me of it often. I could not understand why anything bad was because of me. Almost every day was a warzone growing up between the ages of 6 to 17 years old. Mom verbally and/or physically abused me in a multitude of ways many times each week. I spent much of my early life in continual fear of being physically abused, verbally assaulted, and emotionally traumatized.

Mom's beatings happened so often that I became hardened to the pain inflicted and ceased crying. I'd take whatever punishment she inflicted, but I determined that I would not allow myself to cry. Even as I grew bigger and stronger, I never challenged mom or dad when I was being physically or verbally abused.

Generational Trauma Dysfunctions

I learned that my parents were raised in either alcoholic (dad) and/or highly dysfunctional homes (mom), where screaming, cursing, yelling, hitting, pinching, shaming, etc., was the typical modus operandi as they grew up. I found that both my parents were damaged physically and emotionally by each of their parents (my grandparents) who had exhibited their own generational dysfunctions from the way they were raised by their parents (my great grandparents).

Since they were dysfunctional kids themselves, forced into raising an unwanted child (me), they could only revert to the behavior learned from their parents as they grew up. I was on the receiving end of the following 'physical' or 'emotional' punishments almost daily for most of my early life. My dad was usually at one of his two jobs or hanging out with his post-work excursions to the bars and/or reluctantly complicit in mom's forced beatings of me, whenever he did come back to our house every three or four days.

The Many Bad Days

There were many days where mom would whip or beat me two or more times in a day. And then, if dad came home later that day, mom would badger him to beat me again. Over the years, mom physically whipped and/or verbally assaulted me many hundreds of times – from my earliest memories until I grew too big that they couldn't beat me any longer... but even then, the vicious verbal assaults continued.

Mom physically, verbally, or emotionally abused me in the following ways:

- Pinching me under the inside of my bicep…hard

- Stabbing me with a fork at the dinner table

- Slapping me across the face

- Whipping me with a leather belt or the Kirby sweeper cord

- Slamming my head into walls - repeatedly

- Choking me often to where I almost passed out

- Grabbing me by my ears or hair and dragging me around the house or backyard

- Enduring solitary confinement to our small one car garage or to our unfinished basement

- And the never-ending verbal barrage of swearing, cussing, shaming, bullying, yelling, and the non-stop cursing while getting beat and/or the constant vicious verbal assaults being reigned down non-stop (you're no good, you're a bas***d, a g*d d**n, loser, a s**t head, who will never amount to anything good, you're a lazy bum, just like your worthless drunk father, you're a son of a b***h, a** hole, G*d d**n ba***d, etc.)

Solitary Confinement

As another form of punishment, after getting whipped or verbally assaulted, mom would send me to either the hot, sweaty garage or the damp, musty basement for hours at a time. There was no cable TV, cell phones, or Internet in those days, so there wasn't much for a kid to do for entertainment when locked away in solitary confinement. I was forbidden to listen to the radio, but I was allowed to read books. Both the garage and basement were similar: Concrete floors, bare roughed in walls, only one exposed light bulb, virtually no natural light. This represented the lowest of my personal HELL because I could be confined for many hours. Yet, over time, in a weird way, my banishment became a sanctuary away from mom and the relentless attacks.

I made sure that I always had plenty of books, sports magazines, superhero comics, etc., stashed in the garage or the basement. I went to the library down the street from my grandparent's home, checking books out regularly in anticipation of my hours of solitary confinement. I was left all alone. I figured out that if I had books with me, it gave me something to do besides thinking about my lousy life. Over the years, I had become an avid reader, and enjoyed getting lost in great mysteries or the exploits of my favorite superheroes …they provided an escape from the reality of my dysfunctional home life, even if it was only temporary.

A Few Good Days

Growing up I did look forward to those occasional "good" days. Those days for me were when I played in a sport where I was the hero of the game. When I was the "star" by making the winning TD, or the game saving tackle, or hitting the game-winning home run, or scoring the winning goal in hockey, etc., my parents just seemed to be nicer to me on those days. It didn't make sense at the time, but now I know it was because mom and dad received positive recognition from the other kids' parents when I was the "star" by making the big play to help our team win the game.

As I grew older, it seemed that I would often be the one to make the big play just when we needed it. I didn't understand why; but as I look back, I wanted to be loved and accepted by my parents; doesn't every kid? Without being able to articulate it, at a subconscious level, what I really wanted was to be loved - unconditionally. I wanted to be accepted, to be wanted... just because I was their child. I felt if I strove to be the best in every sport I played, my parents would show something resembling approval and affection towards me. At the very least, they would be tolerable of me, which was a good start in my eyes. I didn't understand why everything was my fault. I just knew deep down that my parents felt that way about me.

Beast Mode Fantasy

As an 8 to 12-year-old, I read hundreds of mystery and superhero books in my extended periods of isolation. I had an active imagination, seeing myself as a superhero, coming to the rescue, to save my family (I felt mom bore a strong resemblance to Lois Lane) or friends. Superman was always a hero to me, but I particularly related to a new superhero that came out in 1962: The Incredible Hulk. I loved when Bruce Banner transformed into "Beast Mode".

I'd often whisper to myself as I daydreamed "Ok Couz, it's Beast Mode time". I thought if I could use my own so-called "Beast Mode" in a superhero-type role, ready to save the day, I'd finally be able *to save mom and dad from all that caused them to be so unhappy with me and ultimately earn their love.* I repeated the mantra, *"Beast Mode time"* to myself, when I needed superhuman strength; even though I knew it was my fantasy world – it seemed to help!

Protecting the Weak

My two younger brothers were never treated the way I was by our parents. It was obvious to all my grandparents, aunts, uncles, and close friends that my younger brother Rick was mom's favorite. He and mom got into very few physical conflicts. Rick and I were very close. He was less than a year younger than me (51 weeks to be exact). Mom would occasionally get upset at Rick for some minor issue, but very seldom to the point of spanking him. But one day, Rick did something so grievous against mom's rules that she got the big belt out to whip him senseless.

What was this egregious offense that Rick supposedly committed? Simply standing-up at the toilet while urinating instead of sitting down – mom found urine on the toilet seat and floor, and there were serious consequences in the Cousino family if mom's strict bathroom rules were disobeyed. That was indeed a rare occurrence. I knew a beating from mom would crush him to the core, so I stepped in between them, (Beast Mode initiated) and said, *"You're not going to whip him, you're going to have to beat me instead! I won't let you hurt him!"* Mom was shocked at my defiance.

I took an absolute walloping for Rick, but I never shed a tear. As mom was whipping me, she pushed me to the floor next to Rick's bed, and I caught a glimpse of a teary-eyed Rick. His eyes said it all: Why? Why is she hurting you? Through the pain, I cracked a slight smile at him. I knew it was going to be okay – I was in Beast Mode. I'd take any beating if it meant it stopped Rick or Mike from getting one.

Outside of the house, any time my brothers were being bullied, I stepped in to protect them, particularly Rick. (Mike was four and a half years younger than me) Rick was smaller than me; even though he was a good athlete, I was his big brother and I naturally protected him.

What I couldn't bear watching was someone else being bullied, hit, whipped, or yelled at, whether it was a total stranger, a classmate, a neighbor, a girl, or lady, but especially if it involved either of my brothers.

Chapter 8
A "Small" Problem

"Life doesn't get easier or more forgiving; we get stronger and more resilient."
                                        -- **Dr. Steve Maraboli**

I became one of the dominant defensive players for our freshmen scout team. I thrived on the positive feedback and praise from my freshmen defensive coaches (Jerry Angelo and Ron Corradini) and was motivated to keep hearing it. As the official scout team for the varsity, our freshmen defensive team had a goal to make the offensive varsity team the best it could be – and that meant that we had to give them our very best to emulate their opponents, so that they could be ready to compete against each team on Saturday afternoon.

That mindset also made our freshmen team stronger. Our primary responsibility was to play the opposing team in practices and help our varsity offensive unit become the best one-possible. However, we also played a mini schedule against five other freshmen teams from colleges within a four-hour drive time. It was a chance to see how we compared against other college teams from the schools we would be playing for the next three years at the varsity level.

During the freshmen games, I wanted to win so desperately that I was like an unleashed lion. I seemed to make big plays when they were needed. I sacked the quarterback and blocked punts, field goals, and extra points. I led the team in tackles, assists, and QB sacks against our freshmen competition. Our freshmen defensive unit dominated all five freshmen offensive teams. We finished with a 4-1 record, playing Cincinnati, Dayton, Bowling Green, Xavier, and Ohio University. We traveled five hours to Athens, OH, for the freshmen game of the year against Ohio University Bobcats – longtime rivals of the Miami Redskins (now called *RedHawks*). Their QB, Richard Beverly, played a great game. We dominated almost all phases of the game. However, our offensive unit gave up three costly turnovers, two fumbles and one interception. As a result, our freshmen team suffered a very disappointing loss.

***

Over the four years I played for the Miami Redskins I practiced daily against three future All-MAC (Mid-American Conference) centers: Mike Poff, Dan Cunningham, and Randy Gunlock. Depending on the year Mike, Dan, and / or Randy and I went to war every day, and I worked hard to help them become even better. (which helped me improve my skills). By playing as hard as I could every day against players of Poff's, Cunningham's and Gunlock's caliber, I furthered my progress as a middle guard in technique, strength, and strategy. Mike Poff was All-MAC center in 1971, Dan Cunningham was All-MAC center in 1973, and Randy Gunlock was All-MAC center in 1975. They were the elite at their position in the MAC! I helped them become better as I became a better player, because I practiced daily against the best of the best – *iron sharpening iron!*

As our freshmen football season ended, *I was voted by the coaches and my freshmen teammates as the defensive Most Valuable Player (MVP) of the freshmen team at the season-ending banquet.* From starting out as a 'non-scholarship walk-on' to be being voted the defensive MVP of the freshmen class was an indescribable feeling. The freshmen and varsity players knew that I was a non-scholarship *walk-on* freshman nobody. But what they didn't know was that Miami had initially rejected me. And for some reason, in desperation, I wrote those letters, begging for a football scholarship, even to the teams that previously rejected me.

What If's...

I've always been one to ask myself rhetorical questions... I call them my "What Ifs":

- *What if... I believed what the 'experts' said... that I was too short, too small, too slow?*
- *What if ... I hadn't hand-written those 25 letters and sent my highlight film?*

- *What if... I wasn't willing to work in the disgusting sewers at $4.50 / hour for tuition money?*
- *What if... I wasn't willing to humble myself as a lowly, non-scholarship "walk-on"?*
- *What if... I didn't jump in to take Kong's place when I was vastly undersized?*
- *What if... I wasn't willing to "go to war" with my bigger teammates and win their respect?*

To me the answers are surreal; yet very real. How different would my life be today? I shudder to contemplate the alternatives. As I was reflecting on the circumstances that led me here, Coach Reublin congratulated me.

"*Cousino, think about how far you've come. What if you hadn't written that letter? Who knows where you would be today?*"

"*Coach, I was just thinking the same thing.*"

"*Take this honor and use it as your motivation to earn the starting middle guard position on the varsity team during spring football. It will be an uphill climb, and it won't be easy. As you know, there are four or five older juniors and sophomores that want Doug Krause's starting middle guard position next season.*

You'll have to work your butt off this winter and spring to get bigger and stronger. Get physically and mentally ready to compete for that starting spot in Spring Ball. It is rare that a sophomore can earn a starting position on the varsity, but you have great potential so don't give up. As for me, I'm taking full credit for recruiting you," he said with a hearty laugh.

"*Coach Reublin,*" I said, "*where would I be if you didn't read my letter and watch my film? I don't think you knew that I sent the exact same letter & film to twenty-five colleges (Toledo, Bowling Green, Ohio U, etc.,) but only Miami responded to my letter?*"

"*I want to thank you and coach Mallory... for helping me get that miserable, but decent-paying job, cleaning out the sewers and then helping get me accepted into Miami!*"

Uphill Battle

Despite my new-found place of respect on the freshmen team, there was still trouble ahead, my lack of size at the varsity level. Prior to leaving for Christmas break, I was summoned to meet with Coach Mallory in his office. *"Cousino, I've never had someone with your lack of height, weight, and speed, be voted as the defensive MVP of the freshmen team. That's why this is very hard for me to say, but I wanted to tell you personally. The thing is, Cousino..."* Coach Mallory hesitated. Something was on his mind, and it wasn't good.

Uh-oh, I thought. *"Is something wrong, Coach?"*

"Cousino...I'm not going to sugarcoat it, but Coach Crum and I think that you're just too small to be a starting Middle Guard on a Division I football team. Your lack of size is a huge disadvantage to our defensive scheme. Our defense needs a much bigger, stronger player to dominate the middle of our defensive line."

"We're just talking at this point," Coach Mallory continued, *"There will be a spot for you on the Varsity team, but it will be as a backup player. As a staff, we believe you're just too small to be our starting middle guard. Now, no final decision will be made until after Spring football, but your lack of size is a major concern, certainly not your abilities or your effort."*

I thought being voted the defensive MVP of the freshmen team buried the belief that I was too small. Here I was, going home for winter break, with a 1/3rd scholarship, now knowing that I would not be given a fair chance to earn a starting position on the varsity team. Does this mean no scholarship? And was it being determined on something for which I had no control?

I was powerless. Thoughts of my childhood started to slither back in. The feelings of being unwanted, rejected, not good enough. And the reality that there was nothing I could do to make myself grow taller or bigger. After that meeting, *I remembered that I was still the 'bastard' child who ruined my parents' lives. Now I was facing the real possibility of having to return to that environment back in Point Place, if I didn't have a football scholarship to pay for my tuition, books, room and board.*

I just didn't want to accept what I had just heard... so I decided that I wouldn't.

I did it before as a walk-on and rose through the ranks to become the defensive MVP. I'll just have to do it again. I cannot go back to that house in Point Place. I must get that scholarship. The coach said it himself: *"You still have a shot to prove your worth during Spring Ball."* Now, it's an even bigger uphill climb because they "as a coaching staff", believe my size doesn't belong on the first-string front line. I was devastated but would never give up!

This wasn't about football at all, but at the same time, it was. Football was a means to my scholarship. My scholarship was my means of escape from my past upbringing. Somehow, someway I had to convince Coaches Mallory and Crum that I deserved to be the starting middle guard so I could earn the full-ride scholarship -- so I could remain at Miami for another three and a half (3 ½) years. I had to prove to them during the upcoming Winter and Spring football season. Otherwise, I'd have to return to Toledo, move back in with my parents, and maybe end up with a job at the LOF glass factory with my dad.

None of those choices were viable options I wanted to consider.

Everything...absolutely everything...
rested on the results of Spring Football!

Chapter 9
Milk Money Bandit

The only person you are destined to become is the person you decide to be.   **-Ralph Waldo Emerson**

I'm broke. I can't work because of football. I am powerless to go out and earn money, and if I don't earn money to pay for tuition and living expenses, I can't stay at Miami. There is no free time for a job. I have classes that I must attend and then there are many hours of study time. Any free time is spent on the field, in the weight room, with my position coach in team meetings, or reviewing film.

This was my new void. No way to earn money. My coach let me know I wouldn't make First Team middle guard, which means NO full football scholarship. Such a foreign concept because I started hustling jobs throughout my early childhood.

Growing up, I began to purchase most of my clothes when I was about nine (9) years old. If I wanted anything that wasn't a hand-me-down from one of my cousins, I had to earn the money to buy the clothes, shoes, athletic gear, team fees, etc. I was also responsible for paying for my own high school tuition at Toledo Central Catholic High School, as well as buying an older used car, auto insurance, gas, etc. when I turned sixteen. Virtually everything that required money, I paid for myself, other than housing and food at my parents' house.

Money provided freedom. Working away from home was a nice bonus of escaping from my mom and her *rage-a-holic* tendencies. This was an even greater freedom. I worked many jobs growing up:

In Grade School:

- Each new spring season: I'd go to our neighbors and those of my grandparents and hustle eight (8) to ten (10) weekly lawn jobs which became long term repeat happy customers and referrals.

- During the fall, I'd rake leaves for the same customers and others that I could pick up.

- In the winter, I shoveled snow for these same customers and their neighbors.

- In early spring, I'd knock on doors and ask to help with "spring cleaning" projects and to clean the neighbors' outside windows.

In Junior high:

- In seventh and eighth grade, I was the primary janitor for my grade school and worked for $0.50 an hour. I worked after school, on weekends, and over the summer. I cleaned classrooms, hallways, bathrooms, windows, stripped and waxed the floors, took out the garbage, and anything else that needed to be done -- except major mechanical repairs, boiler room issues, plumbing repairs, electrical repairs, etc.,

- I had a part-time job working for an elderly blind man (who lived down our street) cutting grass, going to the store, cleaning his house, and doing projects that were too challenging or unsafe due to his blindness.

- In eighth grade, I took on a part-time job at the local gas station a block and a half from home. This job had me on the run because in the 1960s, there was no such thing as self-serve gas. Instead, as a gas station attendant, I would pump the customer's gas, wash their windows, check their oil, and even put air in their tires if they asked.

*** I remember a gas war started up in the Point Place area when gas prices eventually went as low as 18.9 cents per gallon. In 1965, regular gas prices were 29.9 cents per gallon.*

In High School:

- I worked in the cafeteria cleaning up trays and washing the dishes of my classmates' waste to help earn tuition money for attending Central Catholic High School.

- I worked a garbage route one summer and for the State Highway Department on another.

- I worked a part-time job during the school year as a transportation orderly at St. Vincent's hospital about two blocks from my high school on weekends.

- I worked for an asphalt company, as a general laborer, installing new blacktop parking lots, driveways, and neighborhood streets.

- I'd get seasonal work at Christmas tree lots unloading trees from delivery trucks, setting them up on the tree lot, and then helping customers secure the trees on their cars.

Alternative Income Sources

There were other ways of obtaining income, for which I am not proud. I lied and cheated regularly, and I learned this from my early childhood memories of my own parents. I was a product of my environment. My parents cursed, lied, and cheated regularly. They could justify their actions without remorse - *"They won't miss it, so it's not really stealing… they won't even know. We're just taking what we feel is rightfully ours…they can afford to buy another one…They're rich …look at all they have."*

I could rationalize lying, cheating, and even stealing from all kinds of places, such as our local church, school, grocery store, and drug store. Unfortunately, I was starting to become what my mom screamed at me hundreds of times, "that I was a no-good loser, A son of a b***h, a ba***rd, a lazy bum." Here are a few examples of how I followed in my parent's footsteps.

- When I was in grade school, teachers sent students back to the coatroom to sit by themselves for extended periods as a form of discipline. When I was in the coatroom, which was quite often, I would raid my classmates' lunch boxes to see what "goodies" they might have. I took Ho-Ho's, cupcakes, twinkies, chips, or whatever I was hungry for at that time. If I was hungry or bored, I'd act up in class just to get sent to the coatroom.

- We had no cafeteria in our elementary school, but a local vendor provided daily milk for lunch each day at our school. Students ordered and paid a week in advance for those small individual milk cartons. Sometimes the nun in charge made me responsible for collecting milk money from each teacher's classroom's weekly order. On more than one occasion, I'd steal $1 to $2 in quarters from the cash box drawer that I had access to.

- I often padded my weekly school janitor time slip with a few extra hours. I would rationalize that they were only paying me 50 cents an hour. So, by adding a few extra hours, I justified that I was just taking what was rightfully mine…. sound familiar?

- If raiding school lunches wasn't enough to sate my hunger, about three to four times a month, I'd go to the grocery store that was about two hundred yards from my grade school. I'd be hungry and would shoplift items like boiled ham, Swiss cheese, Canadian bacon, candy bars, etc. I'd wear a baggy shirt or coat which made it easy to stuff the stolen items down my pants. Before leaving, I usually bought something little, like a soft drink or candy bar with some of those quarters from the milk money.

- As an altar boy, one of my responsibilities was to collect all the giving baskets at the exits of the church on weekdays. During crowded Sunday services, the deacons would pass baskets up and down each aisle and then count the money after the service. But during the weekday services, there may be only a couple dozen people attending morning mass. Some people left offerings in the baskets located at each exit door as they departed. On those days, it would be an altar boy's responsibility to go around and collect the baskets at each exit. I collected, all right. I'd take a dollar or two for myself. *I justified my actions by telling myself that churches are supposed to help people, <u>and</u> I needed help.*

- Sometimes, I'd return soft-drink or milk bottles at the Food Town grocery store for cash at .02 to .05 cents per bottle, and then lie about how many I returned. There were many times, that I'd walked out of the store with my small, purchased items, with stolen goods down my pants, and still had money in my pockets because of the bottle returns.

Caught Stealing Ham & Swiss

When I was in sixth grade, I got caught stealing Swiss cheese and boiled ham by an undercover officer at the local "Food Town" grocery store. The store manager banned me from being alone in the store without an adult. My mom was called and so were the police. My mom could not come to the store because dad had our only car. So, the police brought me to my house in their police cruiser. As they drove, they advised me that I had better change my ways before I ended up in a juvenile detention center. They wanted to teach me a lesson, so they turned on their sirens and flashing lights as they drove *very slowly* down my street.

I was embarrassed. But mom was absolutely freaking out – she was upset, enraged, and mortified about what the neighborhood would think. Many of the neighbors came out to find out what all the commotion was about. Would the news travel all over Point Place about the perfect Cousino family having issues with the law?

I was a love-starved child that was heading down a very dark path. I was thankful that the police cared enough to embarrass me -- because that experience cured me, and *I stopped stealing from that day forward.*

While my parents were not the best role models, *I knew better and was guilty of being a liar, cheater, and yes, a common thief.*

Chapter 10
Peep Shows

"Twenty years from now you will be more disappointed by the things that you didn't do than by the ones you did do. So, throw off the bowlines, sail away from safe harbor, catch the trade winds in your sails. Explore, Dream, Discover."
-Mark Twain

It had been almost six months since I left Point Place for Miami University. I was the happiest I had ever been up to that point in my life. I was waking up every morning, realizing I'm not afraid today. Yet, I was still flying by the seat of my pants, with no clear solution to pay for next year, other than a possible summer job (which might cover 50% or so of tuition…but then what?).

I returned to my parents' house for Christmas break of 1971, but I rarely spent any time there. Instead, I spent much of my time with some of my high school friends and former teammates. Many of them stayed close to home and attended either University of Toledo or Bowling Green, both less than 30 miles from where I grew up. A few of my high school football buddies tried out for college football at those colleges as walk-ons, but all of them quit within a month. I was the only one from my high school that was still playing at the college level.

I had less than $50 left in my checking account at the local bank at the end of my street, so I decided to close it out. I would open a checking account in Oxford, OH, where Miami University is located, another therapeutic closure from Point Place.

When I walked up to the teller window, I asked to close my account. A teller named Mary called out to the teller next to her.

"Hey, Susie! Look who's here!"

Suzie came over and grinned. *"Oh, hey, Clark!"*

"I think you have the wrong guy, ma'am," I said. *"My name's Brad. Do I know you?"* I inquired.

The two tellers chuckled. *"Oh, we know who you are…perhaps better than you'd like. We miss you here at First Federal Bank. It's been a long time since we have last seen you, and we decided if we ever saw you again, we'd have a story to tell you. You made our day on many afternoons!"* Suzie laughed. *"Right, Mary?"*

I was confused. None of what they were saying made any sense. I thought about it for a moment, then it dawned on me. I was struck speechless and immediately overcome with embarrassment. I could feel my face turning red. *"You mean…?"*

"Yup," Mary giggled. *"The changing room that you fashioned behind our bank's bushes. We were distracted at the teller window many days."*

"But trust us, it was a welcome distraction." Suzie gleefully confirmed. *"I'm pretty sure that whenever our drawers didn't balance, we would always blame you. We called you Superman. 'Hey, Clark! You're supposed to change in a phone booth!'"* The tellers giggled.

"What was that all about? Why were you changing in the bushes instead of at home?"

"It's a long, sad story, but those days are over." I said. But I continued to share...

"When I lived at our house down the street, my mother had some obsessive-compulsive behaviors, one of which was laundry. She could not tolerate clothes left in the clothes chute…ever. Nor was I allowed to hang up my clothes in our only bedroom closet after I wore them. Instead, I had to leave them folded up at the end of my bed. She only allowed me to change my outfit for school on the days when she did the laundry. This meant I would have to wear the same clothes to school for two to three days at a time. As I was getting older, some of the richer kids in my class

would tease or mock me for wearing the same clothes two days or more in a row.

Like most kids, I hated to be mocked or ridiculed. Soon, I figured out a "work around" so I would not be made fun of. Fortunately, I had my own money from odd jobs to buy most of my clothes. I then would sneak some clothes into my bookbag, so I could change my shirts and sweaters each day. I just had to come up with a place where I could change my clothes after I left home.

I eventually started to use the large evergreen bushes surrounding the bank parking lot across the street from the St John's grade school as the best place to change and where I could hide my clothes. On those days I was forced to wear the same clothes, I changed into fresh shirts or sweaters (leaving my clothes in a plastic bag hidden in the bushes), and then switched back to my dirty clothes after school on the way back to the house".

Until that encounter with the bank tellers, I had thought it was a completely private affair. I couldn't see inside the bank windows, and it just didn't occur to my young mind that the teller windows were directly facing the bushes where I had changed. Little did I know I was giving the tellers a mini peepshow every time I used their bushes as a changing room…for years.

In fact, it now occurred to me that I used the bank building full length windows as my mirror to see how I looked after I changed! Each afternoon when I would make my exchange in the bushes, the tellers must have been waiting for me to show up, laughing, I'm sure, while I was posing directly at them, looking at my reflection. Oh, the embarrassment I felt right then!

I closed my account and said my goodbyes. *"We're sad to see you go, Clark! We'll miss you!"* Mary called out as I was leaving. And with that, I walked out of the bank with a smile all the way home, thinking something humorous came out of all that pain & misery.

Grease Ball

Mom's laundry obsessions were not the only problem; she was hopelessly stuck in the '50s when it came to hairstyles. Butch Wax was popular in the 1950's but faded in popularity in favor of the longer hairstyles of the 60's and 70's. Every morning, mom forced me to use Butch Wax with my longer hairstyle, which just made me look like a grease-ball. Butch Wax was supposed to be for short haircuts, not for these new, longer hairstyles that all my peers wore.

Every morning from the doorway to the bank bushes, I was a fashion disaster. After the bushes, I was just a grease-ball until I arrived at school early enough to sneak down to the janitor's closet and wash the greasy wax out of my hair with a bar of soap and water. Then, I dried my hair with the janitor's brown paper towels. There! All better, I fit in now!

On the way home, I'd reverse the process. I stopped at the bank parking lot bushes, and changed back into my 'used' clothes, applied some butch wax I kept in my backpack and greased my hair back, and walked home in shame, hoping no one would see me. Little did I know, I had an audience every afternoon that I changed my clothes in those large evergreen shrubs.

My home life was so broken that I was forced to change clothes in the bank bushes so I wouldn't be mocked. Sadly, I was forced to "deal" with these crazy issues for years.

Chapter 11
Year-Round Cycle

"Football is like life, it requires perseverance, self-denial, hard work, sacrifice, dedication & respect for authority."   - Vince Lombardi

When I returned to Miami after Christmas break, I'd be entering a new phase of my college football experience. I had no concept of what was on the horizon or the intensity it would bring. From my high school experiences, I thought of football as a fall sport. From the spectators' perspective, it is a fall sport. But for college-level players, football is a 10+ month sport consisting of four phases that correspond with the seasons of the year.

Winter Conditioning / Strength Building

The first phase of the four-phase cycle is winter conditioning and strength building (January - April). Winter conditioning was required by all players to compete during phase two: Spring football (April – mid-May).

The first session of winter conditioning and strength building was very intense. For us freshmen players who had never experienced this level of training before, you could say we were going through a bit of college football culture shock. During the first week of winter training and conditioning, we were greeted with five to seven training stations depending on the day's focus.

The training stations were designed by the coaches, and each station was managed by two assistant coaches with help from their assigned graduate students or team managers. The stations were designed for agility drills, speed drills, climbing drills, strength-building drills, etc. There were also hand-to-hand combat drills that required padded floors and walls due to the intense competition between teammates.

These drills would take place in the large varsity wrestling room The graduate assistants or team managers assigned to each coach were tracking every player, detailing every aspect of each player's performance including his attitude and competitive spirit. Strategically, they had an objective to take the players to the very edge. This is what they were hired for. Throughout the training sessions, the graduate assistants roared: *"don't you quit!" ... "you give me your best!" ... "keep going!" .... "don't you dare give up on me now!" They were pounding on floors ... blowing their whistles ... and taking notes of our individual efforts. Even in the winter phase of football, players were fighting for their chance to be a contender for the first team.*

There were groups of giant offensive and defensive linemen who squared off for competition. Hand-to-hand combat-type drills were always an important aspect within these groups. As a middle guard, I was in the group of defensive and offensive linemen the biggest players on the team; however, I was by far the smallest guy in the group. I wrestled in high school, and I excelled in these types of drills by combining my wrestling maneuvers, resolve, quickness, and agility.

Even though I was successful in these drills, I hoped Coach Mallory was not watching my group. Standing next to these big guys, against whom I was competing for the first-team middle guard, would accentuate my small stature. I hoped my results or stats alone would speak for themselves.

The Survival Drill

One of the coaches' favorite drills was a type of one-on-one tug of war between two players. This occurred in the padded wrestling room with a big box filled with pre-cut four-foot sections of thick rope and/or commercial grade garden hose. The coaches called out two players, intentionally matched against each other to test their strength and endurance. The goal was to try to rip the rope or hose out of the other players' hands.

There was only one rule: don't ever give up or coast in this drill-you must SURVIVE. In other words, there were no rules other than NO choking your teammates. I learned that rule only applied IF the coaches were watching; otherwise, it was survival of the fittest!

The purpose was to be quick, aggressive, and resilient – to never give up, and of course, to rip the rope or hose out of the opposing player's grip. Often a player would find himself in a death grip, hanging on for dear life for 30, 45, or even 60 seconds depending on the coaches' desired drill or how long either side could hold on. When the whistle finally blew ending that round, a new group of giants (offense and defense linemen) took the floor, while the exhausted ones tried to catch their breath.

It was a very intense drill for the players participating in it, and disconcerting for those watching and waiting for their turn. Imagine the testosterone level flowing in that wrestling room, with coaches yelling, whistles blowing, and eight pairs of giant men grunting and groaning, trying to rip the ropes or hoses out of the grasps of their opponents.

The winter conditioning sessions started up the week we returned from Christmas break and lasted until Spring break. For Miami's football players, winters were especially *long, cold, and hard*!

Summer Conditioning / Remote Testing

The final phase of the year-round football cycle is summer conditioning and strength building (late May - mid-July). During the summer, coaches had set times to meet groups of players off-campus for conditioning drills to ensure players maintained their strength and agility for the upcoming fall football season. Players needed to show up for fall football season in good shape because it would be too late to try to get an out-of-shape athlete into playing shape and to go through the necessary drills required to play his position.

Spring Football

Spring ball was the Holy Grail for the coaching staff; it is the foundation upon which the next Fall's Varsity team will be built. The whole concept of Spring Ball was another first for us freshmen players. Once the new team was established, the coaches took time to look for strengths and weaknesses in each. Coaches use the strength of the roster to develop the next season's strategy plays, and experiments with these plays are made during the spring scrimmage games.

Spring is the season of rebirth; and the rebirth of the college football roster resulting in a new starting lineup. Every team will lose players due to graduation, injury, or those players who quit during the off-season. Each spring there will be empty spots on the team that need to be filled. Adjustments must be made, and coaches evaluate players to see who has improved, and who is the strongest candidate to fill each hole left by graduating Seniors.

Chapter 12
Spring Ball – Make or Break !

"It ain't about how hard you hit. It's about how hard you can get hit and keep moving forward… how much you can take and keep moving forward. That's how winning is done!"

— **Rocky Balboa**

Division I Spring football started immediately after we returned from Spring Break. For perspective, Doug Krause, was the 1st Team All-MAC middle guard and a major contributor to the Miami Redskin's defense. But Krause was no longer eligible. He graduated, and his departure left an opening for the middle guard position. I viewed it as an opportunity as did at least five other players.

As a freshmen middle guard, I looked up to Krause, even though we did not have any communication. After all, he was a Senior All-MAC First Team player, and I was a lowly walk-on freshman. Being a First Team All-MAC player was a huge achievement for Doug or for any player for that matter. Doug Krause's name now took its place in the Mid-American Conference history book among the best players of the entire MAC conference. Those were some big shoes to fill. I soon learned that I was competing against at least five other players who were bigger, stronger, and older, which meant they had more years of experience than me. Competing to take Doug's place was going to be a monumental task, but I was ready for the challenge.

My last meeting with Coach Mallory was still fresh in my mind. I started to doubt myself. I looked around at the taller, bigger competitors, and felt a brief twinge of envy at their size. However, once I strapped on my helmet and lined up in the middle guard position, I realized I had two choices: I either equated their bigger size to making them slow and clumsy, or I could psych myself out and feel inferior to them just because of their size, and/or doubt myself because of my earlier meeting with Coach. I chose to view my size disadvantage as being a big advantage by viewing myself as quick and agile and them as big and clumsy. It was all a mind game, and it was my choice to pick one or the other.

Since I started spring football listed as #6 Middle Guard (MG) on the defensive depth chart; that translated into minimal practice time for me when it came to getting playing time on the 7-on-7 drills or 1v1 team drills. They usually had the first, second, and third team middle guards on the depth chart get the bulk of playing time during practices and scrimmages.

It was frustrating to have to sit on the sidelines and watch my competition, (the five players higher on the depth chart) get prime playing time against the projected first or second team offensive lines. At the beginning of Spring Ball, I was listed as # 6 on the defensive depth chart for the Middle Guard position. This meant the defensive coaches believed there were five other players who were better suited to the middle guard position than me.

I was reminded of what Coach Mallory had said, that I was just too small for the defensive scheme. The team trainers were specifically tracking my weight, trying to get me to bulk up. I had gained about 7 lbs. of muscle mass but still weighed in at less than 200lbs and was officially measured at 5'11 ¼" tall. There were three Juniors and two Sophomores ahead of me. Each of those guys were older, more experienced, bigger, taller, stronger, weighing at least 30 lbs. more than me.   Even so, when I did get some "reps" in individual drills and team drills, I excelled.

Coaches *love* spring football practice. Coaching philosophies regarding Spring Ball have evolved over the years, and coaches are more protective of their top players and rarely play them during live drills during these months. But in the 1970's, they were not as concerned with players getting hurt. If they did, the coaches theorized the players had several months before the beginning of Fall Ball to heal. Because of these old philosophies, the injured list on the depth chart threw me a bone.

Within a few weeks, I had moved up from #6 to #3 on the depth chart. This was based on my own performance, not because players were on the injured list. I was finally getting more playing time with the better competition on the team. About halfway through the spring season, we held our second live scrimmage. The two middle guards ahead of me got dinged up enough that the trainers pulled them both out for the duration of the game. That moved me up to first team for the remainder of that live scrimmage.

This was another opportunity for me to show what I could do -- and I took advantage of it on the first set of downs as the #1 middle guard for the balance of the scrimmage. This was what I was waiting for... my chance to prove that I was the best choice for the coaching staff. I was already mentally in beast mode.

Below was my first series as the #1 MG.

- *1st down and 10 yards to go for the offense. I broke through the right gap and sacked the quarterback for a loss of 7 yards.*

- *2nd down and 17: I was double-teamed by the center and the left guard, but I was able to split the double team and tackled the tailback for a 2-yard loss.*

- *3rd down and 19: On third down, they ran a counter play, and I flowed down the line and tacked the fullback for a one-yard loss. *****

In my first three plays I made all three tackles. I was playing for my future life. I had this one chance, and I did not know if I would get another. I was on fire for the balance of the scrimmage; I dominated no matter who they put in front of me as the center or the guards on the offensive line. I needed to show my defensive line coach, Ron Corradini, the defensive coordinator, Coach Dick Crum, and most importantly the head coach, Bill Mallory, that I was their best option despite my diminutive stature.

At the end of that scrimmage, my stats spoke for themselves.

I knew that the coaches always pay close attention to the stats, and I hoped they viewed them as more important than my size, because, in the end, all that matters in football is *on-the-field performance*. I led the defense with the most tackles, most assists, and most QB sacks than all the other middle guards that played in the scrimmage – combined!

Red & White Spring Game

The NCAA rules stated that collegiate Division I teams were only allowed twenty days of practice with full contact. On those days we had live drills for short yardage, goal-line and 7-on-7 passing drills and full team drills. Usually, Division I collegiate teams will have three scrimmages over those 20 days of live contact and then end in the final event – the Spring Game! This is the final live game that unveils the anticipated first offensive and defensive teams to their fan base. This is when the rabid fans, local spectators, and even some of the student body could come and see the anticipated new fall team play for the first time.

Typically, the coaching staff splits up. Half of them were the coaches of the Red team, while the other half coach the White team. The head coach was usually sitting in the press box, talking to each team's coaches. The assistant coaches and players are pumped up. It's a big deal! This is the final football event prior to the end of the quarter and represents the first look at next fall's team.

Each coaching staff wanted their team to win as do the players – Red vs White. Normally #1 offense played against #2 defense on the Red team, #1 defense played against #2 offense for the White Team, and so on. But there was a special twist at the very end of the Red and White game ... a fifth quarter that pitted the #1 defense vs the #1 offense... in game-like conditions. It was rare for the #1 defense and #1 offense to "go live" against each other as the coaches don't want to get their starters injured.

But at the end of Red & White spring exhibition game there was a 20 to 30-minute window where it was full go (except you're never allowed to hit the QBs who wore different colored jerseys). The objective for the #1 defense is to stop the #1 offense from scoring – and the objective for the #1 offense was to score on the #1 defense. It was intense; the coaches and players from each team were psyched up. This is where the adrenaline would really be flowing -- long term bragging rights between coaches, teammates, and friends were on-the-line!

Due to some players being injured, I played most of the Red & White game as the #1 middle guard --and my "stats" dominated the game. I led the entire team with tackles, assists, and QB sacks. On the Monday after the Spring game, I received a phone call on the shared wall-mounted phone in my dorm room at 149 Hepburn Hall.

"Is Brad Cousino there?"

"Speaking."

"Brad, this is Lynn, Coach Mallory's secretary. He would like to see you in his office this afternoon; can you come down after your Zoology class is over?"

My knees went weak.

"Okay, I'll be there."

I hung up. It had been quite a while since Coach Mallory called me to see him, and the last meeting was not good news. Did my performance in the Red & White scrimmage stand out enough for him to notice? I'm sure the entire staff had seen the game film and my stats. I didn't want to think about it and get my hopes up, only to be let down. So, I went to my class and then headed to Coach Mallory's office at Millett Hall. I was always nervous when I was called to meet with Coach Mallory. I hesitated before I entered the football offices. Finally, I entered in and knocked on his office door.

"Coach? You wanted to see me?"

"Cousino..." Coach Mallory boomed, "Come on in."

I stood in front of his desk, not knowing what to do or say next.

"Have a seat." he said. "Hey Dick!" he summoned on the intercom, "Can you come in here? Cousino is here!"

Coach Dick Crum, the defensive coordinator entered the room. Coach Crum was the leader of the defense coaching staff and was also the assistant head coach… Coach Mallory's #1 man.

"Hey Brad, how are you doing?"

"Hey, Coach Crum. I'm doing well, thanks."

"Good to hear."

I hadn't sat in this chair across from Coach Mallory in almost five months, and I was hoping for better news than what that meeting revealed.

"Cousino, you're giving our offensive line all kinds of trouble, but the defensive coaches are smiling ear to ear." Coach Mallory said.

Coach Crum interjected.

"We're very pleased with your performance on the practice field and at the live scrimmages; you decimated the centers and guards in Saturday's Red & White game."

Coach Mallory continued. "I've never coached a middle guard as quick as you are. That makes me happy. I've also never coached any defensive lineman as small as you are. That makes me quite uncomfortable, but I can't argue with your stats. You're making me rethink the way we play football."

"With respect, sir, that's my intent."

"Well," he continued, "We gave you quite a challenge, and the way you have played has proved your worth to us. You've moved up from #6 to #2 on the depth chart; now, based on last Saturday's game you are now #1 on our depth chart. That's quite impressive. To make our defense line even stronger, we've decided to move Bill Driscoll from middle guard to right defensive tackle, which makes you the #1 middle guard. You understand that as our first team middle guard, you will be the smallest defensive lineman in the entire MAC, right? And you most likely will be the smallest in all of Division I football. I don't know if that bothers you at all, but it sure makes me nervous."

I stared blankly. I didn't know how to respond because he was giving me a lot of mixed signals.

Ultimate Dream Comes True

"The bottom line is performance, and you have earned yourself that #1 position on the defensive depth chart. And in addition, you've earned a full scholarship, which is what we're here to talk about."

"What do you mean, Coach?"

"We, meaning the entire defensive coaching staff and myself, have decided that you are deserving of a full ride football scholarship. As it stands today, this is a minimum of three years, with the possibility of a fourth year if you get "red-shirted" due to being injured and placed on injured reserve. Congratulations."

I wanted to leap across the desk and give him a big fat kiss, but I maintained my composure, hard though it was.

"I have no words, Coach…thank you."

I stood up and shook his hand as Coach Crum patted me on the shoulder. I turned around, shook his hand, and thanked him as well.

"Congrats Cousino," Coach Crum said. "You've given me a lot of work to do over the summer figuring out how to best redesign our defensive scheme to utilize your speed, agility, and resilience to our advantage. Next fall we play the University of South Carolina Gamecocks. Their offensive line averages over 270 lbs. per man with an average height of 6'5". How do you think you're going to be able to handle being double teamed? That's 540 pounds coming head-to-head against your 200 lbs."

Whoever was going to be Miami's Middle Guard (MG) had to be so dominating that the opposing team was forced to double team the MG. By double-teaming the MG, that means no one is blocking the inside linebacker (LB), which frees him up to make most of the tackles; or if they tried to block the MG one on one with either the Center or a Guard, then the MG was expected to make the tackle. It was drilled into all the MGs' heads repeatedly, especially mine, by coach Mallory.

"You just keep being the quickest guy out there, butt-rolling out of those double teams. Just remember, we expect you to make a big pile when double teamed, so Monos is freed up to make the tackle". (Mike Monos was our junior superstar inside linebacker) "It's a team sport – if everyone does their job responsibilities properly – we will win most of the time." Coach Crum advised. "Do your job and expect each member of our defense to do their jobs on every down. And Brad, you must stay off the injured list," he said with concern.

Coach Mallory interjected, a serious look on his face.

"That's right, Dick. Though your performance says otherwise, Cousino, I am still very uncomfortable about your size and height."

"Coach Mallory, you've made that very clear, and I might be smaller than what you're used to, but that doesn't bother me. I'm not trying to be cocky, but I will do my best to ease your mind so you can sleep at night. I plan on being one of the best you've ever coached. I believe we are going to be a great team over the next few seasons, and I intend to be a significant part of the reason why!"

"Good," Coach Mallory said. "We don't want to see you on that 'injured' list. My secretary, Lynn, will be getting in contact with you regarding the details of your scholarship. You will receive the signed scholarship offer and some other paperwork from the AD office (Athletic Director) over the summer. Dick Shrider, the AD, will explain more about that in his letter of acceptance to you. Once again, congratulations."

"Hey Brad," Coach Crum grinned, "Looks like your days of sewer spelunking are over."

"I'd do it all over again if I had to, Coach."

Coach Mallory chuckled. "Your heart's in the right place, Cousino. In fact, it's never been questioned. But I wouldn't be giving Coach Crum any ideas."

They both laughed. And I just smiled.

My time cleaning out the putrid sewers would become a beneficial memory. I felt that it was an important life experience that would pay huge dividends over my life.

I left Coach Mallory's office, pleased and content that I was able to play Miami football as more than just a placeholder. I now had the financial means to be the first college graduate in my family and play a game I absolutely loved. My scholarship information explaining the offer came in the mail a few weeks later. I showed mom, dad, and my grandpa. They were quite proud of me.

I'm sure Coach Mallory and Crum would never know what that day meant to me. It was one of the greatest moments of my life, and the first time I felt like I belonged to something that really mattered -- a family of sorts.

It was a major "game changer" in my life!

Chapter 13
The Golden Years

"Successful people do what unsuccessful people are not willing to do. Don't wish it were easier; wish you were better."   **-Jim Rohn**

As it turns out, I played at Miami at just the right time... for Miami Football the 1973 & 1974 teams went down in history as *The Golden Years*... the greatest two-year span of football success since football began at Miami in the late 1880's. In addition, the 1974 team (my senior year) has been recognized as Miami's G.O.A.T (Greatest of All Time) for Miami football and for the MAC – (Mid-American Conference). Our number one nationally ranked defense was like a well-oiled machine of which I was the integral component as the middle guard.

In 1972 and 1973, my middle guard position coach was none other than our Head Coach - Bill Mallory for 20-minutes each day. It was rare that the head coach would also be a position coach, but coach Mallory wanted to make sure that the middle guard in Miami's defensive scheme understood just how critical it was to be the difference-maker for the Miami's defensive scheme to dominate the opposing offense. Coach Mallory insured this by being the middle guard coach directly for that one key drill every day.

There was never any doubt of what my responsibility was. And by him coaching me every practice it was drilled into my psyche over and over. He ingrained into all of us middle guards that we were the "tip of the spear" of our defensive unit. I bought into his philosophy hook, line, & sinker. I practiced with the ultimate purpose to be that unstoppable force that Coach Mallory was looking for.

Being the unstoppable force coach Mallory expected, brought back memories to the times I spent hundreds of hours reading superhero books when mom sent me to the basement or garage for hours. Those books helped me create my own imaginary superpowers, which I used to make extraordinary plays to win games for whatever grade school and high school team I was on growing up. As odd as it sounds, I thought that perhaps I could call on those imaginary superpowers from my childhood to help me now. To me, what I called "Beast Mode" was like my personal superpower. It was like an adrenaline surge of rage.

As I looked at my history of playing football, I played angry -- angry at the world, at my parents, my childhood, and that rage became laser-focused onto the center and guards on the offensive team I was competing against. I focused my pent-up anger to make those much-needed game-winning plays - and somehow, someway it often worked!

Power Five Conferences

Not all conferences are created equal. At the time, the top conferences in the country were the Big Ten, Big Twelve, Atlantic Coast Conference (ACC), Pacific 12 (PAC 12), and the Southeastern Conference (SEC). The teams from these conferences get the most national sports media coverage, which equates to big money. College football schedules are made seven to ten years in advance.

We were fortunate that our schedule was packed with bigger and more powerful teams from the top conferences in the country. These included the Big 10 - Purdue Boilermakers ('73-'74), the SEC - South Carolina Gamecocks ('72 -'73), and the University of Kentucky Wildcats ('74), the University of Florida Gators (Tangerine Bowl '73), and the University of Georgia Bulldogs (Tangerine Bowl '74). These teams were all members of the elite conferences in the country. These conferences consisted of the most powerful teams in the country. It was rare to receive a national ranking outside of these conferences, even if the team was undefeated.

Teams like Miami were underdogs in many ways. As a member of the MAC conference, Miami didn't have the years of experience playing against the top echelon teams. The top conferences had larger stadiums, higher ticket sales, and national sports media contracts, all of which equaled more revenue to continue building their football programs. It was customary for the elite team's athletic departments to schedule two to three teams from weaker conferences such as the MAC so they could have a few easy wins. In addition, these were lucrative games for the bigger host teams because they kept 75% to 80% percent of the gate revenue (instead of splitting the gate revenue 50/50 which is the norm when playing bigger name schools in the same conference). The home team always keeps 100% of the concession profits.

Schools in conferences like the MAC might get a $250,000 to $300,000 guarantee plus the team's travel expenses. So, it really was a win/win financial transaction for both the home team as well as for the less known teams such as Miami from weaker conferences.

However, playing Miami was always a double-edge sword for the bigger name schools, and many teams did not want to play a team like Miami on their schedule. Why? Because we had a proven record of upsetting many of those teams. The stronger teams wanted a competitive game, but they expected to win 98% of the time. Miami wanted the exposure, a shot at being ranked nationally if we won, and ultimately a larger payday of a guaranteed amount.

A Defensive Lineman in the Headlines?

People who have read the sports page or watched sports newscasters during a live, televised game likely know that the spotlight is usually on the winning and losing quarterbacks, their respective coaches, and sometimes a running back or wide receiver who was a star that game. It is rare for a defensive player to be in the spotlight, especially a defensive lineman. If a defensive player gets some coverage, it's usually a linebacker or defensive back because those positions are designed to make big plays or intercept passes.

It is extremely rare, almost unheard of, for a middle guard on the defensive line to ever be featured in the news or see his name in the headlines of a paper. Yet I was being covered, interviewed, and featured in sports segments almost every week. Before each game, the opposing coaches and quarterbacks told interviewers their strategies to stop me.

After the game, these same players and coaches were interviewed and discussed how those strategies failed. I was growing the reputation that Coach Mallory wanted...the difference-maker who made the big plays at key times during a game and ultimately over a season.

I had saved quite a few mementos from my college football days, including some newspaper articles, but only if it was a local paper in Oxford, or maybe out of Cincinnati or Dayton. We didn't have the luxury of the Internet back then. I had no way of knowing what was being written about me or Miami in other papers around the country...unless someone in that area sent back an article. Mitch Neu, my co-author, was doing research and it was suggested that he do a 'search' of Brad Cousino on Newspapers.com just to see what he could find.

To my astonishment, when he pulled up "Brad Cousino Miami University" for 1972-1974, I was mentioned over 1,750 times! I was blown away. I had no idea! I started reading about some of the many big games against these top teams in the country. Is it egotistical to say that I enjoyed reading about what was written about me? I say this with a chuckle, but what football player wouldn't enjoy reading stories about himself as the big hero of the game 40+ years ago? We clipped some of the headlines and articles to share their quotes here. (See Appendix #6 Photo Gallery)

David Fuselier, a sports reporter for the Cincinnati Enquirer, wrote in an article titled *"Cousino Just Tries Harder"* on October 11, 1974:

"Coaches have emerged from games with Miami to spend the first few minutes of the post-game interview talking about 'that little kid at Nose Guard'."

These coaches were being interviewed about their defeats. I was the one they wanted to talk about as the reason for their loss in the interviews! I had earned my scholarship, all right.

South Carolina – 1972 & 1973

We played South Carolina on October 21, 1972, during my sophomore year. We were on South Carolina's home field in front of 44,000 fans. This was their Homecoming. It's never a good sign when you're the visiting team, scheduled during the other team's Homecoming. It was common for schools to schedule their Homecoming game against what they view as their easiest game of the season…the one game they knew they could be triumphant for the largest home crowd of generous alumni for the year.

Coach Mallory was quoted in the Journal News before the game, saying, *"This is a prestige game for us",* meaning if Miami wins this, it would be against a much higher-ranked team from one of the best conferences in the country. This would give us a lot of national recognition.

Just as predicted by the local press, Miami was in trouble in the first minutes of the game. We fumbled the ball in our own territory, which was recovered by South Carolina. Fortunately, our defense held them for three plays, forcing them to settle for a field goal from the 19-yard line. Right at that moment, I knew what I had to do…it was time to pull out that imaginary superpower and go into Beast Mode. *At the snap of the ball, I shot through the left guard-center "A" gap and blocked that field goal kick in the first quarter. That was a huge play that changed the momentum in our favor.*

Despite Coach Crum's concerns, I did more than just handle being double-teamed with 540 lbs. crashing down on me. *By the end of the game, I was credited with twenty (20) solo tackles and three (3) QB sacks, plus the blocked field goal.*

As a sophomore, *I was chosen by the Associated Press as the Defensive Player of the Week. I* couldn't believe it! In my first year on the varsity team, at 5'11" 198 lbs., I dominated against the bigger, stronger, older (juniors & seniors) competition. I was discovering how to be a *difference-maker.* I consistently had the "knack" of making big plays, ultimately leading to the underdog Miami of Ohio winning that game against the South Carolina Gamecocks, 21-8…a huge upset!

I made believers out of Coaches Mallory and Crum. From that game on, they knew I could hold my own against the biggest and best offensive linemen as they fine-tuned their defensive scheme to best use my skill-set and competitive nature. This made our defensive team that much better.

In 1973 (my junior year) we played South Carolina again. They were embarrassed and 'ticked off' about their loss to Miami the year before, and they were determined not to let it happen again. It was a real battle, but Miami won this game as well, 13-11.

Paul Dietzel, Head Coach for South Carolina, (also a Miami graduate) was quoted in the Cincinnati Enquirer, calling my performance *"The greatest individual effort I've ever seen. I don't know how he does it."*

He was also quoted in the Telegraph Forum on Oct. 3, 1973, as saying, *"I never saw one player dominate a game the way Cousino did."* According to South Carolina's statistician, *I had seventeen (17) solo tackles and nine (9) assists while being double-teamed most of the time.*

Purdue Boilermakers – 1973

September 22, 1973: A week before the '73 South Carolina game, Miami played against Purdue, a Big-10 team. This time, we were playing to a crowd of 54,000 fans; a record audience for the MAC, and ninety-seven percent were Purdue fans. With less than nine minutes left in the fourth quarter, Miami was behind 19 -10. Miami needed a miracle to happen to score twice. It was fourth down, Purdue had the ball, and they were about to punt. I knew we needed a big play, and I saw myself back in the garage, reading those superhero books about The Hulk, visualizing going into Beast Mode again. My childhood voice came back to me. OK, Couz Beast Mode time!

The micro-second the ball was snapped, I bolted through the left center-guard "A" gap. Time seemed to stand still. I had tunnel vision; all I focused on was blocking the punted football. Nothing else mattered. The punter never got to kick the ball, because I managed to get to him and plow him over before his foot could even make contact.

"Mike Terrizzi was flattened on a punt attempt - before he could get the kick away. Terrizzi still had the ball in his hands when Brad Cousino got there - almost before the ball." The Journal and Courier (Lafayette, IN), 9/24/1973

I had built a reputation for being "lightning-quick" which helped me to sack quarterbacks, block punts and field goals, and make tackles for losses. In the Orlando Sentinel, on Dec 22, 1973, there was an article written about me and that blocked punt that became famous. The article titled *"Cousino Once 'Too Small' For Redskins"*.

"As a starter in 1972 [as a sophomore], Cousino uses unusual quickness and agility to block three extra points in the Toledo game, another in the Bowling Green contest, a field goal against South Carolina, and one punt in another outing. But the blocked punt that he'll be telling his grandchildren about was against Purdue this past September 22, at West Lafayette, Ind., before nearly 54,000 predominantly anti-Miami fans."

Trailing 19-10 with eight minutes left, Cousino darted through the left guard / center gap and hit the punter just before he kicked it." Cousino is quoted:

"After blocking the punt, the ball bounced around. I was able to pick it up and start running toward the end zone. I was hit from behind, but I strained and stumbled about twelve more yards downfield closer to a touchdown, finally getting tackled on Purdue's 34-yard line."

"It was nothing spectacular,' Cousino modestly said of the spectacular play." Jim Warters, Orlando Sentinel; 12/22/73

But deep inside, my childhood voice was screaming in my head, I did it! That was awesome! I am not a bum, I was not worthless, my life means something!

Now it was our turn to score. Miami drove down the field toward the goal line. Our quarterback, Sherman Smith, faked the ball to our fullback, Chuck Varner, who then ran a route into the end zone where Smith threw him a touchdown pass. The gap was closed, 19-17. We trailed by two points and needed at least three to win.

We held the Boilermakers like a brick wall for two plays. Time for Beast Mode I thought. On third down, their QB rolled out for a play-action pass when I hit him just as he was about to release the ball, causing him to fumble. After a mad scramble, I was at the bottom of the pile with the football tucked securely in my arms. It was Miami's ball again, and I had caused the 2nd turnover of the fourth quarter giving us the second miracle we needed to score again to win the game! Chuck Varner finished off the drive with a three-yard dive off the right tackle and into the end zone. Miami beat Big-10 Purdue 24-19! Another upset win for Miami!

Were we better than Purdue? Absolutely - After three quarters, Purdue was ahead by two scores. That's tough to make up for any team in the final quarter, especially on the road as the visiting team. I knew what we had to do to help us win.

In my mind, it was *my job to make the game winning plays* when they counted the most. For this game, I had to do it twice, within a matter of a few minutes… Beast Mode! *But to be candid, I didn't think it was all that special; that was my expectation. I believed I was just doing my job as the middle guard for our team.*

I wished I could go back to the garage all those years ago, to my younger self reading those hundreds of books and superhero comics and encourage him; *"Everything is going to be okay, Brad. One day you will be viewed as a superhero by a lot of people".*

The next week, Purdue handily beat Notre Dame, who was ranked # 2 in the nation at the time they played.

Florida Gators - Tangerine Bowl 1973

December 22, 1973: Miami won the 1973 MAC conference championship by beating Kent State. Our team was undefeated for the first time since 1955; we earned a spot in the Tangerine Bowl, now called the Citrus Bowl. All Bowl games are typically played in neutral territory, and Miami was designated the home team for the game. But this year, the game was moved from Orlando to the Florida Gators' home stadium in Gainesville.

The Tangerine Bowl stadium in Orlando was under construction being expanded and would not be done in time for the 1973 bowl game. As a result, the Tangerine Bowl committee invited the University of Florida Gators to play in and host the 1973 Tangerine Bowl. Florida accepted, which guaranteed the bowl game would generate a much larger attendance which translated into big revenue for both teams due to the national TV exposure. As usual, Miami was a big underdog. Florida was coming into this game on a five-game winning streak. Four of those games were against teams from the powerful SEC conference.

In that article in the Orlando Sentinel titled "Cousino Once 'Too Small' For Redskins," I read a quote that stated, *"Cousino is Miami's Middle Guard who played one of the most vital roles in the Redskins' winning the T-Bowl trip."* To the left of that article, in a much larger bold print, I read, "Greek (Jimmy the Greek) Says Gators by Thirteen", meaning we were predicted to lose by thirteen points.

But the cruelest blow came from Florida QB Don Gaffney, who was quoted in his hometown paper. *"If we lose to a team like Miami, we'll be the laughingstock of the whole South, and I will eat this football."* I wondered if Gaffney wanted eggs with that bacon.

Coach Mallory bought three dozen copies of that paper and passed it out to the team. I cut out the photo of Gaffney and taped it to my locker. I'd be lining up directly in front of his center and him for the entire game. I focused on that picture all week because I wanted to see the face of their cocky quarterback.

I was especially motivated to sack him many times. *The real killer blow I wanted to give him was my signature "helping hand" up as I politely picked him up off the ground after each sack. Then I'd remind him that "**I'll see you again-- real soon.**"* This had become one of my trademarks; extending a hand up to help a quarterback or running back up after I tackled him for a loss.

The excitement ran hot on game day, but the Florida weather was unseasonably cold, and the temperature continued to drop during the game. There were 37,000 fans in the stands, and it was estimated that 34,000 were Gator fans and 3,000 were Miami fans. Prior to the first play of the game, I waited in the center of the defensive line for Florida's offensive lineman to break the huddle and get lined up over the football.

As I was waiting for the Florida linemen to get set, Florida's huge offensive guard looked at me and laughed out loud, asking the center in a mocking voice, *"This is who they're making all the fuss about? He's such a PUNY, little man!* That mocking statement just added fuel to my pent-up fury which I unleashed throughout the game. I sacked Gaffney early and often in the game, the first one resulted in an 8-yard loss for Florida. I then gave him a 'helping hand' up off his back…as promised. Our 3,000 Miami fans cheered! This set up a field goal for Miami. More cheers from the 3,000.

It was getting so unseasonably cold that the field announcer started noting the temperature change. Every time the new temperature drop was announced, there were more cheers from the 3,000. We were still wearing our short sleeve jerseys while the Gators were shivering in their parkas across the field. Our defense was dominating the mighty Gators. Throughout the entire first half, Florida entered our territory only one time, and that was to our 48-yard line.

At the end of half time the temperature had dropped to 30 degrees, and we were up 6-0 when Florida made a huge mistake. At the beginning of the third quarter, Miami attempted an on-side kick resulting in a fumble, which our Special Teams recovered in Gator territory. Within a few plays, Miami had scored a touchdown. 13-0. Our defense continued to punish Florida in the second half of the game.

The television announcer, broadcasting to over forty stations into two million homes bellowed, *"Brad Cousino has earned a letter at Florida. He's been in their backfield all night."* I had three more sacks in the second half. Florida was finally on the board going into the fourth quarter. It was now 13-7. The weather dropped another five degrees by the fourth quarter, plummeting to 25 degrees…in Florida. Even though they had the home-field advantage, I think the weather may have given us an edge in the fourth quarter, and we kicked a field goal. Final score: 16-7.

"Gator Tangerine Turned Sour" was the title of the article in the Orlando Sentinel on Christmas Eve 1973. The writer interviewed Coach Doug Dickey and Florida's center, Jimmy Stephens for the article. *"The Gator coach (Doug Dickey) had proved prophetic earlier in the week, predicting the matchup of sophomore center Jimmy Stephens against Miami's cat-quick nose guard, Brad Cousino, might mirror the game's outcome."*

"Stephens felt he did 'a pretty good job' on Cousino, who nonetheless was in on 16 stops (tackles), pressured Buster Morrison into the short punt that set up Miami's first score, sacked the Gator quarterback four times for losses totaling 37 yards and was voted the game's most valuable defensive player." I guess that wasn't one of Stephens' best interviews.

Bill Clark, Sports Editor for the Orlando Sentinel also wrote on the same page, *"… only 3,000 Ohio fans were on the scene this sub-freezing Saturday night as the Miami Redskins scored what will go down as one of the <u>greatest upsets in U.S Bowl history</u>."*

Chuck Varner, our phenomenal fullback, was selected as the offensive MVP, and I was named defensive MVP of the game. Miami finished the 1973 season undefeated; 11-0 and ranked 15th in the country. And Miami's defense was ranked #1 in the country. In my mind's eye, I was one of the key leaders of the #1 best defensive unit in the country; I had earned my "difference maker" reputation.

It was also the last game played under Coach Mallory. Due to our phenomenal 11-0 season, Coach Mallory was in hot demand as the next great head coach. He was pursued by many teams, but ultimately accepted the position of head coach for the University of Colorado Buffaloes of the PAC 12 conference. He took his entire football staff, except Coach Dick Crum, who was named Miami's new head coach. I would miss Coach Mallory and our assistant coaching staff, but that is the way things work. *You move up if you're good, and you'll be moved out if you're not!* I was elated that Dick Crum, our defensive coordinator – was named Miami's head coach for our 1974 season.

Georgia Bulldogs Tangerine Bowl 1974

December 21, 1974: Miami was now undefeated for two years, and once again secured a spot in the 1974 Tangerine bowl. A few days before the game, on December 19, I was invited to dinner by former Florida Gator Middle Guard Joe D'Agostino (1951-54). He said he wanted to "*meet the youngster who helped up-end his alma mater last year by winning Defensive MVP.*" Someone tipped the press off about our dinner, and they showed up at our restaurant. It ended up in the Orlando Sentinel, under the title *"Feared Cousino Can Be Tame".*

I had to laugh when I read that I bore a striking resemblance to the famous Joe Namath of the New York Jets, known as 'Broadway Joe'. *I couldn't believe I was being named in the same sentence as Joe Namath! He was one of my heroes growing up. The article also said that there are stories about me getting ready for the face-off against Georgia in the Tangerine Bowl by "gnawing on T-Bones and gate posts and tangling with some big cats at Central Florida Zoo." In that same article, they asserted that I had "wrestled alligators over at Gator Alley" to prepare for the victory over Florida Gators in the 1973 Tangerine Bowl.*

Joe Namath? Wrestling gators? I couldn't believe it. How could I have ever imagined that one day when I sat in that cold, dark attic would have led to all this success and media attention?

Miami won our 2nd consecutive Tangerine bowl game. We beat the powerful Georgia Bulldogs, a SEC powerhouse, 21 to 10. I was credited with 16 solo tackles, 8 assists and 3 QB sacks. I was selected as co-defensive MVP along with our superb inside LB, John Roudabush, who miraculously came back from what our head trainer Ken Wolfert said was a season-ending knee injury). Our record remained the best in the country - undefeated 23-0-1. We finished the 1974 season as the #10 team in the country, the highest end of season ranking ever for any Miami team; AND the highest final ranking for any M.A.C. team – ever!

I often wondered what I would be doing now in life? Where would I be living? What kind of work would I be doing? Did I attend college? How could I have ever known that the catalyst of my football success stemmed from one split-second decision to spend a few hours handwriting letters literally begging for a football scholarship?

I had everything to gain...

and nothing to lose...

but a life of misery!

Chapter 14
The 'One'

"A person who truly loves you will never let you go no matter how hard the situation is."
--Anonymous

While I loved all the media praise, pats on the back from the coaches, and cheers from the fans, I can remember wishing I had someone who really cared about me to share these moments. My whole life, I had been devoid of the love and compassion I so desperately craved. Calling home at night would be fruitless; dad would be drunk or absent, and mom would be violently angry because he was drunk or absent. So, my conversations with her would be solely about how horrible and neglectful he was.

Many nights I tossed and turned endlessly. Often, I lay awake at night wondering why I wasn't fulfilled or happy or content, even though I was away from my miserable existence with my parents. This had been happening a lot – why now? Considering I was away from my parents, I thought I had everything I could ever want. But why was I so lonely?

It was the fall of my sophomore year, about midway through the season, after one of our home games. I left the locker room and started walking back to my dorm: *when I saw THE one! The most beautiful young woman I had ever seen walked through the door. She was tiny, petite, and professional model gorgeous.* My jaw almost hit the floor. She was wearing a Shakerette uniform, which indicated she was a dancer with the marching band during halftime. A few days later, I found out she was a member of a popular Miami sorority: Pi Beta Phi. A sorority girl to boot! I have got to meet her!

Over the next few weeks, I went out of my way to catch a glimpse of her whenever the defense was on the sidelines. In my room, I'd often rehearse how I would introduce myself to her, ask her name, she'd act shy, etc. I played this scene over and over in my head.

But, as it turned out, I used up all my courage on the field, leaving none for this mystery girl who stole my heart. I didn't know anything about her: not her age, where she lived, what year she was in school, what she was studying...not even her first name. I had to do something to get her attention. But, like any kid who experiences love at first sight, I was afraid of being rejected. What was wrong with me? How could I be so aggressive on the field, but weak and helpless when it came to asking a pretty girl out on a date? I had a growing positive reputation on campus, so I figured my name alone would make a positive first impression with her. I was wrong once again!

Rejected in front of 25,000 Fans

It was the final game of the 1972 season – the weekend before Thanksgiving break. Our long-standing rivalry with the University of Cincinnati Bearcats had reached a fever pitch. This year's game was an away game at University of Cincinnati. The distance between the Miami and UC campuses was a little more than an hour drive time on our game buses. If we lost, it would be a much longer drive home.

Personally, I was having a great game. Our defense dominated the Bearcats. When I came off the field, I had this thought - maybe *she* would come to our end-of-season party!

During the season, Coach Mallory had a team rule: no one on the football team was allowed uptown in any establishment that sold alcohol. So, after the last game of the season, a big party had been pre-planned.

I scanned the sidelines for her. Sure enough, there she was, warming up with the other Shakerettes, getting ready for their halftime show. I couldn't just leave our sideline and go over and start a conversation with her. That was not an option. I had to get back onto the field and focus on the game. I know! I'll see if I can get one of our student managers to pass on a message to this lovely shakerette!

I sought out one of our best football student managers – Terry Martin-- and asked him to do me a big favor – could he ask the beautiful blond Shakerette (I didn't even know her name) that I pointed out to him, if she'd like to go to the big season-ending party this evening after the game with Brad Cousino. "Oh, yeah, and can you also find out her name?" I said as I put my helmet on and ran back into the game. Two minutes later, it was halftime, and our entire team went into the visitor's locker room.

When halftime was over, I got back to the bench and Terry Martin, the manager, came over to me. "Well, what did she say?" I asked as I was anxious for her response. I really hoped he did follow through and speak to the young lady -- and give me a positive response.

Terry responded with a little chuckle. He explained that he asked her what I told him to,

"Would you like to go with Brad Cousino to the big end-of-season party later this evening?" Her response, to my shock and surprise:

"I don't know who this Brad Cousino is. Which team does he play on?"

The manager then shared.

"I explained to her, *"He's one of our young star football players"*, and she said, *"OK, that's great to know, but I can't say yes to someone I've never even met. Sorry."*

"Couz, you've been blown off. Looks like you're going to have to work for this one. Oh, almost forgot... I did catch her first name – one of her friends called her Tami."

I was crushed. This sweet, lovely lady, in her own naivete, had rejected me. I hated to be rejected. Considering that she had no idea who I was, she must have been clueless about anything related to Miami football. Based on that response, we did not meet up that night; but the season-ending party was a good consolation prize!

What was I going to do? Give up trying? Not me! If I'm motivated - I'm not one to give up easily. Two months later, in February 1973, I was behind the scenes setting up a blind date with this same Shakerette; the mystery girl, miss Tami. One of her sorority sisters (Cheryl McFarland) was dating my teammate, Bobby Williams, our outstanding All MAC senior linebacker. So, Cheryl and I arranged to set up a *blind date* with miss Tami.

That is how I officially met Tami Netzly. It was a blind date for her, but thanks to her sorority sister, I knew exactly who I was going out with. As I would come to learn, Tami was a junior ten months older than me. She was from the small town of Orrville, OH (corporate headquarters of Smucker's Jelly). She was somewhat shy, but very confident in who she was as a person. I was nothing short of mesmerized by her beauty and her sweet personality. Our first date was a success-- which led to more dates.

Let the Mind Games Begin

As we continued dating (though not exclusively), she played "hard-to-get" mind games with me. I found out one of her favorites was getting her roommates to tell me she was out on a date; while she was sitting in the room listening. This happened many times. As a classic example, I'd call her dorm room, and one of her two roommates would answer the call.

"Hello?"

"Hi, Debbie, it's Brad!"

"Oh, hey, Brad! You looking for Tami?"

"Ssssshhh! Tell him I'm not here!" Tami whispered urgently.

"Ummmm -- hang on for a minute, Brad, let me see if I can find out where she is." She turned to Tami with her hand over the phone. *"What are you doing? I thought you liked him?"* she whispered.

"I do," Tami grinned, *"but I'm doing what my mom told me to do - playing 'hard to get'. Tell him I'm on a date."*

"Clever girl!" The three roommates giggled softly. Debbie took her hand off the phone and answered.

"Hey, Brad! I asked around and found out that Tami is on a date with one of the Betas. Sorry."

"Oh, she is? Okay, no problem. I'll see you around."

This happened more than a few times, and it drove me crazy. She was indeed a clever girl. I found out months later that she was putting into practice what her wise mom, Betty Netzly, told her to do when she was dating someone she liked; "play hard to get!"

Tami was masterful at this! She acted as if she wasn't all that impressed with me – who I was or my growing reputation as being an up-and-coming future star player on Miami's football team. I couldn't figure her out; she was totally different than any other girl I had ever dated. *While I couldn't understand why, it made me want to win her heart even more.*

I always treated the ladies I dated extra special. But I went out of my way to do even more for Tami. I was the perfect gentleman, holding the car door open for her, and always walking her to the front door of her MacCracken Hall dorm after bringing her home from our dates and never, ever allowing her to pay for any of her food or drinks on our dates -- despite my very limited funds.

Clash of Two Realities

In the summer of 1973, Tami asked me to come and meet her family. I felt like I was moving up on Tami's *depth-chart* of dates. While I was thrilled to meet her family and see where she came from, I was also aware that I might have to reciprocate, which in my mind was never going to happen. Nonetheless, I agreed, and when I journeyed to her house in Orrville, I was met with something I never thought I'd see.

I met a happy, loving family, like something out of the popular "Leave it to Beaver" 1960's sit-com TV show... except Tami's family was even better– they were the real deal. Tami's parents, Howard & Betty Netzly, were the perfect parents: Tami loved being around them and her siblings. I sensed that everyone loved and respected each other by the way they dined together, laughed together, and teased each other.

Tami's parents made a big deal of Orrville being the home of Smucker's Jelly because several members of the Smucker's family graduated from Miami. I couldn't help but compare this family, and their respect for one another, to the squeaky-clean reputation of Smucker's Jelly. Like Smucker's reputation, they oozed pure sweetness.

Every night I was there, we spent time around an outdoor fire, and hand-cranked homemade ice cream as I listened to them regale me with heartwarming funny stories of past vacations, school trips, camping, etc. This was a foreign culture that I had never experienced, nor did I think even existed. I felt like I was visiting a fantasy kingdom, or that they were from an alien planet, or that I was in the perfect dream from which I didn't want to wake.

To me, those nights were magical. I'm glad it was dark outside, because several times during their storytelling, filled with love and joy for one another, I was moved to tears. I didn't think they'd understand these tears, nor could I explain them. These people had touched my heart in a way that I never would have imagined.

After witnessing their relationship and how they all interacted with each other, I just knew that what Tami experienced growing up was the absolute opposite of how I was raised. Without knowing how to do it, I was determined to have that kind of relationship be my reality for my future family. Right then, regardless of who I'd eventually marry, I knew I was going to try my best to raise my family like Tami's parents raised theirs. (*Deep in my heart, I hoped it might be Tami... but it was way too soon in our relationship to be thinking those kind of thoughts*)

The reality was, at that point in my life, I wasn't ready to tell Tami anything about my family. *How do I bring up the subject of my alcoholic dad, my rage-a-holic mom, the lower-middle-class status we lived in, the verbal and physical abuse I endured since I was a young child? What if she ran the other way?*

I couldn't put into words that my football life wasn't about football at all. It was my escape from my traumatic life to go to college and make something of myself. In fact, to me, football was both everything...and nothing.

On the last night of the best few days, I'd ever experienced, we were sitting outside near the fire. Tami was resting her head on my shoulder. Everything was perfect...until she asked the question I prayed would never come.

"When can we go to your home so I can meet your parents?"

I had just been roused from my perfect dream.

****

Jocks And Frat Boys

As Tami asked that dreaded question, my mind flashed back to a few months earlier, before I officially met Tami, and to the circumstances that contributed to it. Even though I was a division I football player who enjoyed a growing, positive reputation on campus, I did not want to be one-dimensional. So, in January of my sophomore year (1973), I checked out the "Greek" fraternity system that Miami offered. I knew next to nothing about "fraternity" life. I'd investigate the fraternity scene during the annual "winter" fraternity rush. My primary reason was that it would open a new group of friends that were not involved in college sports.

I asked around to find some of the more popular fraternities on campus, and I found that the *Betas, Sigma Chi, Phi Delta Theta, Sigma Nu, SAE's, FIGI's, etc.* were all recognized as "good" fraternities. As an athlete on a football scholarship, I knew I'd not be allowed to live off campus in the fraternity house... as my scholarship funding was only good to live in the dorm and to eat in the dorm cafeteria. But I could still become a "social member" and not live or eat at the fraternity house – but could attend their social functions which I thought might be a good place to start.

I visited those six fraternities in the winter rush period. I did hear the horror stories about the long-time tradition of "hell week" in nearly all the fraternities. This *"hell week"* was an intense initiation period of sorts into the fraternity brotherhood. Based on what I heard from first-hand witnesses, it caused me to rethink joining a fraternity. I had enough torture growing up from my parents and then again on the scout team practicing against the giants. I couldn't fathom why a group of fraternity guys would want to abuse me (or anyone) physically, emotionally, or verbally in order to join their fraternity. *Based on my dysfunctional background, that would be a deal-breaker for me. If hazing and hell week was standard operating procedure for fraternities, then I would pass on the whole idea of joining a fraternity.*

Phi Kappa Psi

Not long after I mentally opted out of becoming a member of a fraternity, I learned of a new fraternity that started up on Miami's campus a year earlier in 1972... Phi Kappa Psi or "the Phi Psi's". Based on what I was told, they had a different mind-set. I learned that one of the younger guys instrumental in getting a Phi Psi chapter on Miami's campus, was a former fellow "walk-on" on our freshmen football team last season. Paul Apyan was also a "walk-on" that played on the offensive scout team as a running back during our freshmen season. He eventually quit the football team (as over 95% of "walk-ons' usually do), but we shared a similar bond as teammates and fellow non-scholarship walk-ons.

I made contact with Paul, and we met at the Boars Head Bar in the quaint college town of Oxford for lunch. There I was able to ask a bunch of questions regarding the Phi Psi chapter -- and the ways the Phi Psi's were significantly different compared to the rest of Miami's fraternity system. After our meeting, Paul arranged for some of those men instrumental in the startup of the new Phi Psi chapter to make a time where we could all meet. What I really appreciated, was there seemed to be a sincere interest in me as a person... not because I was rising star player on the Miami football team.

I was even more intrigued as I listened to each guy give their reason why they chose to go with a startup Phi Psi chapter verses the other more secure fraternity options available to them. I liked what I heard, and it was refreshingly different compared to my interaction with the 6 fraternities I visited a few weeks earlier. Besides Paul, I had the chance to spend quality time with many of the guys that were now the active leaders of Miami's Phi Psi chapter. Many of these young men had an impact on my life at a critical time – good, sharp young men such as Larry Larson, Carl Bennett, Bill Zimmer, Mike Elliot, Nick Miller, and Mike Waller, to name a few.

While I really liked the guys I met, what impacted me far more, was what separated the Phi Psi's from the other fraternities I visited. These young leaders had a vision to build-up the character of the young men that wanted to join the Phi Psi's, in order that they would become better versions of themselves! Even more impressive, the local chapter leaders made a bold decision at the time; they would not conduct a hell week for the new recruits, nor would they revert to any "hazing" of their new pledges. Instead, they came up with a fresh, innovative approach to the fraternity initiation called "**help week**" -- instead of the traditional "**hell week**" concept.

The entire Phi Psi house, plus the new 'pledges', got involved and provided resources, manual labor, work projects, transportation, etc., to 'help' those who needed it throughout the Miami campus...even to the "townies" who lived near the Oxford area, but were not students of Miami. What I witnessed inspired me to want to join these young men in their endeavor. I resonated with everything I learned about Phi Kappa Psi. When I decided to join the Phi Psi fraternity, Larry "Lars" Larson was my sponsor and "senior brother", and we became good friends.

To be candid, I was not and could not be involved in most of the many events and projects that the Phi Psi fraternity undertook. As a Division I college player on a full football scholarship, I had limited time for anything other than my classes, studying, and football. I had mandatory early morning lifting, classes to attend, study sessions, team meetings reviewing film before practice, two-and-a-half hour daily practices, team meetings after practice, review of practice session film, training table, required study time in the evening, etc., In Division I football, there is very little free time!

Even though I could not spend much time at the Phi Psi house because of my football obligations, I did bond well with most of the guys, especially Larson, Zimmer, Apyan, Bennet, Johnson, and Miller.

Secret Revealed

Do you remember the blind date I arranged with the pretty Shakerette, Tami? Fact was, I was trying to decide if joining the Phi Psi fraternity made sense considering available funds were always an issue. Paul and Larry invited me and my date to the next Phi Psi fraternity party, to take a trial run, even though I had not joined yet. Tami, being a sorority lady with the popular Pi Phi sorority, attended many fraternity/sorority beer blasts and theme parties. If she agreed to go with me, she would be perfect to provide feedback at what she thought of the Phi Psi's. Tami would know a lot more about on-campus *Greek life* and what the sororities thought of the reputation of this new fraternity than I ever would.

As a result, I took Tami on our 'blind date' to the new Phi Psi fraternity house in mid-February 1973. Tami fit in well and knew several of the ladies that were dates of the Phi Psi members. For a first date, we got along great. Tami gave a positive review of what she noticed and the overall feel of the Phi Psi men and the fraternity. She liked the guys she met. Tami thought it would be a good fit for me to join the Phi Psi fraternity – even if it could only be as a "social" member.

Here is another secret revealed! *Later that same night of our initial blind date, at the Phi Psi fraternity house, in Larry Larson's apartment, playing a serious game of "spin the bottle" with five other couples, Tami and I had our very first kiss. It was like a dream...the best dream I ever had*!

In March 1973, just before Spring break, I joined the Phi Psi fraternity.

Chapter 15
All-American / MVP

"It is not the critic who counts; not the man who points out how the strong man stumbles, or where the doer of deeds could have done them better. The credit belongs to the man who is actually in the arena, whose face is marred by dust and sweat and blood; who strives valiantly; who errs, who comes short again and again, because there is no effort without error and shortcoming; but who does actually strive to do the deeds; who knows great enthusiasms, the great devotions; who spends himself in a worthy cause; who at the best knows in the end the triumph of high achievement, and who at the worst, if he fails, at least fails while daring greatly, so that his place shall never be with those cold and timid souls who neither know victory nor defeat. — **Theodore Roosevelt**

During my junior and senior years at Miami, (1973 and 1974 football seasons) we had the longest winning streak in the country for Division I football, at 23-0-1. Of the seven games we played against the highest-ranked conferences in the country, our record was 6-0-1. While our undefeated streak was a big deal, our seven victories against Power Five conference teams put us in the spotlight. They helped us earn respect from the NCAA and fans alike.

- Miami finished #15 and our defensive unit finished #1 in the country for major Division I colleges in 1973, my junior year. That included beating Purdue Boilermakers, South Carolina Gamecocks, Cincinnati Bearcats, and the Florida Gators.

- Miami finished #10 in the country and our defensive unit finished #3 in the country in 1974, my senior year... that included playing Purdue Boilermakers, Cincinnati Bearcats, Kentucky Wildcats, and Georgia Bulldogs. By the end of my senior season, we had four more Power

Five victories, plus we tied Purdue 7 – 7 a Big 10 team and a grudge match for Purdue. Miami remained undefeated.

For the first time in the history of Miami football (since 1888), Miami finished in the top 10 teams in the nation. That kind of national ranking is unheard of for a school the size of Miami playing in the MAC. **This #10 ranking was, and continues to be, the highest final ranking of any Miami team... <u>ever!</u> It was also the highest final ranking of any Mid-American Conference (MAC) team...<u>ever!</u>**

And of all my honors and awards bestowed on me, being chosen as the MVP of our 1974 team (voted on by my teammates and coaches) is the one award I'm most honored and humbled by; to be selected by my coaches and teammates as the team's MVP on Miami's G.O.A.T. – (Greatest of All Time) team – the best Miami team ever is an amazing feat and one I cherish!

I often think about how different my life up to this point could have been. I had so many "what ifs" spinning around in my head, which were left to the hands of fate. What if I didn't play with all these talented players as my teammates? After all, we were undefeated and won our conference both years as a team. What if I didn't play for some of the best coaches in the nation? Both Mallory and Crum were named the "Coaches of the Year" by the MAC in 1973 and 1974.

These weren't the only "what if's I thought about. *What if I never wrote those letters to the 25 coaches begging for a scholarship... or was unwilling to work in those sewers... or I didn't jump in to take Kong's place despite being undersized... or what if I never maneuvered behind the scenes to set up that blind date with the cute Shakerette... Miss Tami?* One thing I knew for sure, If I had not made the effort to change my future, much of my life would be dramatically different.

1st Team All-MAC... Defensive MVP... All-American

At the end of every football season, each head coach of the MAC conference teams voted for first and second-team players of each position, meaning the top two players in each position in the entire conference. They then voted on the two MAC Most Valuable Players (MVP) of the year: 1) the best offensive player, 2) the best defensive player. They also voted on the MAC head coach of the year, which was won by Coach Mallory in 1973 and Coach Crum in 1974.

In 1973, my junior year, I was the unanimous selection for 1st team middle guard and was also awarded the *1973 MAC defensive MVP of the year as a junior, unseating the returning 1972 defensive MVP, the great Jack Lambert from Kent State. (Fyi: Jack Lambert played middle linebacker with the Pittsburgh Steelers and was voted into NFL's prestigious Hall of Fame)* In 1974, my senior year, I was again unanimously selected first team middle guard and was honored as the 1974 MAC defensive MVP of the year for the second year in a row. I also played with some of the best collegiate players in the country. I was surrounded by great teammates. (See Appendix #3A and #3B)

While I made first or second team All-American on many of the organizations, there was something unique about one of the committee's selections. Even though middle guard was the only position I played throughout my college years, *I made the 1974 Coaches All-American FIRST team as an outside linebacker.* I never played a single down as a linebacker! The committee stated that my defensive stats were so strong, yet they couldn't justify honoring me as their first-team All-American middle guard due to my lack of size for the position.

Stats that Matter!

I'm listing the following stats and awards received only to provide context against the overwhelming odds of what I was able to accomplish as a former *non-scholarship walk-on* who benefited from great coaching and playing on the G.O.A.T football team composed of my outstanding elite teammates.

Here is a listing of my stats in my junior year ('73). Miami was undefeated 11-0 finished #15 in the country and our defense was #1 in the nation:

As the middle guard on Miami's #1 defense, I...

- had 39 Tackles for Losses (TFLs = QB Sacks). If a defensive player had twelve to fifteen TFL's over 10+ games, it would translate into all-American recognition.

- led all defensive linemen in the country for most solo and assisted tackles at 205... an average of 20.5 tackles per game.

- led all defensive linemen in the country for most blocked punts and field goals.

- was selected as the Defensive MVP vs. the Florida Gators in the '73 Tangerine Bowl.

- was selected a unanimous first team selection as Middle Guard for the MAC as a junior

- was selected as the defensive MVP (Most Valuable Player) of the MAC 1973 as a junior

- was selected to many major All-AMERICA teams.

******

Here is a listing of my stats in my senior year ('74). Miami was again undefeated **11-0-1 - finished #10** in the national poles for the country and our **defense was #3 in** the nation. As the middle guard on Miami's defense, I...

- had 23 TFL's or QB sacks, despite being double-teamed over 50% of the time

- led all defensive linemen in the country for most solo and assisted tackles at 195, or an average of 19.5 tackles per game despite being double teamed over 50% of the time

- led all defensive linemen in the country for most blocked punts, field goals, and/or extra points.

- was again selected as the Defensive MVP vs. Georgia Bulldogs in the '74 Tangerine Bowl.

- was a unanimous selection first team as Middle Guard for the MAC as a senior

- was again selected as the 1974 defensive MVP (Most Valuable Player) of the M.A.C. as a senior

- was voted the MVP of the 1974 Miami Football team; the all-time best team in Miami history as well as the **best final ranking (#10) of any M.A.C. team ever.**

- was selected to nearly every major All-America team.

The Game of the Ages vs 1974 Kentucky Wildcats

I've been told by many sportswriters, coaches, and players that the best game I played at Miami was against the University of Kentucky, where I faced their great returning All-American center, Rick Nuzum. The Kentucky Wildcats plays in the powerful SEC. There were a lot of stories in the Lexington newspapers talking about the big match-up. They didn't give me much of a chance, considering that Nuzum was 6'4" and weighed in above 240 lbs.

The game was a night game, a beautiful warm fall evening with a full moon. The stands were packed with Kentucky fans. The date was October 5th, 1974. No SEC team expects to be beaten by a MAC team...ever. Miami was jacked up because it would be another prestige game against a higher-ranked conference team. Kentucky was just as pumped because they were on a mission to break the nation's longest unbeaten winning streak at 17-0. At the time, Miami was ranked in the top fifteen teams in the country by the Associated Press.

The game started off fast, as Kentucky scored twice within the first seven minutes. On their first score, our offense fumbled, and they were able to score quickly with a field goal -- 3-0 - Kentucky.

Our #1 ranked defense was struggling with the speed and agility of their backfield, especially their excellent quarterback Mike Fanuzzi. He gave a great fake to the tailback and then ran outside our defensive end for 30 yards... He ran that same play three times and scored a touchdown with about eight minutes remaining in the first quarter. Kentucky 10; Miami 0.

As a key leader of the defensive unit, I gathered everyone in the huddle.

"Defense, huddle!" I roared. *"It's only the first quarter, and I can see the frustration in your eyes. Now is not the time to panic at the score, guys. We've been behind before, and we just need to play our game, and we'll come out on top. They think they've already got this game in the bag. Now's the time to take it to them - no more cheap yards - we are better than that!"*

Kentucky, known for their quick, powerhouse offense, was the best team we would face until the 1974 Tangerine Bowl. I was in a battle with the best center I had faced in the last three years. He wasn't dominating me, nor I him. Without question, our defense had to stop Fanuzzi and their running game – we had to break their momentum. We came out after half-time with a revised game-plan. Our defense needed to take pressure off our offense by making one or more big plays. *We needed a difference-maker to make a game-changing turnover. I was acutely aware that if we hoped to win, I needed to step up and be that difference-maker.*

It was fourth and long on Kentucky's 22-yard line. Kentucky needed to punt, and I knew what I had to do, it was "beast mode" time. I lined up over the long-snap center, who would be snapping the ball to the punter. I faked going to my left 'A' gap just before the snap of the ball, and then used my agility to quickly slip through my right-side 'A' gap between the center and left guard. The center took the bait and neither he nor the guard touched me as I raced to the punter.

Knowing that the fullback, the last line of defense, would be assigned to block the first defensive player up the middle I catapulted over him and was able to block the kick just as the ball came off the punter's foot. The ball hit my upper left arm and shoulder pad with such force the sportswriters said you could hear the "thud" throughout the stadium as the ball traveled about twelve yards backward all the way into Kentucky's end zone. This caused a mad scramble to recover the loose ball by both the offensive and defensive teams. There was a big pile. Our defensive end and my former roommate, Brad Miller, was at the bottom of the pile where he recovered the blocked punt in the end zone. TOUCHDOWN, MIAMI! Amazingly, *our first score of the game was made by our defensive line!*

10-7, Kentucky.

The momentum changed dramatically - our entire team was revitalized. In the blink of an eye, we were only down by three points. *Each of us knew we were in a battle, but it was a battle that we could win!*

During the rest of the third quarter, it was a defensive struggle for both teams, but our defense was superb against their talented offense. In the fourth quarter, Fanuzzi continued to make big plays. He was quick and used play-action fakes better than anyone we had played against. Late in the quarter, I sacked Fanuzzi; that resulted in a fumble, which I was able to recover.

Miami's ball on Kentucky's 40-yard line. On third and six, our offense came through with another first down. On the next third down, (third and goal) Miami scored! 14-10, Miami was now ahead. It was a team effort, and I was able to come through with two big turnovers that resulted in our two touchdowns.

How Legends are Made

There were several key plays in that game that are still talked about after 45 years. Two of those plays were the blocked punt I made for a TD and the QB sack and fumble recovery I made that led to the second TD. But there was a series of plays that have been deemed legendary in Miami football lore.

There were approximately eight minutes to go in the game. Our offense continued to have problems with Kentucky's defense, which meant that our defense was out on the field for long periods – with little time to rest on the sidelines. Fanuzzi was on a drive where he was able to get three first downs in a row. Our defense was exhausted! I was exhausted! I whispered to myself – *"OK, Couz – it's Beast Mode time!"* Our defense could not have a breakdown. The ball was on our 48-yard line. It was third down, and Fanuzzi needed five yards to make a first down or be forced to punt on fourth down. Fanuzzi faked to the fullback to the right side of the line and ran off the right tackle. He made the first down, broke a tackle, then veered back to his left and sprinted down the far-left sideline; the sideline near his own Kentucky team bench, which was going nuts.

I was initially blocked by their great center -- Nuzum, but instinctively, I began to sprint in pursuit of Fanuzzi.; who was far faster and had a serious head start. I repeated my mantra in my mind - *Beast Mode* - as I sprinted in pursuit. Under normal conditions, as a defensive lineman, I would never be in pursuit 40+ yards downfield. But for some reason, on this one play, I ran like a possessed maniac to try and protect Miami's 4-point lead.

Fanuzzi couldn't see me, as I was well behind and running at an angle, and he was outrunning our defensive backs. I adjusted my pursuit angle and kept sprinting, thinking that if he wasn't tackled by my teammates, maybe I could intercept him before he got to the end zone. My pursuit angle was right on target. I dove at Fanuzzi and hit him from the side with a touchdown-saving tackle as he landed out of bounds at our 5-yard line. I had chased down a faster man 40 yards downfield. It was a huge Beast-Mode play.

But now, it was first and goal on the 5-yard line. Our 17-game winning streak was in jeopardy. I was heaving to catch my breath from that 45-yard sprint. Our goal line defense huddled up. Many of us in the huddle had been playing together for two or three years. We had not lost a game over two years... and currently had the longest winning streak in the country.

The Goal Line Stand of the Ages

We came together in the huddle holding hands. We knew what we had to do. I reminded those men in the huddle... '_We each had to do our specific job with excellence and trust that each player will do his particular job._' We had become a "band of brothers" that weathered many battles to have the longest undefeated streak in all of Division I College Football. It all came down to Miami's defense stopping a bigger, stronger, more experienced offensive team from gaining just five (5) yards in four (4) downs... it came down to an epic "do or die" showdown!

First and goal on our 5-yard line.

On the first play, they ran their fullback right at me, seeing that I was gasping for air. I used my agility to burrow underneath the double-team block of the center and guard and made the tackle along with our captain and inside linebacker Chuck Varner; Kentucky gained one yard.

Second and goal from the 4-yard line

They ran a fake into the right side of the line, and Fanuzzi tried the same QB option play that he used multiple times in the game. I was triple-teamed. But our defensive tackle (Jim Feucht), linebacker (Chuck Varner), and defensive end (Jay Fry) stopped him for a one-yard gain

Third and goal from the 3-yard line.

Fanuzzi faked to the fullback up the middle, and then sprinted to his right, looking to pass to his tight end for the TD - but the pass was defended by our Free Safety, John McVay... incomplete. A field goal would not help Kentucky because they were down by four points. Kentucky needed a touchdown. So, they had no choice but to go for the touchdown. _In the huddle, we encouraged each other and again re-committed that each of us was going to do our job... to the best of our abilities we would complete our individual assignments. If we each did our specific responsibilities, we would stop them._

Every Kentucky fan was on their feet screaming as loud as possible for their Wildcat team. But as Kentucky broke their huddle,

Fanuzzi quieted the crowd, by waving his arms slowly up and down... and the crowd hushed to a whisper.

Fourth and goal from the 3-yard line.

Both teams knew that either a win or a loss was on the line. Each team was very determined to win. Fanuzzi came to the line and barked out the signals hoping to draw the defensive line off-sides. Not able to do so, he called "hike" and faked to the fullback off left tackle, and then sprinted in a bootleg out to his right. He had the option to either throw the ball or run it in if there was an opening. Fanuzzi couldn't find an open receiver. Our defensive backs covered their receivers like ants on honey. He had only one viable option: run for the goal line.

At the snap of the ball, I had penetrated my left 'A' gap and was trailing Fanuzzi down the line of scrimmage. Once Fanuzzi knew he had no one to throw to, he had to find a seam and cut up the field toward the goal line. I saw him cut up the field and I accelerated and hit him hard as I wrapped him up just below the waist to keep him from leaping into the end zone. A micro-second later, our defensive tackle Jeff Kelly and defensive end Jay Fry joined in and together gang-tackled Fanuzzi and all four of us came crashing down on the three-yard line... no gain.

Our # three rated defense held an SEC team to only two yards when they needed five yards for a game-winning touchdown. Miami's defense had held! Miami's offense was coming onto the field. It was indeed a HUGE goal-line stand. From Miami's perspective, this was '*the goal-line stand of the ages.*

Miami ball first down on our 3-yard line. This was not the time to celebrate - there were still about five minutes remaining. A lot can happen in five minutes when the opposing team has all three of their timeouts available. Our offense took over on our 3-yard line... 97 yards to a TD. But we didn't need a touchdown, what we needed was for our offense to move the ball down the field away from our end zone while running down the clock by running the ball and getting a few precious first downs.

But our offense never gave them that chance. They were able to control the ball down the field for the remaining five minutes. *Sherman Smith, Rob Carpenter, Randy Walker, and the entire offensive line were masterful.* They continued to run the ball and make first downs. They burned up valuable time on the clock, and Kentucky was forced to use all three of their timeouts. Kentucky could not stop the clock.

Our offensive unit, who struggled in the first half against Kentucky's defense, started at our own 3-yard line and drove the length of the field ... 94 yards to Kentucky's 3-yard line... With no timeouts remaining, the clock counts down....5... 4... 3... 2... 1...zero.

Our sideline bench and our fans were going nuts. - MIAMI WINS! Our 17-game unbeaten streak is still intact. After the game, reporters crowded around each of the head coaches in their perspective locker rooms.

The Lexington Herald-Leader and the Cincinnati Enquirer reported on the Kentucky - Miami University game the next morning and stated the following:

"Kentucky coach Fran Curci and Miami of Ohio coach Dick Crum were in complete agreement: *Cousino was the difference*".

And then quoted coach Curci: *"Here's my assessment of the game,* Curci said. *"That Cousino kid. I don't think I've ever seen a more competitive kid. That was a tremendous display of courage."*

Chapter 16
Family Secrets Revealed

Being deeply loved by someone gives you strength while loving someone deeply gives you courage.

-- Lao Tzu

Despite spending only a few nights in Point Place since I enrolled at Miami, the tiny bungalow house at 2934 123rd Street still loomed over me like a haunted house out of a gothic horror novel. I dreaded this day like no other, but a part of me knew it had to come eventually.

Tami's query about going to see my family had been a hard one to answer. I couldn't outright refuse, but I also didn't want to give Tami too much of my past that I prefer to forget. *Her family life and mine were about as different as night and day. Would she understand?* Still, it was one of those things that had to be done to allow our relationship to grow.

Tami, a grade ahead of me, graduated from Miami in May 1974. That summer, I secured a job with a construction company in the Toledo area but chose to live with some of my high school buddies who were students at Bowling Green University, about 25 miles away. I invited Tami to visit me in Bowling Green on the weekend that I knew mom, dad, and my siblings were away on a week-long camping trip to Traverse City on Lake Michigan. With my family out of town, it was a perfect opportunity for an impromptu (but secretly planned) day trip for us to Point Place in my family's absence. I planned to show her around my house, and then take a quick tour of Point Place, and then stop in to surprise my maternal grandparents. We would then eat lunch out on the pier of a popular local seafood restaurant, do some laundry, and then head back to Bowling Green. I figured we'd be there less than six hours. My plan was for Tami and me to spend as little time as possible in my childhood house.

We left Bowling Green around 11:00 am and drove to Point Place about 30 miles away. As we exited off the I-75 freeway, the last exit in Ohio before entering the State of Michigan, we passed the sign that read "Welcome to Point Place". Tami smiled. *"So, this is where you grew up, huh, Brad?"*

"Yeah", I grumbled, barely paying attention. I was deep in thought about how to answer any questions she might have about why my parents weren't there.

As we turned down my parent's street - 123rd street, we passed the bank where I changed my clothes all those years. Tami perked up as she looked at the identical tiny houses we passed. "The neighborhood looks nice. I love the cute little cottages." she said. (They were actually small two-bedroom bungalows) I knew she was searching for something nice to say to avoid offending me.

"Come on, let me show you around,"

We got out of the car and walked around to the back door of the house. I tried to hide it, but I felt repulsed. It was like I was returning to the scene of many vicious, horrendous crimes. So much trauma and horror happened here, and I was revisiting some of the worst memories as I entered the backyard and saw the garage that I spent so much time in. Nonetheless, I had to just grin and bear it. I opened the back door and let Tami walk in first.

"Well, this is just about everything. You can see almost every room in the house just from here." I spoke.

"Come on, Brad, just show me around," she smiled.

As we walked through the house, I gave her a guided tour, room by room. Everything was on one floor, the kitchen, living room, the two bedrooms, and our only bathroom. We then went downstairs to the dark unfinished basement with a concrete floor, walls, and exposed ceiling joists. I noticed that mom finally got a clothes dryer for her laundry area. There was also a small utility sink and our makeshift "shower", consisting of a shower head and faucet above a basement drain in the concrete floor, with a plastic shower curtain hanging from nail hooks dad attached to the exposed wooden joists. There was also an old gas furnace (no air conditioning), and an empty back room where dad hung up makeshift clotheslines so mom could hang clothes to dry if the weather outside was raining or too cold. I then took Tami upstairs to the unfinished attic (which was blazing hot) and showed her where I spent many hours writing those 25 letters to the college coaches, begging for a football scholarship.

"Mind if I use the bathroom?" Tami asked. *"I didn't have time to get ready this morning, and if we're going out later, I'd like to freshen up by taking a shower, if that's OK?"*

Here was the other reason why I picked this weekend: My mom had issues related to the bathroom. No one was allowed to use the bathroom sink or bathroom tub/shower except my mom. *We boys could only use the toilet if we **sat down** (no standing to urinate ensured we wouldn't pee on the seat or floor). I bet no one on Miami's entire campus had to deal with a rule like that.* The rest of us (dad and us 3 boys) had to use the make-shift shower in the unfinished basement and brush our teeth in the kitchen sink; we never were allowed to use our bathroom sink. That was the way it had been ever since I could remember. No one dared violate those rules…or else.

As I showed Tami to the bathroom, it felt as though we were about to walk through *"Danger Ahead - BEWARE NO TRESPASSING"* signs. I went to the hallway closet and grabbed her the best towel we had. *"Here"*, as I winked, *"is our one and only guest towel"*. I'm sure she thought I was kidding. I wasn't!

I was having some reservations about allowing Tami to use the bathroom shower. Then I thought, seriously, Tami is not taking a shower in the open basement with concrete walls and floors with one plastic shower curtain hung by nails into the basement rafters... no way!

"Thanks, babe," Tami said, *"I'll be out in about 20 minutes."*

She kissed me on the cheek and walked to the bathroom, leaving me alone. I grabbed my dirty laundry bag from the car and took it to the basement. As I loaded it into the washing machine, I remembered the hundreds of times I was sent down here or out to the garage after my beatings to tend to my wounds in solitary confinement. As these thoughts entered my mind, I felt sick to my stomach. *Geez, I was just a kid.* I walked around to some of my former hiding spots and found a few old mystery books I had stashed down here to read during my punishments. To escape my harsh reality, I would lose myself in these mysteries. Sherlock Holmes, The Hardy Boys, The Boxcar Children…I read them all as a kid.

While Tami was in the bathroom, it hit me. *I'm 21 years old, this is the only house I can remember living in, and I've never taken a shower in our only bathroom.* Then another thought flashed through my mind: *My girlfriend was taking a shower in my own house before I ever did. And what is so sad is that I'm freaking out because I had allowed Tam to use our bathroom sink, tub, and shower. That is so not normal, who thinks like that? What kind of parents would raise their kids this way?*

After Tami got out of the bathroom, she changed into some fresh clothes. Even with her hair still damp, she looked like a beautiful, glowing princess. She really was a very beautiful lady….and still is. I could only grin. I then made a brave and bold decision; I was going to take my first shower in the forbidden bathroom. Why now? I did this for a couple of reasons, but primarily because I thought I could clean the sink/tub/shower combo to mom's perfection when I was in there to make it look like it hadn't been used. You'd think I would somewhat enjoy this act of rebellion, but it caused me some anxiety. I showered as quickly as I could, so I could spend my time getting everything back to the way mom left it.

Despite my concerns, I never let on to Tami about my inner turmoil. She had no idea that I let her cross the threshold and violate the rules of mom's weird obsessions. I took time and effort to wipe down the tub, polish the faucet, clean, and dry the tile walls of the tub/shower combo, the bathroom sink, faucet handles, medicine cabinet mirror, the toilet handle…. even the doorknob and shower head were wiped free of any fingerprints or water spots. I then took the "guest" towels and threw them in the wash with my clothes. I double, triple, and quadruple-checked every aspect of the small bathroom to make sure that everything was where mom left it... precisely where it belonged. I realized covering my tracks had become my obsession.

As Tami watched on, she said, *"I had no idea you were such a neat freak. Your mother taught you right."* She had no idea how wrong she was.

OK Brad, Operation: Spic & Span is complete. I think all is well. I dodged that bullet. Or so I thought.

****

I looked at my watch and saw that it was around 1:15 pm. We hadn't eaten anything yet, so I asked-- "Tam, do you want to go get something to eat?"

"Sure," Tami agreed. "What's good around here? You lead the way."

I said, "I'd like to take you to Weber's Seafood House, an excellent seafood restaurant on the water. I went to grade school with the owner's kids, and the restaurant has some great outdoor seating along the waterfront. It serves excellent seafood, but it's most famous for its awesome Fish 'n' Chips; and is one of the most popular restaurants in the area. Let's eat there and then we'll come back to get the clothes out of the washer and into the dryer when we're done. And I'll take you around to see all the places that I told you about, then we'll head back to Bowling Green."

We went to Weber's and had the best of times as we enjoyed the sights of being on the water. I explained some history of this place, as it sits on the Ottawa River right where it dumps into Lake Erie. *"The Ottawa River froze every winter, and my friends and I played hockey almost every afternoon from early December through late March."*

"Is there any sport you didn't play?" she asked.

"Yes, there is. In fact, I wasn't a synchronized swimmer. I just didn't have the talent for that."

Tami chuckled.

Tami seemed to enjoy watching the speed boats and cabin-cruisers that cruised in and out of the marina, many of them docking right next to where our table was on the pier and having lunch and happy hour drinks. It was a fun, busy place with a great atmosphere. We both ordered the specialty of the house -- their *famous Fish & Chips*, fresh-caught perch, potatoes thinly sliced, seasoned with their secret recipe, and flash-fried in a seasoned deep kettle that resulted in super thin crispy chips served piping hot with their distinctive dipping sauce and their made-from-scratch coleslaw. It was an awesome combination.

"Hey Tami, do you see that sign up there?"

"Yeah, why?"

"Do you see what it says?"

"'Welcome to the Great State of Michigan.'"

"I grew up less than half a mile from the Michigan border."

"Well, I'm glad you're living on this side, otherwise, you'd have gone to a Michigan state school, and we would have never met."

"Yes. Yes, it is." What a lovely thought.

As we ate this late lunch, she kept smiling that wonderful smile of hers. *How did a guy like me end up with a classy, foxy lady like her?* I thought to myself. That might sound corny, but it was a common term we used back in the day. This day couldn't get any better.

Oh, how quickly things can change.

I paid for lunch, and we drove back to the house, where I removed the wet clothes from the washer and popped them into mom's new dryer. I didn't want to spend any more time inside the house, so Tami and I jumped in my car where I acted like a paid tour guide showing her all around Point Place; where I went to kindergarten and then grade school where I was the part-time janitor, the Food Town grocery store (where I stole the ham and cheese), the A&W root beer stand near my grandparents, which was across the street from the Point Place library I spent a lot of time in, and then we drove by my maternal grandparents home (who were not home) and showed her the Dairy Queen, which was directly across from the gas station I worked at on and off while in high school.

Super Cool?

As I pointed to the gas station, I remembered something I did more than ten years earlier that I decided to share with her. "Tam, both my parents smoke cigarettes. In fact, dad smokes up to two packs a day."

"Oh, I'm so glad you didn't pick up that habit!" Tami exclaimed.

"Well, it wasn't for lack of trying," I said.

"What? Really?" Tami asked.

"Yup. When I was about 10-years old, I sometimes hung out at this local gas station. One day, when the manager went to the bathroom, I stole a pack of my parents' favorite cigarettes, Pall Malls. I shoved the pack of cigarettes down my pants. When you're young, seeing other kids smoke, you think it looks cool. Back in the '60s, it was 'cool' to smoke. And I always wanted to be cool."

"You? Cool? You don't need to try to be cool." Tami smiled. "You ooze cool." I squeezed her hand.

"Later that afternoon," I continued, *"I headed home by running down the back alley directly behind our house. I stopped at our next-door neighbor's garbage cans, sat down on the ground, and pulled out the stolen pack of cigarettes. I lit one, smoked it, and did it again... and again. I chain-smoked cigarette after cigarette. I was now officially 'cool'. I quickly learned how to inhale and exhale. I tried to blow those neat 'smoke rings' like my dad. I even held the cigarette between my fingers the way my dad did."*

"Even though I thought I was now very cool, I didn't feel so cool after I smoked about a dozen cigarettes in a row. My head was spinning, and I started coughing, gagging, and choking as I became sicker and sicker. In less than thirty minutes, I became woefully sick and started vomiting repeatedly. I threw up everywhere...into the garbage cans, over my shirt, pants, and shoes. I was a mess. I could hardly walk and ended up dry heaving for the balance of the day... and into the next morning... I was in sheer misery, but I couldn't tell my parents what caused me to become so sick."

"Have you ever smoked any cigarettes since?" Tami asked.

"Nope, not a one. I learned my lesson.

And I've never even been tempted," I said. *"Looking back at how foolish that was, I'm thankful that I learned that lesson. Even when a bunch of 'macho jock' guys get together to play cards or attend frat parties smoking their Cuban cigars, I always declined. I was usually teased, but I didn't care. I had no desire to ever smoke a cigarette (or even try a cigar) ever again."*

I pulled in front of my house just as I finished my stolen cigarette story. Then I saw it.

My parents' car was in the driveway. *Oh, no! What are they doing home a day early?*

I slowly turned to Tami. She had been the last one in the bathroom. I remembered that she was putting her makeup on before we left for the restaurant. *"Tami, I need you to listen to me very carefully. Is everything exactly where it was in the bathroom before you started putting your makeup on? Like, nothing was out of place?"*

"Ummm...yeah, I think so. I did leave my makeup and hairbrush on the bathroom sink. I was going to clean it up when we packed up to leave. Why?"

My stomach flipped. It was too late now. I knew as soon as mom saw that someone had been in the bathroom, she'd go ballistic.

"Tami, I'm in the mood for a hot fudge sundae. How about you? You want to grab a sundae?" I asked her. *"Let's go to the Dairy Queen across from the gas station I worked at."*

Tami nodded. *"Yum! Why don't we split one?"* she said.

"Deal," I agreed.

When we got to the Dairy Queen, we walked up to the counter. "One large hot fudge sundae with two spoons, please," I asked.

"Would you like some crushed nuts on that?" The cashier asked.

"Tami?"

"No nuts for me, thank you," she said. *"But how about whipped cream and two cherries?"*

We received the sundae and we sat at the picnic table with a big red umbrella and started eating our sundae. After a few minutes of awkward silence, I took a deep breath and started the conversation I never wanted to tell her.

"Tami, there is a reason why I brought you here, and why I picked this weekend to bring you to my parents' house."

"Yeah, I've been wondering about that."

"You probably didn't notice this, but I saw my parents' car in the driveway when we came back from our sight-seeing tour of Point Place. I decided to bring you to DQ because I need to explain things to prepare you for what's about to happen when we go back to the house."

"Uh-oh, what's going on? Brad, what haven't you told me?"

What I thought would take fifteen minutes to explain took over an hour, as Tami had questions. I told her everything I went through in that house growing up until I left for college. I started with the reason I was so stressed about keeping the bathroom in the most pristine conditions. Then I told her that today was the first time I had ever taken a shower in our only bathroom in my life. Tami couldn't understand the life I was describing to her. How could she?

"One of mom's oddest habits for me to deal with was her cleaning habits. She took the phrase 'neat freak' to such an extent that it nearly drove us all mad. We were forced to sweep and hand-wash the kitchen and bathroom floors multiple times a day to make sure there wasn't even the smallest speck of dust noticeable. Next, we cleaned the back door area and the steps leading into the basement by hand two to three times per day. We weren't allowed to wear shoes indoors... ever! As crazy as this seems, we weren't allowed to sit on our one couch or chair in our small living room. We always had to sit on the floor. Everything had to be perfectly clean…spotless…as if no one lived there. There was no 'living' there, just 'existing' and washing away every trace of living.

If there was hair or dirt on the floor, or a bar of soap that was an inch out of place, or a cobweb in the corner of the ceiling, you would think that the world was coming to an end. A clean house is never a bad thing, but her incessant need for cleaning was nothing short of an obsession. The amount of cleaning we kids did would go on for hours before we were allowed to go out and play every day. It was pure unfiltered insanity, and it is the only life I had ever known.

Growing up, I never had one single friend come over to my house...ever! Not in grade school or even in high school. I had a fear that mom would lose it and start shouting and hitting me if I ever did have a friend come over, or my dad would come home drunk and a verbal and physical fight would ensue between my parents. I didn't trust that either of them wouldn't drop their filters around my friends if I had the chance to invite them over. I always went over to my friends' homes to have fun and to escape from my parents – 100% of the time."

"I can't imagine growing up in a home that you're describing". Tami said: "I'm so sorry!"

Chapter 17
Cousino Fantasy Exposed

"People who succeed have momentum. The more they succeed, the more they want to succeed and the more they find a way to succeed. Similarly, when someone is failing, the tendency is to get on a downward spiral that can even become a self-fulfilling prophecy."   - Tony Robbins

When mom was with her friends or talking to the neighbors, she'd always paint us as the perfect family. As an example: She could be in the middle of whipping me, the phone would ring and she'd calmly answered it, and then proceed to tell her friend on the other end of the phone, of just how great we kids were, how much we helped around the house, or the game winning touchdown I came through with, etc., and that dad was working two jobs, and she was in the midst of a project to do for the school's PTA; and then proceed to hang up the phone and pick up where she left-off by finishing whipping me.

It was all a sham, our family's deceptive lie. It was our deeply guarded family secret, and my parents would go to great lengths to make sure no one ever found out. Mom was perceived as being a wonderful, loving person. She was very active in the school's PTA and volunteered for many school functions. None of her friends had any idea of what occurred in our home, the verbal and physical abuse was kept top secret. My parents never let anyone know about the general feeling of loathing, shame, disappointment, and resentment they felt towards me from before I was even born, especially how trapped they felt because of their mistake.

"What do you mean by their 'mistake'?" Tami asked.

"Mom got pregnant with me at age fifteen – dad was 16," I said. "They both were forced to drop out of high school and get married, and

mom & dad blamed me for their own miseries. No one had any idea what went on behind closed doors. "This was what I came to call 'The Cousino Fantasy' or 'The Cousino Lie.' Mom wanted our family to be viewed as the perfect family by our neighbors, friends, and relatives; but it was nothing more than a smokescreen. Everyone who knew mom thought we were the upstanding family of the neighborhood on the outside. But when no one was looking, the family dynamic reverted to how it always was for us. To the outside world, she would never say a cross word or show anything other than what she wanted people to see."

There was no hiding it from Tami now, though.

I bared my soul and told her everything that I went through for the past eighteen years. My deepest family secrets had finally been unearthed. Tami hung on every word as her eyes teared up. When I finished, I thought she would walk out right then and there... because I knew that what I had just told her was too much for her to grasp. How could she? She had no frame of reference because of the wonderful parents and family environment that she was raised in.

"That's the kind of situation we're about to walk into. So, be ready. If you don't want to be with me anymore afterward, that's okay." I said. *"I understand. You don't deserve this. No self-respecting woman would want to stay with such a messed-up guy like me."*

Her eyes were as big as saucers, but she didn't say a word.

"Okay. Let's go get our stuff and get back to Bowling Green." She nodded her head in agreement.

Tami was seeing a whole new me. I wasn't about to let my mom berate me or her for something as simple as using the shower. As we parked behind my parents' car, I could hear mom screaming and ranting to dad. Tami inched closer to me as we walked, using me as a shield. I realized at that moment what was important to me. We walked into the backyard, and I braced myself as I opened the back door.

We were immediately met with my *mother's seething red face.*

As soon as she saw Tami, her whole demeanor changed. She forced a smile and was cordial. She had reverted to "perfect mom" mode. It was like she could change her personality at the flip of a switch. My goal was to get my clothes out of the dryer and Tami's belongings from the bathroom. I walked past mom and into the bathroom (with my shoes on) and retrieved Tam's brush and a bag of toiletries. *"Tami, please go out and wait in the car. Let me get my clothes from the dryer and talk to mom and dad for a bit. I'll be out in a few minutes and then we'll be leaving to head back to Bowling Green."*

The spell had been broken. I was no longer under my parents' control – and they knew it. I paid my own bills, including college tuition, and I was recognized as one of the top football players in the country. They saw me being the football "hero" on campus and read dozens of articles about me, their 'bastard' son. I knew that I had a bright future ahead. In the past, I took whatever punishment that mom could throw at me as a kid. But I was no longer a kid... I was a young man. Fact is, they hadn't financially supported me for many years. I wasn't going to allow mom to demean me or bully anyone I truly cared about, especially Tami – that was not going to ever happen because Tami did nothing to deserve this.

Tami was shocked. Everything I told her about mom's demeanor had happened just as I said it would. The instant personality changes to cover up the Cousino Lie was happening before her very eyes. Even after what I had shared with her at the Dairy Queen, she wasn't prepared for this. She never had to experience a confrontation with her parents. And I didn't want her to witness my mom losing it. I knew she was ready to explode. Tami was still at the back door. I needed to get her out of this toxic environment as quickly as possible. I turned to her again and repeated firmly, but with affection, *"Tami, please go wait in the car. I promise I'll be there in a few minutes, and I will bring all your things."*

Tami nodded. I could hear her footsteps receding as she walked back to the car.

Now that Tami had vacated the scene, my "real mom" showed back up. Like a volcano, she erupted with a fury that had been building since Tami and I walked in the door. I knew she would try to push all my buttons over the next few torturous minutes.

She blurted out, *"How dare you use my bathroom, you SOB? You're a worthless, no-good bum! You and your cute little girlfriend!"*.

It took everything I had not to forcibly stop her from comments like that. No one insults Tami. But somehow, I had the strength to maintain my composure and said nothing. I walked right past her downstairs to get my clothes out of the dryer. She followed close behind, raging about how I might be a football stud, but I was still a no-good loser; and that I'd still end up like my deadbeat dad, etc., as she was flailing her arms about like a banshee.

Of course, dad, who was meekly hiding in their bedroom, said nothing in my defense. I treated her ranting as business as usual as I grabbed the now-clean clothes out of the dryer and stuffed them in the laundry bag. Mom tried to hit me, but I stopped her immediately. I was far too strong and was not going to allow her to strike me ever again. Not anymore. I grabbed her firmly by both wrists as I looked directly into her eyes and told her calmly but with steely conviction:

"You are never going to hit me again…and there is nothing that you can do about it."

Though she was still in a banshee-like rage, she was taken aback. That was the first time I had stood my ground to her. She couldn't believe I had said something like that. She followed me upstairs in shocked silence, but I could feel her temper boiling over. As I left the basement, she stood in the doorway behind me.

I walked out the back door, with my laundry bag and Tami's make-up bag in hand. As I placed both bags in the backseat of the car, the gravity of what I had said to mom sunk in. Did I just stand up to mom? Wow! When I got back in the car, I noticed Tami, sitting wide-eyed in shock over the truth she witnessed behind the Cousino Lie. There was nothing more I could have done to prepare someone as sweet and innocent as her for something I dealt with daily for most of my life.

"I'm so sorry that you had to witness this babe," I said, tears in my eyes. *"I purposely tried to keep this part of my life away from you."* I wiped the tears from my face. *"I guess you got your Sunday with 'nuts' after all!"* I exclaimed. Even though it was no laughing matter, the irony soon sank in, and it prompted a little chuckle from both of us.

Tami tenderly caressed my right arm. *"Brad, it's okay that you didn't tell me about this sooner,"* she said.

After hearing that, I knew that things were going to be okay between us.

Chapter 18
The NFL Draft

"Keep away from people who try to belittle your ambitions. Small people always do that, but the great can make you feel that you, too, can become great."   **- Mark Twain**

As my senior football year ended in December 1974, I had serious aspirations of continuing my football career. Since I had proven myself as one of the best players at the college level, the next logical step, was to play in the NFL. Dreams of a pro football career were on my horizon. I was more frustrated than ever with the "experts" telling me that I wasn't big enough, tall enough, strong enough, or fast enough to play in the NFL. I told myself, I proved them wrong before…I'll just have to do it again. This time, however, it would be an even bigger uphill battle. I felt I had a shot at testing my skills at the professional level, and yet I knew that the NFL would be a real long shot considering that everyone in it is the 'best of the best'!

My first step towards a possible pro career was to interview several sports agents to see if they could offer any guidance or insight. No matter how each one said it, they all basically said the same thing:

"Brad, you had a phenomenal college career. Better than 99% of all college players. But there is no place in the NFL for a 5'11" 200 lb. defensive lineman or linebacker. If you were able to run a 4.5 40-yard sprint then maybe you could be a strong safety, but you don't have that kind of speed. Those are the facts."

Despite the bad news, the agents tried to get me an invitation to a Pro Day. What is a Pro Day? It is when the scouts measure potential players to see if they really have what it takes: strength tests, endurance tests, timed sprints, agility drills, long/high jumps, defensive coverage drills, etc. I really wanted to attend the Pro Day. Unfortunately, I wasn't even considered by any of the scouts.

A few days before the draft, I received a phone call from my agent, Jimmy Jones.

"Brad? This is Jimmy Jones."

"Hello, Mr. Jones, what's up?"

"Brad, call me Jimmy, - things might be turning around for you. Bad news, you aren't going to get drafted immediately, but you already knew that."

"Well, that's what they tell me." I shrugged.

"There is some good news. I wouldn't sit by the phone on the first day of the draft, but there is a possibility that you could receive a phone call during the later rounds. I would stay by your phone on the second day, around the eleventh to twelfth rounds."

"Really?" I inquired. *"What have you heard?"*

"Well, after the top 10 rounds have passed, that is when teams take chances on players who don't have all the tangible traits such as size, height, speed, strength. etc., but have shown great potential despite not having the numbers. This is where some of the top tier players along with the All-Americans who were not already drafted start showing up because of their stats."   *"I see..."* I spoke. *"Thank you for letting me know."*

"Cheer up, man," Jimmy said. *"There's bound to be a spot for someone with your abilities somewhere. Why don't you go get something to eat, take your mind off it for a while?"*

"Come to think of it, I am a bit hungry. I just might do that, thank you, Jimmy."

"No problem. Have a good day, and keep your ears peeled." Jimmy hung up. I decided to go to Mac & Joe's restaurant in downtown Oxford, well known by the Oxford community for their awesome burgers.

As I chomped down on my sandwich, I pondered the circumstances that led me here. The only time my parents showed me any sign of approval, not to be confused with affection, was when I performed well in sports. My parents often received accolades for how well their son performed. When I got to college and earned the reputation of an up-and-coming "star player", as it were, the adulation of the many fans and classmates I crossed paths with on campus and on the field served as a sort of substitute. True, those people would never give me the unconditional love that I desperately craved on a personal level from my parents, but at least it was something. If I wasn't picked by a team to go pro, what was I but a love-starved child in a twenty-something's body?

I barely slept that night. These pre-draft conversations were like a dangling carrot. I became more determined than ever to go pro.

442 Rejections

The 1975 NFL draft finally began. There were 17 rounds. 442 players would be selected out of a giant pool of exceptional college athletes. Like a lot of other potential players, I hoped for a miracle. That morning, I went out for a long run to calm my nerves, which were firing on all cylinders. The agony of waiting for something that might never come was overwhelming. I thought to myself, *Brad, you're a first-team All-American. All-Americans get drafted.*

When the second day of the draft came, I sat by the phone. Its silence was deafening. I was never called…not even in the later rounds, as my agent had predicted. Surprisingly, two big husky basketball players were chosen in the fourteenth and sixteenth rounds of the draft. *Yes, it's true, two (2) college basketball players, who never played a single down of college football were drafted. And I'm a 1st team All-American... and I still didn't get drafted!*

I was crushed.

There I was at the end of those two days, staring at the wall-mounted phone…rejected. I couldn't believe it. I dared to hope, *I dared to even pray.* I felt unwanted, just like when all those colleges rejected me for a football scholarship 4+ years earlier. Now I came face to face with the cruelty of being rejected 442 times over the past two days.

I didn't want to be seen by people at Miami – because everyone would be asking if I got drafted and by which team and in what round. I felt embarrassed, small, weak, forgotten because I wasn't drafted. Just like that, I was old news, and it was on to the next star player.

What would I do now? There was no chance that I'd return to Point Place. Too much had happened, and I had now experienced life on the other side. But I had no plan B. I thought that at least one team would draft me in the later rounds. My mom's voice in my head seemed to mock me... *"I told you that you'd be a loser... a failure... a deadbeat."* I was frozen in my own personal hell. I went to bed that night feeling lost in an endless void. I tossed and turned until it was almost dawn.

A few hours later, I woke late to the phone ringing. Confused, I picked it up. *"Hello?"*

"Yes, hi, is this Brad Cousino?"

"Speaking."

"Hello, Brad, this is Paul Brown of the Cincinnati Bengals."

Chapter 19
West Point Lab Rat

"The greatest glory in living lies not in never falling, but in rising every time we fall."
- Nelson Mandela

Paul Brown was the legendary coach of the Cleveland Browns and the founder of both the Browns and the Cincinnati Bengals. At the time, he was the Head Coach of the Bengals, and he was calling me!

I did my best to hide my excitement. *"Hello, Coach Brown?"*

"Brad, I can imagine yesterday was a tough day for you."

"Well, Coach, that's being generous."

"You were on our list; we really wanted you. I'm a Miami alumnus myself, so I've been following Miami football, specifically, your career. I've been reading about your successes in the local papers and watching you on the news for a few years. I spoke to Bill Mallory and Dick Crum, and they both had nothing but good things to say about you."

"Thanks, Coach, I'm flattered. They are great coaches!"

"Let me tell you, Brad, we were all very impressed with your play. But, as the draft progressed, and we saw players getting drafted across the board based on size over college stats, everyone followed suit and we drafted bigger players of our own to match up against the competition, size for size. But we see a lot of potential in you, young man. I just wasn't happy about passing you up. So, I'd like to ask you if you'd be willing to try out with the Cincinnati Bengals as a Free Agent."

I couldn't believe what I was hearing. This was a dream come true! *"Yes -- but how does that work considering that I wasn't drafted by the Bengals?"* I said.

"Brad, you play with a lot of heart, and everyone knows it. We want to give you a fair shot in the tryouts. But let me be frank...we don't

normally sign-up undrafted rookie free agents. In fact, you are the first Free Agent I've considered in seven years. We see great potential in you. Of course, you will have to earn a spot on the team based on your own efforts during tryouts. You will be up against everyone else trying out for a spot, and we just drafted four linebackers plus seven returning veterans. You will have to convince us on the staff that you deserve it more than they do."

"Thank you, I will definitely consider it."

"Talk to your friends and family. Think it over for a few days. I don't think you're going to receive calls from other teams, but we'd like you to consider us. I can't promise you anything other than to give you a fair shot. You have my word on that."

"That sounds fair, Coach. You really renewed my hopes to become a pro football player. Last night, I thought it was time to bury my dreams of going pro, but you have resurrected them." I beamed.

"Well, let's just see how tryouts go, Brad. I wish you the best of luck."

"Thanks, Coach," I said, and hung up. This was the second time in my life that the phone rang with the opportunity I had hoped for in my darkest hours. When all hope seemed to be lost, the phone rang. Paul Brown would later say in the Cincinnati Enquirer:

"Cousino should have been drafted. That was my mistake."

A Call from the Super Bowl Champions

But there was more. Later that day, I got an even bigger surprise: a call from Chuck Noll, Head Coach of the reigning 1975 Super Bowl IX champion Pittsburgh Steelers, asking me to join them! I couldn't believe it. To think that two future Hall of Fame coaches called and wanted me to be on their team on the same day was already an achievement on its own. While the struggle was far from over, I look back on what happened that day as one of the more memorable moments of my life.

I didn't want to make a big deal out of either of those calls because I didn't want to get my hopes up too soon. All my friends were constantly asking me "Did you get drafted? What round did you get drafted in? What team did you get drafted for?" I got sick of hearing these questions. Of course, when I told them all, "No, I didn't get drafted," they offered their sympathies. When I got called by Coaches Brown and Noll, though, there was one person I wanted to tell right then -- Tami. I called her immediately after the call with Coach Noll.

"Tami," I said.

"Hey, babe, you are feeling any better today?"

"Well, maybe. I've got some good news."

"Oh, my gosh! Tell me some good news, tell me!"

"I got a call from both Paul Brown of the Bengals **and** Chuck Noll, head coach of the Pittsburgh Steelers. They want me to join their teams as an undrafted free agent."

"No way! Oh, Brad, that's wonderful!"

"Well, don't congratulate me yet. Nothing's set in stone. I haven't picked which one I want to sign for yet."

"Still, I'm so happy for you! Who do you want to play for?"

"I'm still thinking about it. For whatever reason, I'm leaning toward the Cincinnati Bengals. Maybe some of my college coaches could help me to make the best choice."

"That's a great idea!"

Even though both coaches wanted me to try out for their teams, they told me that it was better to not have been drafted in the later rounds because I would be in a better position to choose which team, I had the best chance of making the team. I found that *being an NFL free agent in 1975 was far more challenging than being a "walk-on" at the collegiate level. Why? Because NFL scouts have 3 to 4 years of collegiate film to review and compare. With 17 draft picks per team in 1975, it was rare to try out and make an NFL team as an undrafted free agent.*

Regardless, my head was spinning from these two calls because I was still in the game. This is just like college all over again, just at a much higher level; but I'll take it! I thought. I may have been rejected for the draft, but at least I now had a chance to show the coaches what I could do! But which team to choose, either the Cincinnati Bengals, or the Super Bowl champion Pittsburgh Steelers. The thought of wearing my own Super Bowl ring at the end of the next year had me thinking -- Look at me now, mom!

Before I made my final decision, I reached out to my college coaches to get recommendations from them. After talking to them and considering the options, *I felt I had a better chance of making it with the Bengals than the Steelers. I liked that Paul Brown had talked numerous times to my college coaches... and that he had strong ties as a Miami University graduate (1930). But I really felt that I could trust him when he stated: "**I can't promise you anything other than to give you a fair shot. You have my word on that.**"* That's all I ever hoped for; nothing more, nothing less.

On paper, the Steelers were a better team with a lot of young talent. They won their first Super Bowl earlier that year, in January 1975. Odds were, if I was able to make the team, I would rarely get any playing time, if at all. Considering all the factors, I signed a contract to be a Free Agent with the Cincinnati Bengals. I received a $500 signing bonus, and if I made the final team roster, I'd get an additional $1,000. I was offered a league minimum of $21,000 salary, plus play-off money if we made it to the play offs. I had finally begun my climb out of the abyss. I was clawing my way back to the other side. I was ready to be a "somebody" again.

218 or Bust

Before signing the Bengal contract, I was reminded that there was a "catch". Even though Coach Brown said he would give me a fair chance, he also told me in no uncertain terms that if I signed with the Bengals, I had to come to summer camp at a minimum of 218 pounds. I then weighed 198. I had to gain at least 20 pounds of muscle mass in four months. But how? I'd been trying to get bigger during my whole college career. Several times, I was successful in gaining seven or eight lbs. but I couldn't keep it on. I had no control over how tall I was, and I could only gain so much muscle mass by the time camp started in a few months.

I knew any weight gain had to be muscle – it could not be useless fat. That would be like trying to play with a 20-lb weighted vest under my shoulder pads– of no benefit to playing football. If I couldn't bulk up fast, there was no way I was going to qualify to be allowed into preseason camp by Coach Brown. This was a huge problem because Paul Brown was a man of his word. If I didn't get to at least 218 lbs., he wasn't going to allow me to come to preseason camp... I'd be out of the Bengal organization and the NFL.

Fortunately, Coach Kim Wood, the strength coach for the Cincinnati Bengals, took a special interest in me because of my relationship with Miami University. And as it turned out, Miami University was one of the first "clients" of Coach Wood, who represented a relatively new company called Nautilus in the Midwest during the off-season. He installed new Nautilus strength equipment at Miami before the fall of my sophomore year, and Coach Wood was on-site quite often to make sure we used the equipment properly. As such, he already knew me, my work ethic, and the success I achieved.

Major Decisions

Now that I was officially a new "Bengal rookie", Coach Wood helped me get placed into a very intense strength training program with Nautilus. The special training program was being held in upstate New York... at the West Point Military Academy.

For me to participate, I would need to stop going to classes and forgo most of my winter and spring quarters of my senior year. It was a difficult decision and yet again it wasn't. If I had any hope to play in the NFL, I had to gain 20 lbs. of muscle, and I needed to devote all my energies to that end – to even show up at the Cincinnati Bengal's camp. I wanted to graduate from Miami and also go to West Point, but that was not a feasible option. I had to put myself in the strongest position to make the Bengals' roster. At the time, it did not seem like a bad decision to temporarily leave Miami to train 600 miles away at the West Point Military Academy.

For context, I was originally enrolled in Miami's Pre-Med program. I wanted to be a pediatrician. For a "jock" I had good grades, but not good enough to qualify for med-school. In addition, my career aspirations and education had taken a much different path, and my dreams of entering the medical field had become a distant memory as I achieved significant success on the football field. So, in my Junior year I changed from Pre Med to a Zoology major. Even so, I still needed eight credit hours of Organic Chemistry and eight credit hours of Inorganic Chemistry to graduate.

Back in the 1970's, only those players that were struggling with courses and grades to remain eligible were given an academic advisor's guidance. Because I was a solid 2.9 to 3.0 student, I did not qualify for an academic advisor's help with my courses or grades like many scholarship athletes required. Since I got solid grades, I did not have issues of trying to maintain eligibility to play football. However, each quarter, I foolishly kept delaying (procrastinating, dreading) registering for those Chemistry classes. I knew Chemistry was going to be exceptionally challenging for me, so I avoided the inevitable pain quarter after quarter. I had every intention to take the necessary courses to graduate in the next year or two off-seasons. ***But then life happened!***

The West Point Project

My training regimen would take place at the same facility as the West Point Army cadets. Coach Wood arranged for all my expenses to be paid and a hotel for me to stay near the West Point Academy. As the

Bengal's strength coach, he convinced Paul Brown to cover the cost of my hotel room and food during my extended stay at West Point. The Bengals and Coach Wood were in my corner...and I didn't want to let them down.

After signing my Bengal contract, I was off to West Point. I left the Miami campus in the middle of the winter quarter and missed most of the spring quarter of 1975. Mentally, I was in an extended 'Beast Mode' period. I had ten weeks of pure hell that Coach Wood designed specifically for me. A training regimen customized to fit my needs that were far more intense than the traditional regimen Nautilus created for the West Point cadets. Coach Wood and I became good friends as he fine-tuned the training regimen and demonstrated how to best use it.

This was going to be a much bigger deal than I expected. I found out later that the West Point Protocol would be turned into a national study, sponsored by Nautilus. I was one of the first "lab rats" in their program, so to speak. Each day, I was hooked up to all kinds of sensors and machines that continually monitored my heart rate, oxygen intake, calories burned, fluid loss, blood sugar levels, etc. In essence, anything that could be monitored that had to do with conditioning, strength building, weight gain, and cardiovascular systems was charted meticulously during every workout. Part of the study was to see how far I would go before I broke down due to muscle failure. I was, in essence, a mouse on a wheel that never stopped moving. They were testing to see how long their mouse would last before the wheel threw him off.

As part of my training, I had the honor of working alongside the great Dick Butkus, Hall of Fame MLB of the Chicago Bears. He was a celebrity endorser and investor with Nautilus early on and was very involved in the whole West Point project. He was a big man with a great heart! If the program that incorporated Nautilus equipment was intense enough for someone of my size and could assist me in growing bigger and stronger (unfortunately not taller) in a relatively short duration of time, that would have huge implications for future high school, college, and even pro athletes, which proved to be the case.

They also regimented my diet, which was supervised heavily by a dietician. Specifically, my calorie intake was monitored, as was my water intake, protein, carbohydrates, and fats. I was weighed each morning at 9:00 am and each evening at 9:00 pm...for the entire ten-week period. During my daily workouts, I would run sprints, quarter miles, or up stadium steps to increase my speed, quickness, and endurance. I would then transition to the strength-building phase. I was monitored while utilizing a variety of strength-building Nautilus machines. There were times where my entire body felt like it was on fire due to the intensity of my workouts that day.

Fortunately, I had 48 hours in between workouts to let each body part recover. But that didn't mean I had two days off. For example, I did my leg routine one day, and then, while my legs were resting for 48 hours, I did my chest and back the next day, and my arms and lower legs the next. Then the routine would start all over. When I wasn't working out, I was able to study the defensive playbook, so I could learn my new linebacker duties. Every waking moment was spent preparing for the Bengal's training camp... where Coach Brown and Marv Pollins (Bengals head trainer) would be checking to make sure I reached the *required* goal of 218 lbs.

Chapter 20
Bengals Training Camp

"Nothing in the world can take the place of Persistence. Talent will not; nothing is more common than unsuccessful men with talent. Genius will not; unrewarded genius is almost a proverb. Education will not; the world is full of educated derelicts. Persistence and determination alone are omnipotent. The slogan 'Press On' has solved and always will solve the problems of the human race." —Calvin Coolidge

By the time summer camp started in mid-July 1975, I had surpassed my goal of 218 pounds, reaching 220. It was the most intense physical experience of my life. The net result: when I reported to pre-season camp at Wilmington College, I was bigger, faster, stronger, more flexible, and agile, than I had ever been. I was now in "Beast Mode", both mentally and physically. Now, given a fair chance, I could prove to the coaches, scouts, and the world in general that I was indeed worthy of being in the NFL as a Cincinnati Bengal.

Thank you, Coach Kim Wood! Thank you, Dick Butkus!

****

1975 Bengal's Training Camp

My rookie year training camp with the Bengals was eight weeks long, and I had to learn a new position as a middle linebacker quickly. An NFL team normally keeps six to seven linebackers, and I was #12 linebacker out of 12 on the depth chart. I was dead last, but I was used to starting this way. This meant I had to beat out five or six other players to earn a coveted spot on the team's roster. I had to rise to the challenge, but I was used to running the gauntlet at this point.

There were seven returning Bengal veterans and four drafted rookie linebackers drafted in rounds #1, #3, #7, and #12. At the end of the line was me...an undrafted rookie Free Agent. And even more daunting, I never played a single down as a linebacker in college. Not only was I competing against some of the best college and pro linebackers in the country, but I also had to do it with no prior linebacking experience.

Making an NFL team as a low-round draft choice is exceptionally difficult... but to make the team as an undrafted Free Agent was rare - almost unheard of – far rarer than becoming a starter as a non-scholarship "walk-on" at the college level. In college and even more so in the NFL, you either produced results or you didn't. I would have to showcase my skills on a much bigger platform to a much larger audience.

In 1975, all NFL teams played six exhibition pre-season games. But the 1975 AFC Cincinnati Bengals played an additional pre-season game because it was the Bengals' turn to play in the traditional "kick-off" to this year's NFL season – the nationally televised Hall of Fame game held in Canton, OH against an NFC team – in 1975 it was the Washington Redskins vs the Cincinnati Bengals. The defensive coordinator decided to "sit-out" two of the veteran middle linebackers, (MLB) Jim LeClair and Tim Kierney, who were ahead of me on the depth chart. They were both somewhat dinged up. The reality was the coaches didn't want to risk them getting injured for an early preseason game.

The good news for me was that I was given significantly more playing time as the #1 MLB for the Hall of Fame game. I took advantage of the opportunity and had a phenomenal game on national TV. I led the team in tackles. I was responsible for covering running backs out on the backfield and caused a fumble when I tackled the receiver I was covering. I also didn't make any glaring 'rookie' mistakes, which is expected from a rookie. After the game, on national TV, Coach Brown specifically mentioned my abilities to play in the NFL when talking to the reporters. I graded out very high by the Bengal's defensive coaches -- who were quite pleased with how far I had come, considering I had only been playing MLB for about three weeks.

Dominate the Special Teams

But I knew that for me to have any legitimate chance to make the final roster was that I had to be the dominate player on all the special teams. My personal goal was to lead the team in the number of tackles, assists, blocked punts, fumbles caused, and fumbles recovered on special teams, and that's just what I did. I was the dominant special team's player for the Bengals during those seven exhibition games. I excelled as the team's best special team's player.

I survived the final cuts and made the roster of the 1975 Cincinnati Bengals as an undrafted "Free Agent". Against overwhelming odds, I was the *only undrafted Free Agent rookie that made an NFL roster in 1975.* Back in 1975 they did not award "All-Pro" for special team players, except for field-goal kickers, punters, and kickoff & punt returner specialists. The NFL changed that policy in the early 1990's. They now name All-Pro Special Team Players from kickoff and punt teams.

As a rookie, I led our special teams in most tackles on the kickoff team, most tackles on the punt team, and led the team in blocked punts and field goals. In addition, I was recognized as one of the best special team players in the NFL, my stats were off the charts. I was also credited for most fumbles caused. In 1975 I was in the top echelon of special teams' players in the NFL. It was a sweet victory for me. But I still hoped to get playing time as a middle linebacker.

Coach Brown promised to give me a fair chance to make the Bengal's team. I promised to give him my best.

We both came through on our promises!

The Speech

I was now officially a professional NFL player. We had our first official team meeting before each player's individual meeting with the coaches. My heart pounded in my chest as I made my way to the meeting room. Even though it was a short walk to Riverfront Stadium, I had to stop myself momentarily just to contain my excitement. I was a professional football player, getting paid (what I thought) an exorbitant amount of money — to play a game I loved in the NFL!

I was excited, and nervous. I felt I couldn't just be good on the field, but I had to be outstanding. As I walked into the team meeting room, I was reminded that I was now on the official 1975 Bengal's roster. No doubt all the other rookies were just as excited as I was to achieve their similar lifetime goal. Among the forty-eight of us were current and future NFL legends: quarterback Kenny Anderson, wide receiver Isaac Curtis, center Bob Johnson, running back Boobie Clark, tight end Bob Trumpy, middle linebacker Jim LeClair, safety Tommy Casanova, and linebacker Ron Pritchard, just to name a few. I had watched these men and many others over the years on TV; and now I was sharing a locker-room with them, as teammates! It was a surreal experience, to say the least, and I didn't want to take this greatest of honors for granted.

Paul Brown was never one to waste time. He was a man held by all who knew him in the greatest respect. He was a living legend, and he liked keeping things on point. "All right, gentlemen!" he boomed. After his initial introduction, welcoming everyone to the 1975 Cincinnati Bengal's team for the new season, he went straight to business.

Over the next sixty minutes, he gave us what the veterans referred to as "*The Speech*". He told us what to eat, what to wear, who to befriend, and who to watch out for. Whatever Coach Brown said went completely unchallenged. He made it clear, "*I'm the last word. You do it my way or hit the highway.*" Coach Brown spoke from his many years of experience.

He reminded us that in January 1975, the Pittsburgh Steelers won their first Super Bowl (the first of four Super Bowls over six years). Since Pittsburgh was in our division (which meant we would play them two times each year), Coach Brown was giving us an overview on how we were going to beat Pittsburgh this year. He shared with us the necessary steps to position the Bengals in such a way that we could make a serious run in the playoffs.

Once the meeting was over, reality hit -- fast and hard. The rookies needed to secure housing, which the veterans, of course, already had. During the pre-season, everyone lived in the dorms at Wilmington College, where we held camp. Now that I made the final roster, we had to move out and find our own housing.

Chris Devlin (a 7th round draft pick), a fellow rookie linebacker from Penn State, needed a roommate, so we decided to lease an apartment together. Chris was a great athlete and an all-around good guy. We were set up with a real estate agent who would make recommendations based on where we wanted to live, how much we wanted to pay, what part of town, etc. Chris and I ended up renting a decent two-bedroom apartment in Montgomery area, about 10 miles from our practice facility at Spinney Field, which was less than one mile from Riverfront stadium.

Meeting with an NFL Legend

After the team meeting ended, all rookies were instructed to meet with Coach Brown later that day for an individual meeting. I was one of the first to meet with the legendary coach one on one. Coach Brown was recognized as one of the best team builders of all time – his stated goal was to build a culture of winning championships. Vince Lombardi and Paul Brown were the standards for head coaches in the 1950s through the mid-1970s.

"Hi, Coach Brown" I said as I walked in.

"Ah, Brad, come in," Brown said, firmly shaking my hand. *"How are you?"*

"Well, Coach, words can't express how happy I am that I'm now a member of your team. Thank you for giving me this chance. This is what I wanted to happen – to play in the NFL." It was nearly impossible to hide the grin growing on my face. I was standing in the presence of one of the

best coaches ever. I quickly turned serious. I didn't want to look like I was in awe of him – even though I was!

"I'm glad to hear it," he said. *"Here's the thing, though…"* he continued, *"you proved that you deserve to be in the NFL. Your special team's production during the preseason was some of the best I've seen – very dominant… and you made some great plays that helped us win two of those exhibition games. You're now a professional athlete – in the NFL. Things work differently around here compared to college ball. Every player at the NFL level is one of the best of the best. But…"* Here it comes…

"Considering your size, you're going to have to continue to show results as we go up against some formidable opponents."

"That is exactly my goal, Coach," I said. *"I won't let you or any of my teammates down; I promise you. I will be one of the top contributors to our special teams. That is my goal."*

"I like your spirit, Brad." Coach Brown stated: *"But, as I told you after the draft, I promise you a fair shot. It will be up to you to show that you continue to belong in this league… and based on your stellar stats, you are well on your way."*

"And you were true to your word!" I responded. *"Thanks, Coach".*

Our meeting ended shortly thereafter, and I told Chris I'd see him back at the apartment as I walked out of Coach Brown's office.

I walked down to the locker room and began putting my equipment in my newly assigned individual locker with my name and number at the very top. (*Brad Cousino #52*) Considering the path I traveled to get here, it brought a happy tear to my eye… to see my name and number in an official NFL locker room.

I carefully unpacked my new gear that was placed in each locker. I was amazed that each player was given two pairs of new Adidas cleats and a whole bunch of free stuff from nationally known companies. I had to pinch myself. I was experiencing one of the perks of being an

NFL player. Later that night, I lay in bed, confident and relieved that I had finally found a home. It was the best sleep I'd had in a long time.

Who is Chaplain Wendel?

Chris Devlin and I got along great. He was a quiet guy. And he seemed to have already built some friendships with a small group of veterans and rookies – usually with one guy who always seemed to be around in our locker room. His name was Wendel Deyo, the Bengal's Chaplain. I found out later he was also the Cincinnati Red's Chaplain. I didn't know then what a Chaplain was or did. I just thought he was a part of the front office staff.

Chris told me that Wendel oversees conducting the weekly chapel service, very early every Sunday morning of a game before the pregame training table. It was totally optional, but it seemed that about 60% of the players and virtually all the coaches would attend those early morning services. He invited me to attend, but I chose not to. Chris and Wendel seemed to click, and he and some other Bengals (Pritchard, LeClair, Curtis, and others) seemed to become good friends. I knew that Chris confided in Wendel a lot. About what - I didn't have a clue.

Wendel was a good guy. He invited me to attend a "couples" Bible study about three or four times over the next month or so. I didn't know what that meant but attending a weekly couple's Bible study... sounded a little bit too religious for me. Besides, I never knew anyone who read the Bible. I thought it was just a big fancy book that people like my grandparents kept out on their coffee table.

Special Teams 'Kamikaze'

All the rookie linebackers like Chris and myself, along with the tight ends, fullbacks, and defensive backs were usually the primary combatants on every special team...Kickoff, Punt, Kickoff Return, Punt Return, Field Goal, Extra Points, and Field Goal teams. In essence, any time a football is kicked it requires a "special" team. Special teams are one of the most underappreciated among all the others because it is neither a defense team nor an offense team. Rather, it is always based on when a ball is kicked or punted. Often, rookies or non-starters are placed on these special teams, to give a break to those who are starting on the defensive and offensive teams.

Moreover, being on special teams is incredibly challenging. For starters, because of its oblong shape, a kicked football takes crazy bounces and can lead to many turnovers. In addition, running full speed for 40 to 50 yards and trying to maintain your lane of responsibility is quite the undertaking because the opposing special teams' players are also running full speed at you in their own lanes of responsibility, ready to block you from making the tackle. As such, there are significant collisions, more serious injuries, and turnovers on special teams than on either the defense or offense teams – because the velocity of the hits is so much greater.

It takes great courage to run full speed for more than 40 yards at a big blocker running full speed toward you. Both sides *must stay* in their designated lanes of responsibility to make sure the entire field is covered with no running lane gaps. However, the kick-off or punt return specialists are looking for an open running lane. As challenging as it was, I became one of the best special team warriors in the NFL because I overcame the natural inclination of fear by focusing on my goal of being the 'difference-maker' on special teams. I became a fan favorite because I played with all-out intensity and resilience, making a high percentage of tackles, assists, and turnovers on the Bengal's special teams.

According to Coach Paul Brown, *I was a "gamer"*, or as he put it, *a "puh-layyy-er"*; someone who seems to be involved in making big plays at just the right time. One of a handful in the NFL that make a significant number of tackles, causes and/or recovers fumbles, blocks punts & field goals as a part of being a key player on the special teams.

Chapter 21
NFL Off-Season

"Obstacles don't have to stop you. If you run into a wall, don't turn around and give up. Figure out how to climb it, go through it, or work around it."
-- Michael Jordan

In 1975, the Bengals got off to a phenomenal 6-0 start and completed the regular season at 11 wins with only 3 losses. An NFL regular season then consisted of 14 games, and 8 teams qualified for the playoffs. So, having 11 wins under our belt in that season was a sure playoff qualifier. We finished one game behind the Pittsburgh Steelers, who were 12-2.

We played the winners of the AFC West Division, the Oakland Raiders (now known as the Las Vegas Raiders), in the division playoffs at the Oakland Coliseum. The Raiders were a dominant team at the time, with John Madden as the head coach and Kenny Stabler as their All-Pro quarterback. Sadly, despite our best efforts, we lost that game 31-28. The Bengals lost a chance to move on to play in the conference championship against the Steelers. The Pittsburgh Steelers later defeated Oakland, then went on to beat the Dallas Cowboys in Super Bowl X.)

Every loss hurt, but losing a playoff game is especially crushing, because the losing team's season ends immediately, while the winner is still in the running for the Super Bowl. In the playoffs, only one team ends the season happy – the Super Bowl winner. It was a long, depressing flight home. Even so, my first season in the NFL was a great success.

Just the fact that I, a rejected "walk-on" nobody, could make an NFL roster being paid to play a game I loved – even ending in a playoff loss against John Madden's Oakland Raiders proved that I could make it as a professional football player. My position coaches were all optimistic about my future, and my stats showed that I displayed great success in my first year as a leader in tackles and assists for all the special teams plays.

1975 NFL Income

In my rookie year, I played in the NFL for about six months. I earned what I considered to be a rather large sum of money ($33,500); but compared to other players, I was at the lower 5% of the pay scale. My dad confided in me that the most he ever earned at the LOF glass factory was $11,000 a year, including overtime – and that was in 1975. So here I was 22 years old, and I made 3x as much as my dad but in less than 6 months. And doing what I loved! I surely wasn't complaining!

In preparation for pulling my records together for filing my 1975 taxes I was shocked at how much I had to pay in taxes. However, based on almost everyone else in the NFL, I was only paid the league minimum from the beginning of the season to the end (about five months of pay). But compared to what my father made in a year, or what I made in the sewers, I thought I was paid generously... playing a game I loved while entertaining millions of people around the country.

My 1975 W-2 showed I was paid a little more than a total of $33,500**. This included eight weeks of preseason weekly pay as a rookie plus the following breakdown.

- $500 signing bonus

- $1,000 for making the final team roster.

- $21,000 salary + summer rookie income of $4,000 for eight weeks

- $7,000 additional for the playoff game vs the Oakland Raiders

What I appreciated most was I finally had my own income that didn't rely on bouncing back and forth between a bunch of different jobs like I did in my younger years, and I wasn't cleaning out sewers at $4.50/hour

*** FYI: $33,500 in 1975 dollars would be an equivalent of $161,000 in 2022 purchasing power based on compounding inflation*

In college, I often wondered what it would be like to be a TFB (Trust Fund Baby) running around campus, flaunting money, and expensive toys. My dad, after 20 years on the job, could never earn that kind of money as a laborer at the glass factory. I was finally a "have", instead of a "have-not".

****

I knew that the nature of the NFL was to continue to try to replace me with bigger and faster players via the draft due to my being so small for a linebacker. Pondering what I was going to do, I read some inspirational words from an NBA player:

"I thought I would make it (to the NBA). But I had a Plan B. I was going to get my master's degree at Tulane University had it not worked out. I think the pressure of making it wasn't on me as great as some other players that had no other options. I was going to do something special in life, and I wanted to play in the NBA. Even though I had a backup plan, I went full speed ahead with my Plan A." -- Avery Johnson

These words really opened my eyes, and I decided to start investigating other things to do in the off-season, my future 'Plan B'. I wanted to find something I enjoyed during my NFL days that I could turn into a career once my playing days were over. I held out hope in my heart to play in the NFL for many years, but I knew I wasn't going to be a Terry Bradshaw, Kenny Anderson, or a Mean Joe Green with over twelve years playing or more under their belt. I was very aware that the average NFL career lasts less than three years.

Football careers for a Free Agent like me end abruptly at any time because there is no long-term contract. If you got hurt and could not play for that year, they would pay you based on your contract. However, if or when you got released / waived / cut – then your income ended immediately. So, like Avery Johnson, I narrowed down my Plan B post-football career quickly. I was fortunate to become friends with some very successful real estate investors – men I looked up to. I decided, at least for my first off-season, to follow in their footsteps; to learn how to become a successful real estate investor and entrepreneur.

This was the first time that I started to think of the long-term end goal. I wondered if I could begin a career as a real estate investor / manager while I was still playing in the NFL and then transition full time after my time in the NFL ended?

Nautilus Spokesmen / Keynote Speaker

In the meantime, as my off-season progressed, Coach Kim Wood and I continued our relentless Nautilus training to bulk me up even further (or at the very least, to keep me in top shape). During my first off-season, I started speaking and promoting Nautilus equipment at various high school and college coaching clinics and conventions across the country. I was a product of what I was endorsing, as my Nautilus history with Miami University and the West Point program was vital to my increased weight gain, muscle strength, and quickness.

Many people love to listen to a *true underdog story*... and mine was compelling and verifiable. Because of my success in making it in the NFL after not being drafted and being a walk-on in college who became a two-time All-American, I began getting more and more requests to speak at many different events. I was amazed at how fast word spread. I received rave reviews.

One speaking engagement led to another, and the ball continued to roll. I would speak to a group, which would then recommend me to even more groups looking for a compelling true-life story with a purpose. I spoke to a variety of groups at dozens of different size venues...from over 4,500 people in Charlotte's Coliseum to small events with only a dozen people, and everything in between.

I spoke to small businesses, colleges, high schools, and big companies at major corporate events as a keynote speaker. I even spoke to large motivational rallies for organizations like Amway. Sometimes I would donate my time because it was for a great cause. Other times I'd speak, without a guaranteed amount, and receive an *honorarium,* usually between $500 and $3,000 per speech. It was everything that an NFL rookie like me could have wanted at the time.

The Legendary Paul Brown Retires

In the spring of 1976, during the off-season, Hall of Fame legend, General Manager, Head Coach, and founder of both the Cleveland Browns and the Cincinnati Bengals Paul Brown, decided to retire as Head Coach. However, he continued to keep his ownership shares in the team and served as the General Manager of the Bengal organization. He promoted the Offensive Line Coach for the Bengals since 1967, Tiger Johnson, as the new Head Coach for the Bengals beginning in the off-season of 1976.

At that time, many people thought that Coach Bill Walsh, the quarterback coach and offensive coordinator for the Bengals, should have been named the Head Coach instead of Tiger Johnson. When Coach Walsh didn't get the job, he left and became the Head Coach of Stanford University and eventually, had a very successful career as the head coach of the San Francisco 49ers...winning three Super Bowls under his leadership.

With the change of the Head Coach came changes in our routine. Coach Tiger Johnson made it a point to have a private meeting with each returning player from the previous year. The purpose of these meetings was to give his vision and then to give each player a chance to respond and ask his own questions. Together, they could come up with a strategy to achieve the goals outlined over the off-season. I specifically wanted to ask Coach Johnson for a fair chance to play as a middle linebacker (MFLB) on defense in addition to being a leader on the special teams. While I loved special teams and considered it an honor to be a recognized leader, I still felt I could help the team even more if I was also used as a middle linebacker.

When I communicated my wishes to him, he simply let me know that he wanted me to be the leader of the special teams.

"Brad, you are too small. You are four inches too short, and you weigh about 35 lbs. less than what we want our MLB to be… I mean, we are amazed at how well you do. But we still don't think that you could play even half the season without getting hurt. Your primary spot on the team is to be our special teams' leader and captain."

It was like I was hearing a broken record. Internally, I was rolling my eyes and screaming *come ON! You've got to be kidding me! AGAIN!?* I tried to hide my irritation, perhaps unsuccessfully. I stood my ground, and I reiterated that I was more than willing to be the special teams' captain, but I also felt that I could help the team even more by playing as a Middle Linebacker (MLB). We ended the meeting not long after that, but I wasn't happy with the results.

I now knew I had no chance of being given a fair shot to be a middle linebacker with the Bengals. My lack of size was a definite reason why, but I reasoned that my stats were deserving to at least be given a fair chance to earn the #1 MLB position.

It was a major mistake on my part; I was thinking of what was in my best interest instead of what was in the team's best interest. This was a life-lesson I would soon learn – ***the hard way!***

Chapter 22
Traded

"The greatest test on earth is to bear defeat without losing heart."   —**Robert Green Ingersoll**

About two months after my meeting with coach Johnson, the Bengals co-sponsored a kid's charity event at Kings Island Amusement Park, just north of Cincinnati. This was a special event for underprivileged orphan and foster kids at a special picnic. Since this was for a great cause, I volunteered my time (as I often did for these kinds of events) signing autographs and posing for pictures with the kids. Hundreds of fans who had read about me in the papers or heard me speak at numerous engagements were recognizing me in public and wanting autographs and pictures with me.

There was about a month to go before the 1976 pre-season would begin. I was riding high, maybe a little too high. It didn't occur to me in the slightest that I was about to be knocked down a few pegs.

As I was signing autographs, one of the foster parents came up to me and inquired if I had heard the news.

"Did you hear the announcement?"

"No - what announcement?" I was confused.

"I just heard on the news that you (Brad Cousino) have been a part of a three-person trade with the Chicago Bears."

I was shocked. I had no clue that there was a trade in the works. The Bengals never called me to let me know I was in the process of being traded, which is usually the norm. To be fair, back in 1976, there were no cell phones, and since I was at Kings Island, there was no way that anyone could have reached me in time when the news came out. In my head, I considered the Bengals as a surrogate family. Once again, I felt *my family* had betrayed me.

I just stood there, shell-shocked and in disbelief of the situation. Here I was, signing autographs as an ambassador for the Cincinnati Bengals, only to find out from a stranger that I was no longer a Bengal, traded to the Chicago Bears. I couldn't understand why they would trade me when I had a great rookie season, far surpassing most of the other rookies as far as getting results. It just didn't make sense to me. I was the low man on the totem pole again. As Paul Brown told me after the draft, *"Brad, at the pro level, everyone is a good athlete. In the NFL, every team will continue to draft bigger, stronger, faster, and younger athletes."* That was and will continue to be the prevailing philosophy in the NFL.

As I found out later, Tiger Johnson traded me because he had three middle linebackers on their roster, future All-Pro Jim LeClair (6'4", 240lbs), first-round draft pick Glenn Cameron (6'3", 240lbs), and undrafted Free Agent Brad Cousino (5'11", 210 lbs.) with no college experience as a linebacker.

Glenn Cameron was a first-round draft pick. A significant amount of money was invested with him, and the new Head Coach (Johnson) didn't want any unnecessary pressure on him. Their line of thinking came down to: *what is best for our team and the culture we are trying to build?* Even though I was the leading special team's player, Coach Johnson decided to stick with the prototypical linebacker that is taller and bigger, removing me from being a potential distraction. Coach Johnson projected that Cameron as the Bengals #1 draft choice would become the Bengal's starting middle-linebacker in the near future. I understood Coach Johnson's reasoning, even though I disagreed with it.

I drove to Riverfront Stadium, home of the Bengals and the Cincinnati Reds for what would be the last time. I returned my defensive playbook, cleaned out my locker, and handed in the key to the locked workout room. I then had a final meeting with Assistant General Manager Mike Brown, Paul Brown's son. (Coach Brown lived in La Jolla, CA, an elite suburb of San Diego, CA in the off-season) Mike apologized to me for not getting the message to me in time and thanked me for what a great job I had done with my time on the team. He also reiterated that *he and his dad were big fans of mine*, and loved my attitude, and what I brought to the team.

However, as the new head coach, it was entirely Tiger Johnson's call on all player decisions on who made the final roster, who was cut or traded. Deep down, I think part of the reason Johnson traded me was because of the way I responded to my recent meeting with him. I pushed the envelope to become more than the Bengals' third-team middle linebacker. I wanted more than just being a role-player on special teams. Understandably, he made a deal with the Bears and got a future draft choice.

Once again, I was without a family. I wasn't completely out of the game, but still…I knew my Cincinnati teammates. I was going to have to get accustomed to a whole new group of teammates and fans who knew me about as much as I knew them in an unfamiliar city. The last five years I came to know Cincinnati because it was the biggest city nearest to Miami University in Oxford. Nonetheless, I had to shrug it off and get used to the fact that I was no longer part of the Bengals.

This was a huge wake-up call for me, telling me that my time in the NFL would likely be short-lived. I realized a long time ago that I wasn't going to get any taller or bigger than I was already – at 5'11" and just barely 205 lbs., by the end of the season. ** I was a Chicago Bear now. I either reported to Chicago or I would have to quit the NFL. There was no other option based on the trade, and there was nothing I could do about it.

** It was a common habit for many NFL teams to exaggerate the height and weight listed of many of the smaller players in the official game programs, case in point, I was usually listed in the program at 6'1" and 225 lbs.

Chapter 23
"Play Me or Trade Me"

"When they discover the center of the universe, a lot of people will be disappointed to discover they're not it." — **Unknown**

In the past, I usually could take defeat without dwelling on it for too long. When I was traded to the Bears, though, I exhibited a poor attitude that wouldn't go away. It wasn't like me to whine or pout over even the most severe of losses. Yet, here I was, wallowing in a sea of self-pity. I wanted Coach Johnson to realize that he had made a big mistake in trading me, and at the same time, prove that the Bears had made a great trade deal-- the steal of the decade!

Throughout high school, college, and my first year in the NFL, I was always the underdog with a "watch me prove them wrong" mentality, but also with a good attitude. This time was different. I was angry, frustrated, tired of the same old underdog fight. I had proven the NFL draft was wrong with my time on the Bengals, which the media and fans repeatedly confirmed. Yet, I was traded anyway. Once again, I was the outsider working my way in.

In a way, I wanted revenge by becoming the best Chicago Bear the fans and coaches had ever seen. Only, this time, I wasn't known in the Chicago marketplace, nor did I have the friendly ear of a legendary Head Coach who happened to also be a Miami grad that had followed my college career. When I got traded, the media only had a few articles which then became a few paragraphs worth of things to say about me and the trade to Chicago, but that is the nature of the media. Every day was a new "news-cycle", and I had become "old news" within a matter of a few days.

Three weeks from the time of the trade, I was to report to the Chicago Bear's training camp, held at Lake Forest College in the northern suburbs of Chicago. The team would be housed in one of the dorms of the college. I continued to work hard to be in the best shape when I arrived at camp. I left Cincinnati the day before I needed to report. I felt an extreme sense of Deja-vu like I was going to the Bengal's camp all over again. Like my first day at the Bengal's training camp, I was going to meet a whole new group of players and coaches. Hopefully, they would accept me for what I could do on the field. I was more determined than ever to prove my worth to this team, to any team. I was determined to be a real difference-maker, like I was in high school, college, and as a special team leader for the Bengals.

When I got to camp, I discovered that the Bears wanted me because of my proven abilities on special teams. No problem there, I loved special teams, but I also hoped to be given a fair shot to play middle linebacker. Unfortunately for me, they already had a high drafted veteran from the previous year, and a new high draft pick rookie as well to fill both the starting and backup linebacker positions. I was once again the odd man out. In training camp, I didn't get much playing time at MLB with the first-team defensive unit. Regardless, I gave my all in every practice, despite my "backup-to-a-backup-to-a-starter" status. Even though I had limited time on the field, I often led the team drills and scrimmages with the most tackles, assists, and/or caused fumbles.

It was very frustrating. Why was I not being considered as a starting linebacker when my "stats" provided the evidence that I was a better option for the team? I had better stats on those ahead of me on the depth charts. I had more tackles, more assists, more interceptions…more of everything. So, why wasn't I getting noticed for that? Every time we went through the film of practice that day, my good plays were ignored. I still stayed in the same place on the depth charts. Are the coaches blind? Maybe I need to turn up the volume and point out to them what they are clearly missing. Here I was, 23 years old, working my rear end off, with better results than most of the starters, and not getting recognized for it. I needed a fair chance to play.

Attitude Problems

My poor attitude showed up after a practice or scrimmage when I was ignored. I often moped around after practices and voiced my disappointment to one of my new friends and teammates, the great Walter "Sweetness" Payton. He was already recognized as one of the best running backs of all time. By his retirement, he would be named all-pro nine times and was a unanimous choice for the NFL Hall of Fame.

Walter had a lot of wisdom and shared with me that maybe it would help if I talked to Chuck, the team chaplain. I soon learned that Walter was a man of faith, a Christian, and I was surprised at how transparent he was about God. I usually kept a safe distance from religious people, as I had many negative experiences growing up in a religious environment. Even so, there was something about Walter that was refreshingly different. He was authentic and transparent.

The longer I was in camp without opportunities to demonstrate my abilities, the more I chafed on the inside. One day, after a typical practice, I took Walter's advice and set a time to meet with the Bear's chaplain, Chuck. I was more annoyed than ever. Between the morning and afternoon practices, I sat down on a bench outside the players' dorm, prepared to pour out my heart to Chaplain Chuck.

"What's going on, Brad?" Chuck asked as he sat down next to me.

"I feel like I'm being wasted on this team," I grumbled.

"Why is that? You're good out there on the field."

"That's practice and scrimmages. I want a chance to play middle linebacker – for more than a few plays here and there. Ninety percent of the time, I'm watching from the sidelines. I know the more I play, the better I can help the Bears. I've proven myself with every drill and scrimmage. Yet I'm still not getting a chance to compete on a level playing field for the middle linebacker position. Why did they trade for me? I'm a member of this team, aren't I?"

"Of course, you are, Brad, calm down."

The nerve had been pinched.

"Why am I not being evaluated as a middle linebacker in games!?" I hissed. *"I'm just as good, even better statistically, than the two guys ahead of me! Why aren't I being used? I deserve to be given a chance to compete like the rest of the team! I know I could help the Bears even more if I was more than just a special team player."*

"Easy, Brad, easy. We're all on the same team here," he said, raising his arms. *"If I had a crystal ball, I'd tell you why you aren't out there more. Before you vent your frustrations to anyone else, consider this: you're asking to take another player's spot on the field while he takes your seat on the bench, because you think you're better than him. The coaches have a plan that might be different than yours because they are trying to build a team. Every person has a specific job to do on a well-constructed team. Even if you are better, you need to remember that the Head Coach and his assistants are responsible for building a positive team culture that will lead to a winning organization. This "every man for himself" kind of talk isn't good for developing a winning team. Sure, it's a competition for time on the field, but we're still a team."*

"Well, this 'team culture' isn't giving me a chance to earn a spot on the team," I growled. *"Back on the Bengals, I had a chance to play more than just special teams. It wasn't all the time, but it was at least something."*

"This isn't the Bengals – this is the Chicago Bears, one of the oldest, proudest, and most revered franchises of all time. Everyone gets their chance with us, too, Brad." the chaplain said. *"But, in your case, you might have to be patient and wait for an opening.*

I bet you know what I'm talking about. You will need to be ready when one of those guys ahead of you gets dinged up, or seriously hurt. Then you will have your chance to show them how you can dominate despite being too short, too small, and yes, even too slow in their eyes. That way they can evaluate you not based on a few plays but over an entire game, or even better, over a couple of games. It will happen if you don't force it."

As he was speaking, I thought back to Miami and my Kong experience, and knew that he was telling me what I needed to hear. He looked me directly in the eyes. *"You have a lot of heart, Brad, we can all see that. But heart alone doesn't guarantee success. Don't rush this process, or you will be the one who will suffer."*

I looked at my watch and knew that we needed to stop. Afternoon practice would start in forty-five minutes, and I needed to get taped and dressed. I thanked Chuck for his time and then walked off. I didn't want to hear another rehash of what I had heard before. Chaplain Chuck's words, though true, were not what I wanted to hear. Just as before, my concerns had been ignored. The conversation had changed nothing. While I saw the wisdom Chaplain Chuck offered, I was still ticked off that I was having to fight these issues as an NFL player. After another week of "waiting for my chance" passed by, I knew the Bears were set in their ways. I was tired of waiting to get a fair shot. It wasn't long before my temper and immaturity came back to bite me in a big way.

The Ultimatum

Disregarding the wise advice of Chaplain Chuck, I felt I could convince Coach Jack Pardee myself. I asked the coach's secretary for a short meeting and got it. As I walked into his office, I was polite in greeting him. At the same time, I got right to the point. I asked him why I wasn't being given a fair chance to play as a middle linebacker. No surprise here, he gave me the same speech that every other coach has given me time and time again.

Coach Pardee explained: *"Brad, your MLB play has been consistently good. You are a very good linebacker with great instincts. However, this is the Chicago Bears, home to the legendary Dick Butkus. That's the prototype middle linebacker we want for our defensive scheme. And that's not you. You're not what the Chicago Bears want as our Middle linebacker(MLB). It's amazing how well you perform. We can't figure out how you do so well. However, you're never going to be six foot four and 245 pounds. And because of that, you have little to NO chance of being our starting MLB. You'll be able to get in and be a backup when someone gets hurt or when we substitute. But you're not going to ever be the starting middle linebacker for the Chicago Bears. To be brutally frank, that's never going to happen in the Bear's organization."*

As context, the Chicago Bears were renowned for their great defense. They were known as the "Monsters of the Midway", anchored by one of the best middle linebackers of all time – Dick Butkus. Butkus had been their all-pro middle linebacker through the '60s and early '70s. He retired years earlier and was voted into the coveted NFL Hall of Fame (Even though I knew Dick Butkus from my time at West Point, I didn't feel it was the appropriate time to bring that up.)

Additionally, Coach Pardee acknowledged that they traded for me because of my special teams play. That was the assigned role they wanted me for. I still tried to hold my ground, and I remained firm in my stance. *"Coach, I want to play special teams. I will be a great special teams' player for the Bears. But at the same time, I really believe in addition to the special teams, I can help the team even more by playing some situations as your middle linebacker."*

Try as I might, Coach Pardee wouldn't budge. His decision was final. I was frustrated. This was not going the way I hoped. I couldn't hold back anymore. In my arrogance, immaturity, and "my way or the highway" mentality, I calmly but firmly stated:

"Coach Pardee, either play me...or trade me."

It didn't quite come out as I planned; it came out as more of an ultimatum than a request. Everything fell silent. With those words hanging in the air like a mushroom cloud after a nuclear detonation, I thanked him for his time and left his office.

Chapter 24
The Scars You Can't See

"From every wound, there is a scar, and every scar tells a story. A story that says, 'I survived'."
- Craig Scott

As I walked back to the team dorm, I was still fuming. I couldn't believe I was still dealing with the "weight/height" issues when I had a track record of disproving it every time. Based on my stats, I was just as good, if not better, than the other linebackers in camp despite being the smallest one on the roster.

Then, it dawned on me. The realization of what had just happened hit me like a MACK truck. What did I just do? I had just given an ultimatum to the head coach of the Chicago Bears. Should I turn around and apologize, taking it back? How would I even say that? I started pacing back and forth, not knowing which way I should go.

I felt nauseous, breaking out in a sweat standing in the summer heat. *Why couldn't I just be content with the role they wanted for me? Why did I have to complain about not having a fair chance to earn a starting position?* That was it. I was done for sure. That was not a smart move at all. I'd be lucky to play football with any other team ever again.

The next morning, as I was getting ready to go to our team meeting at 8:30, I heard a knock on the door. When I opened it, it was one of the team's managers. He held a grim expression on his face. Uh-oh. I asked him what I could help him with.

"Coach Pardee and the General Manager want to see you – now! Bring your playbook."

Yep. I had really done it now. I was about to be waived by the Chicago Bears.

In the NFL, if a player was asked to see the coach and bring his playbook, it meant that the player was getting released, waived, and/or cut, and must turn in his playbook immediately to protect the secrecy of the team's plays. They call it being put on "waivers", where players go through this cycle and every team in the NFL can "claim" the player off the waiver wire, in essence, agreeing to pick up their contracts. If no team does, then the player is released, or "waived."

I knew right then when the team manager asked me to bring my playbook to see Coach Pardee, that I was in that process of going through the waiver wire format. I had made a huge, ego-driven mistake the night before. I should have held my tongue and followed the wise advice of Chaplain Chuck, biding my time as I waited for the next "Kong" opportunity like I did back in college.

Arguably, if I hadn't pushed the envelope with Coach Pardee with my *"play me or trade me" ultimatum*, I could have stayed on the Bears for at least another three weeks before the final cut deadline. In that time, I either could have had another chance to prove myself to them, or they could have traded me to a different team, where I could prove myself there. Either way, it would have been a much better prospect than what I did.

Reluctantly, I picked up my playbook and walked down to the coach's office. By this time, all my soon-to-be-former teammates were starting to go into the team meeting room. I stepped in to say goodbye and good luck to Walter Payton. I would miss him. I liked him as a person and respected how he was so open and transparent about being a Christian. I knew he was destined to be one of the best players of all time! I was heartbroken by what I knew was coming. I silently whispered my farewells to the rest of the team and walked into Coach Pardee's temporary office.

The Immediate Fallout

When the news was finally broken to me that I was getting waived, I felt my entire life come crashing down around me. I knew it was coming, but that didn't stop it from hurting unlike anything I'd ever felt before. The Chicago Bears were in process of waiting to see if any team had an interest in me. If so, I go to that team, if not then I'm released from the contract, and I'm a free agent once again. I shambled out of the Bear's temporary office at the college at a snail's pace. I was a zombie, with no purpose. All I could do was wait for another team to contact me, but it could be days, weeks, or even months depending on the needs due to injuries on other teams.

I don't remember the walk back to my dorm room. I just remember trudging through my dorm room door about a half-hour later, falling face-first onto my bed. I was angrier at myself than sad at the situation. *Why did I have to go and shoot my mouth off again? I believed another team would pick me up because I had an excellent reputation as a special team's player, but there was no way to know how long I'd wait.*

Then, after wiping away the tears, in my quiet reflections, I heard it. It was far back in my mind, but it was there.

"Look at yourself. You're a loser and no-good bum. You are a S.O.B. You ba***rd, you're a poser, someone who will never amount to anything worthwhile."

After all these years… mom was back!

*"I told you... you'd be a loser... a bum. A G*D D**N A** H**E. A has-been! A never-was."*

Though it was only in my head, I heard my mom's voice as if she was in the room shouting at me. *"You'll never amount to anything." she echoed.* This was all I needed. The voice in my head didn't let up.

Repeatedly, I heard mom's insults reverberating through my cranial cavity. I tried to shut her out, denying that she was even there, but the voice only grew stronger and louder. Finally, I again fell on the bed and surrendered to my mental agony. I was too exhausted to vent anymore.

I dealt with these feelings of depression and worthlessness for a long time after being cut from the Bears. It was like I was back in Point

Place all over again, with mom hovering over me like a vengeful specter, endlessly tormenting me. Was there no end to this madness? I was alone...more alone than I'd been in years. And then a traumatic nightmare from my past flashed into the forefront of my mind.

***

Most Tender Memory with Mom

It was an unseasonably cold night in early May when we arrived at the bowling alley. I was about 10 or 11 years old, and my dad was in a Saturday night bowling league with some of his work buddies. Often our whole family would go to the bowling alley. The Dads drank and bowled while the moms talked and mingled. The younger kids, meanwhile, would run around the huge bowling alley playing hide-and-seek or tag, as the older boys would end up forming teams pretending to be big-time wrestlers. The bowling league usually lasted two and a half to three hours. Then the parents would mingle for another thirty to forty-five minutes before leaving.

The "wrestling" room was an unused playroom in the back section of the bowling alley. The older boys would separate from the other kids, so we could commence the big-time wrestling match.

I noticed that there was a new kid, older and bigger than most of the other kids, and he was causing all kinds of trouble. He picked on the smaller kids and even bullied some of the girls who were also in the same playroom. He was a real piece of work. No one wanted to be around him, yet no one could escape his cruelty. Then, the new kid made a big mistake. He started to bully my younger brother, Rick. I told him to stop. Instead, he ratcheted it up by pushing him off the chair he was sitting on.

I was livid and immediately came to his rescue. A fight erupted between Bully-boy and me. As we wrestled to the ground, I ended up on top of him, pummeling him relentlessly. Then Bullyboy grabbed my new sweater by the collar, pulling it over my head, and IT happened.

I felt my sweater being savagely ripped apart around the zipper and neckline. I went crazy! It was a "Beast Mode" moment, but not necessarily in a good way. I lost it and fought with such fury that after a minute or so, Bullyboy ran out of the room with a swollen right eye, a bloody nose, and a fat lip. I never saw him again, not that I cared.

I was now focusing on much bigger problems. Upon inspecting my sweater and seeing it badly ripped and stained with Bully-boy's blood, fear gripped me immediately. I could only imagine how much trouble I was going to be in with mom. Even though I was in a fight protecting my younger brother from Bully-boy, it wouldn't matter.

I tried to hide the badly torn sweater under my coat. When mom saw me, she instantly knew something was up. She was suspicious as to why I'd put my coat on inside and zipped it all the way up to my neck, especially since I was sweating from all that wrestling. Before we left the bowling alley, as dad was getting the car, mom had me unzip my coat. Immediately she saw my badly ripped sweater with the bully-kid's bloodstains all over it. The color immediately drained from my face as mom's eyes widened in rage.

Mom absolutely erupted, like the volcano Mount Vesuvius, which destroyed the entire city of Pompeii without any warning. Only this time, it was "mom Vesuvius", bringing her flaming wrath down on me. Our house would become Pompeii.

She pinched the back of my arm with her long fingernails with all her might and marched me out to the curb, where dad had just pulled up. For most of the 15-minute drive home, mom was leaning over the front seat to get at me crouched in the back seat. She was cursing and yelling at me, hitting me around the head, and telling me that I was really going to get it when we got back to the house.

Dad didn't say a word. He was fully concentrated on just getting us back to the house because he had had too much to drink, as usual. When we got back to the house, I was sent to the basement. Mom went to the coat closet and brought out the heavy-duty, rubberized sweeper cord retrofitted from an old Kirby vacuum cleaner. She referred to it as

"The Kirby" and it was only used for "special occasions" -- because it *inflicted far more damage during a whipping compared to a normal belt.*

She then started yelling at dad, *"You better whip him good."* Dad didn't want to do anything of the sort. He just wanted to go to sleep. Mom kept nagging him, telling him to be a man and "take care" of me. She started to push him and tried to slap him in the face, but he grabbed hold of her hand so she couldn't hit him.

Both of my younger brothers, Rick and Mike, were on the basement stairs crying in fear. Rick kept telling mom that I was protecting him from bully-boy, but that didn't seem to matter. The screaming and physical abuse my two younger brothers witnessed in the past was simply too much for them as they wailed away. They knew what was coming! Mom screamed at Rick and Mike to go to your room, or they would be next.

Mom was relentless as she continued to badger dad, who was still buzzed from drinking. After another minute or so, he screamed and cussed at mom that he would deal with me. He took the "Kirby" from the chair and forced me to strip down to my underwear. He then began to whip me as mom was prodding him to hit me harder and longer. The lash of the Kirby hit my butt, upper legs, back, arms, and shoulders. At one point, dad missed my arm, hitting my face on the left cheek and neck with a wicked swing of the cord.

This thrashing seemed to go on for an extended period. Finally, dad dropped to his knees, exhausted. He was sobbing in great heaves, like a blubbering whale, when he shouted at mom; *"Is this enough? Are you happy now, you evil b***h?"* He looked toward me with sorrow, pity, and guilt. Dad had never beaten me that hard and long before. No doubt he had to be thinking, *what did I just do – why did I let this lunatic woman make me do this to my son*? He then stormed out of the house in tears, got into our only car, and left. True to form, dad wouldn't return home for another four days.

I was in a catatonic state. Mom Vesuvius's cataclysmic eruption had finally subsided. After all the volcanic-level carnage and pain she had brought down, there was only silence, with ashes floating solemnly down on the barren wasteland. I was the sole survivor, wondering what I had possibly done to deserve this. I was simply trying to protect my younger brother from being bullied. I had stopped crying much earlier and was curled up into a corner of the room physically and emotionally spent. I was covered in welts, even a few on my face and neck. The lash of the Kirby broke the skin in some places, leaving blood to seep through the open wounds.

After dad left, mom looked back at my battered, broken carcass. I think she got scared because I wasn't moving, talking, or crying. I just stared blankly at the floor. Mom got a pan, filled it with cool water, took a washcloth, and had me lay on my stomach as she wiped the blood off me. Though I was in shock, I complied. The whole time she was apologizing profusely as she moved the washcloth over my skin. Next, she put ointment on the open wounds.

I was confused. Mom had never once shown an ounce of compassion towards me before. Was she remorseful for the brutality she forced dad to inflict on me, or was she selfishly scared that neighbors or teachers would report her to the police upon seeing my battered, bruised body? I didn't really care. But as crazy as this sounds...

This memory represented my <u>most tender</u> moment with my mom.

It was moments like these, in all their visceral savagery and unrelenting brutality, that I thought of after I was released from the Bears. There were many other "similar" memories that flashed helter-skelter in my mind – they came and went... <u>sad, sorrowful, hurtful memories</u> from the many past bouts of physical and verbal abuse.

But after waiting for two hours, I knew that no team had picked up my contract, so there was no point in staying in Chicago. With a heavy heart, I packed my things. When I finished packing, I cleaned up the dorm room, and it looked like I had never lived there in the first place. I walked down the stairs, through the lobby, and out the main door. I turned and took one long last look back at the huge Chicago Bear's logo on the front window of the dorm, cognizant of what I was leaving behind.

I got in my car, preparing myself for the long, lonely drive back to Cincinnati. Unfortunately, I had company the whole trip... mom! She was in the backseat shouting at me... "*I told you were a no-good bum. You're a G*D D**N loser, a poser, who has disgraced this family. She cussed and cursed as she turned up the volume. Look at you... already a has-been! You'll never amount to anything, just like your father.*"

Though it was only in my head, I heard my mother's voice as if she was in the backseat shouting at me. Those thoughts ricocheted in my mind for six hours and more than 350 miles.

Chapter 25
Free Falling

"A word of encouragement during a failure is worth more than an hour of praise after success."
-- Anonymous

On the six-hour drive back to Cincinnati, I thought about what had transpired. I was devastated after I was released from the Bears, but I had a major part in my own undoing; a costly "self-inflicted" wound.

Yet, everything was still the same. My former teammates all looked and acted the same. I drove the same car. I had the same amount of money in my bank account. I dressed the same way. My football skills were still the same. Tami was still my girlfriend. Life seemed to go on as if nothing had happened, but I felt as though everything had changed. I had caused the life I wanted to be taken from me. It slipped through my fingers like dry sand held in a tight fist until nothing was left but an empty palm, staring back at me like an inescapable white void.

Tears blurred my vision, making my drive home even more difficult. Just three hours earlier, I was an NFL player, a VIP. I was important, a "somebody". Now, everything in my life seemed to be dark and in absolute chaos. My self-esteem was built up while being a college football star and then as an NFL player. I loved being a titan on the field, worshipped by legions of adoring fans. I received high praise from Paul Brown and Chuck Noll -- two of the greatest coaches of all time (both inducted into the NFL Hall of Fame), as well as getting rave reviews from teammates and opposing coaches & players for the way I played.

Now, I felt that I was less than nothing -- if I didn't have a number on my back or a helmet on my head, what was going to happen to me? Who was going to want to be around me if I wasn't a star football player?

Who Am I... Really?

Due to my football success at the college and professional level, I thought I had escaped my abusive past, but did I? No! It was just hidden below the surface. While it did fade somewhat as a distant memory, it was always lurking deep within. I didn't know how to face my traumatic past, to stop running from it. Even though football, for me, was a means of escape from my abusive childhood, it had taken hold of me and began to define who I was. My self-esteem was directly fed by my success on the football field.

I was dating a beautiful lady and enjoyed the recognition and respect from thousands of fans. I loved my popularity, and believed I owed it all to my football skills, certainly not because of my worth as a valuable human being. I hadn't experienced any thoughts like that in the last five years. During my time at Miami and with the Bengals, I was an up-and-coming star, a former walk-on who despite overwhelming odds aspired to join my idols in the NFL Hall of Fame.

I dreamed of earning wealth and status, as I intended to play in the NFL for the next 10 to 15 years. Despite my size limitations, I couldn't see myself as anything but successful. Failure never crossed my mind, until a few hours ago. This was the first time I officially had to come to terms with the potential end of my football career, which, in many ways, had become my life! Sure, I could pursue my real estate backup plan, but at this point, all I could think of was my lost chances as a future great player in the NFL. Without realizing what was happening, football had become my everything, my self-esteem and self-worth was a direct result of how well I performed.

Recognition:
I craved it... I wanted it... I needed it...
It became my god!

****

I fully expected to make the Chicago Bear team, as such, I subleased my Cincinnati apartment to Steve "Smitty" Smith, a good friend from my Miami days before I left for Chicago. Now that I was back in Cincinnati, he was going to need to find another apartment, but that would take some time. Chris Devlin, my rookie roommate, found out I needed a temporary place to stay and mentioned it to Wendel Deyo.

Chaplain Wendel called me and graciously invited me to stay at his home with his family for a few weeks until I could move back into my apartment. Wendel married his high school sweetheart, Cindy, and at that time had two girls, about six and four years old. Wendel had a guest room in their lower level, so I had my own space, but I got an actual glimpse of how a real family interacts on a day in day out basis. Just as Tami was raised by great parents with unconditional love; so too, I saw Wendel and Cindy model the same kind of love in action. The absolute opposite of how I was raised. I made a mental note... that is the kind of relationship that I wanted for my future family.

*****

I didn't handle being out of football very well. Far too much of my self-esteem was based on how good of a football player I was, not because I was unconditionally loved by my parents, or anyone else for that matter. I locked myself away for days at a time feeling sorry for myself. I knew I had many friends in my former teammates, coaches, and of course, Tami, my soon-to-be fiancée. But how can I face any of them? I was a failure in my eyes, why wouldn't I be a failure to them?

Tami noticed that I was quieter, more aloof, more distant than I had ever been. I turned away anyone who reached out to me out of concern. To avoid any possible rejection from my friends, I decided, "If you can't beat rejection, be the rejector." I hid in my apartment, seldom leaving unless necessary. I was a recluse in every sense of the word. I stewed in my own emotional misery like a petulant child, blaming coaches, my parents, me, and everyone else for my lot in life.

I was at the beginning stages of recognizing all the effects of the trauma inflicted on me from my earliest childhood. I knew this was not healthy for me. I needed to get out of this emotional funk. I decided to put my old childhood reading habits to good use by seeking out motivational, self-help, and Christian books and tapes by the most famous authors of the genre: Earl Nightingale, Dale Carnegie, Napoleon Hill, Stephen Covey, and Claude Bristol, to name a few.

These authors provided some light in a very dark time of my life, and a beginning of a foundation of truth that was missing in my life that ended up being instrumental in my growth as a human being. I was forced to face some very unpleasant truths from my past, but they were necessary for me to endure, to grow as a person. Mom's taunting voice however, tormented me the entire time.

I was hoping that either reading books or listening to cassette tapes would overcome the dark words I heard over and over from mom. The tapes really helped me. Even though mom's voice was still in my head, telling me I'd never amount to anything, I also knew what I had accomplished in the last five to six years was amazing. I wasn't worthless. What I did mattered, regardless of what mom's voice said.

While I was listening to these tapes and reading these books, I knew I needed to implement step two of my "*Life Goes On*" plan: stay in good shape and keep busy, any way possible.

*****

On Thin Ice

While I was trying to progress out of my emotional pit, I also wanted to stay in good football shape. I really felt that I would be playing in the NFL again – I just didn't know when. While NFL football was out of the picture for the moment, I needed to stay in great shape, because whenever the call came from an NFL team, I'd have to pass a grueling physical tryout before I'd be asked to sign a contract. I couldn't go to the gym or Nautilus facility like I used to. Why? I was still dealing with my emotional fragility. I didn't want to face all the people who knew me asking all the questions about what I was doing and dealing with the fears of being recognized and then the rejection from the pressing questions people might be asking me.

So, what did I do? I turned to possibly the most unlikely vehicle I could at the time: ice skating – hockey ice skating to be exact. The fact was football was not my best sport in high school; it was ice hockey. I was an outstanding defenseman and played on many All-Star traveling teams growing up. (Few Colleges in the US had a varsity hockey program in 1971 – so full college scholarships were rare) Now, though, I had nothing better to do, and I hadn't skated in over six years, so I thought, why not? I found my old pair of hockey skates.

It was a warm mid-September afternoon as I laced up my skates at a local indoor ice rink near my apartment. I went right out onto the ice and within a few days, I had my hockey legs back in no time. I was staying in shape, doing something I enjoyed, and I guess it was a way to avoid the public, too. I decided to skate every day for at least 90 minutes or longer to stay in top football shape. Each day I'd do skating drills, sprinting, puck handling, shooting on an empty goal, etc. I was surprised that my dormant hockey skills came back quite quickly.

Once I was on a football scholarship, none of my football coaches would allow me to play hockey during the football off-seasons. (I know because I asked permission to play during the off-season). Since I was on a football scholarship at the time, they were afraid I'd get hurt, compromising my performance on the football field.

Skating provides great cardio exercise, and it helps to stretch muscles. I also liked that no one knew who I was while on the ice, and it kept me from thinking anything negative. It was a win-win situation for me! As I skated over the next ten days, I noticed that one or more people would watch me skate. I asked around and found out that one of them was the majority owner of the ice-skating rink. He was an overweight man, made even portlier by his puffy navy-blue coat, chomping on a Cuban like it was a candy cane. One day, he came down near the ice where you enter and exit onto the ice.

"*Excuse me, young man, got a sec?*" as he waved me over.

"*Yes sir, what can I do for you?*"

"*You're a darn good skater, kid. What's your name?*"

"*Brad Cousino.*" "Wait...*THE Brad Cousino? Some of my employees told me that they thought that you were the former Bengal football player,*" he said with a puff on his cigar. "*Did you know that the Cincinnati Stingers practice here every morning, and I'm good friends with their head coach, Terry Slater?*"

I blinked in surprise. I had no idea that the Stingers trained here, of all places. I *knew* Terry Slater. He used to be the head coach of the Toledo Blades semi-pro hockey team. In high school, I played with a traveling all-star hockey team that used the same ice rink (Toledo Sports Arena), as it was the Toledo Blade's home venue. I'm sure he watched some of our games because we would often play before the Toledo Blade's home games.

Without getting my approval, the owner of the rink, arranged for Coach Slater to show up one morning and watch me skate from high above. I didn't even know that he was there until he came down near the ice, and the owner introduced us. I could tell that the owner of the rink had already talked to Coach Slater about me. I played along because I didn't think anything would come of it. The 'tryout' was very low key. It was just me. I skated for Coach Slater and completed some stick-handling drills.

He knew that I hadn't skated or played hockey since the winter of 1971, 5+ years earlier. I must have piqued his interest enough, that he inquired if I would like to try out for the Stingers as a defenseman. Playing hockey wasn't something I intended to passionately pursue. I was convinced that I'd be back on the gridiron soon, but, considering that no football team had called me yet, I agreed to the tryout, but on one condition: *if an NFL team called and wanted me to join their team, then I would be free to go.* Coach Slater agreed, and that was how I found myself in a Cincinnati Stingers uniform a few days later.

My time with the Stingers lasted about three weeks. Considering I had been away from an ice rink for more than five years, I played very well. It didn't matter, however, because I finally got the call I coveted – a call from an NFL team: the New York Giants. I immediately let Coach Slater know, thanking him for the tryout. He told me he understood, loved my competitive spirit, and wished me success with the Giants.

I wanted to be back in the NFL far more than I wanted to play professional hockey. Then why did I try out for a hockey team? There were two primary reasons that I agreed to try out for the Cincinnati Stingers:

- I wanted to see if I could do it. I didn't want to look back and say "I wish I could have done this when the opportunity came."
- At a subconscious level, it was another way to prop up my fragile self-esteem. While it wasn't my intention, I had no idea the amount of press coverage it would generate from newspapers, radio, and local TV. *"College all-American and former Cincinnati Bengal now with the Cincinnati Stingers – going from football to ice hockey in a matter of weeks?"* From the press' perspective, this kind of noteworthy news sells a lot of newspapers and advertisements.

After being out of football for six weeks, I was back in the NFL, playing a game I loved! I was chastened and learned some valuable lessons. I would not make the same mistake again. I learned I need to fit into the game plan of the coaching staff, be patient and wait for my opportunities like I did with "Kong".

Even though I was back playing NFL football -- my mom's voice wouldn't fade away. Her voice wasn't as loud; but it was still there. That really disturbed me now especially since I was back playing in the NFL.

I needed to embark on my most critical life mission.
- *Find out why I was so negatively affected when released by the Chicago Bears?*
- *Why was I still being haunted by the ghosts from my past?*

Chapter 26
Back in the NFL

"Our greatest glory is not in never failing, but in rising every time we fail." — **Confucius**

After being out of football for nearly seven weeks, I was back in the NFL. When I got the call from the New York Giants (in mid-October 1976), my attitude had changed 180 degrees compared to the poor attitude I had with the Bears. The Giants had lost all their games in the first half of the season in 1976 (0–7). Coach John McVay was named the new Head Coach of the Giants, replacing Coach Bill Arnsbarger, who was fired in mid-season.

Coach McVay had seen me play in college many times because his son (John McVay, Jr) and I were good friends, (he was a groomsman in our wedding) and teammates at Miami. John Jr. was our superb All-MAC Free Safety on our #1 nationally ranked defense.

Coach McVay had another coach on his staff that knew about me as well. Coach Jay Fry, the defensive line coach for the NY Giants, had a son on the same team, Jay Fry Jr., our outstanding All-MAC defensive end. Coach Fry saw me play many times as well. Both coaches played football and graduated from Miami and are members of Miami's nationally recognized "cradle of coaches."

When Coach McVay called, he impressed upon me exactly what my role was to be for the Giants. He wanted me to be a difference-maker, to be a key player on special teams, and to be a backup MLB to their rookie MLB, future All-Pro Hall of Famer -- Harry Carson. I let him know that I would relish the chance to be used as a key role player for him.

Upon arriving in New York, I had to pass the physical and go through several drills. I passed with flying colors. I was placed on all the special teams right away - Punt, Kickoff, Punt Return, Kickoff Return, etc. I learned that the Giants had lost a key special teams' player, Danny

Lloyd, to a season-ending injury. He was the leading guy on their special team's unit and his loss drastically weakened their special teams, which prompted Coach McVay's call to me.

Six days later, I was in the home dressing room of the *Giants, wearing my new #57 New York Giant jersey with "Cousino" imprinted on the back.* I was sitting next to football legend Fullback Larry Czonka, soon to be playing in front of 75,000 fans in the brand-new Giants Stadium in the Meadowlands, NJ.

One of the first games I remembered playing as a New York Giant was against the Detroit Lions. I was pumped... mentally, I was in full-out Beast Mode. I was relishing the moment of being back in the NFL. In that game, I made two tackles on the kickoff team and two tackles on the punt team.

At a crucial point in the game, I blocked a punt that I also recovered and ran to the 4-yard line. Two plays later, the Giants scored a touchdown and took the lead. Early in the fourth quarter, I recovered a fumble on a kickoff. I was in my element: making tackles, blocking kicks, and having a blast.

The New York Giants won their first game of the 1976 season, and I knew that I had achieved what Coach McVay wanted: for me to be a difference-maker. Those plays had a lot to do with their first win of the season. I was on a high from being back in the NFL, and my successful role in it. I knew I was instrumental in helping Coach McVay** win his first game as an NFL Head Coach. And the ever-present New York media was equally thrilled.

** Coach John McVay, a Miami University Alumni, became the general manager of the San Francisco 49ers where Bill Walsh had been hired as head coach and together, they won four Super Bowls. McVay was inducted into San Francisco 49er Hall of Fame.

FYI: Coach McVay is the grandfather to Sean McVay, also a Miami Alumni, and the Head Coach of the Los Angeles Rams (the youngest NFL head coach) who led the LA Rams to win SuperBowl LVI vs. the Cincinnati Bengals

For the remainder of the season with the Giants, I was the top producer on all the special teams (Punt, Kickoff, Punt Return, Kickoff Return, and Field Goal Block). The Giants finished the season with 3 wins – 11 losses. But I was a contributing factor to all three games we won of the 6 games I participated in, which was a huge turnaround for the Giants. Coach McVay* and my defensive coaches (Jay Fry and Marty Schottenheimer) gave me glowing reviews.

My Toughest Coach... A Ballet Instructor*?

In the final game of the 1976 season, I reinjured a minor tear in my right hamstring which resulted in developing a lot of scar tissue. I needed to get it rehabbed or I'd never be able to pass the physical before the Giant's 1977 summer camp began. I signed up with Annelieze von Oettingen, a German lady who was a renowned Ballet instructor. She had a proven reputation of helping other pro athletes (e.g., linebacker Ken Avery) who experienced similar hamstring injuries. I never liked stretching in high school, college, or in the pros. Stretching was always very tough work for me. Annelieze was a tough '*taskmaster*' who pushed me very hard. She gave me NO slack. She also happened to be one of the toughest "coaches" I ever had.

It was a bizarre scene, as she would be teaching a class of 10 to 12 petite ballerinas that could range from 15 to 20 years old. And I would be off in a corner of her studio, dressed in sweats, grunting, and groaning, trying to do all the stretching drills she concocted for me. I had developed so much scar tissue on my right hamstring that it limited my mobility by over 33%. It should have been a career ending injury, but due to the innovative stretching routines she developed, I avoided surgery and increased my speed and quickness to where I was the quickest and fastest, I'd ever been – and most importantly was able to continue playing in the NFL.

** I was featured in the July 11, 1977 edition of Sports Illustrated, with a ¾ page picture of me and a young ballerina along with the story of my ham string recovery that enabled me to continue playing. See Appendix #8 Photo Gallery for a print of the Sports Illustrated Photos & article.*

Chapter 27
Building On Sand

The true test of a champion is not whether he can triumph but whether he can overcome obstacles."
- Garth Stein.

After the last game of the Giants' 1976 season, I was anxious to get back to Cincinnati. I was engaged to Tami, and our wedding was coming up in early April, and I was way behind the curve on my assigned duties. In addition, I had previously agreed to a major speaking engagement in early January in Charlotte, NC.

It was a 12-hour drive back to Cincinnati, which allowed me a lot of alone time to reflect on all that happened to me within the last six months. I had many mixed emotions. Even though I was now playing again in the NFL, which made me happy, lingering doubts were always close by.

Doubts that transformed into fear after each season, because every NFL team would look for younger, bigger, and stronger players to draft onto their team from the college ranks. That was just the way it was at the NFL level.

I finally accepted that fact as my ongoing reality. I would always be on the *bubble* due to my size-related issues – not because of my results on the field. I learned my lesson after the Chicago Bears debacle, and I was OK with that.

NFL football was big-time business. The team owners provided the resources, the General Managers were responsible for building the infrastructure and hiring the Head Coach, and the Head Coach was responsible for hiring his coaching staff, scouting staff, trainers, etc. to build the best team possible and develop a winning culture. They all had their marching orders. And if for whatever reason, I didn't fit into their plans – or prove as best I could that I was a better option – then they were going to proceed accordingly.

Coming To Terms with Myself

I knew the NY Giants would draft one to two linebackers that would be bigger, stronger, and faster than me in the upcoming 1977 draft, and those drafted players would be given every opportunity to take my place. Because of my lack of NFL numbers (height, weight, speed), I was resigned to the fact that I wouldn't have a long NFL career. Even so, I intended to play for as long as I could. Every aspect of football appealed to me: I loved the rivalry, the competition, the idea of becoming a member of a team, the money, popularity, and ego gratification it provided. It was like a drug, and I was addicted to it.

In fact, what scared me the most was how much I loved all these things, and I lived in fear of losing them. I loved it to such an extent that it became my "fake" identity, which is why I reacted the way I did after being released from the Chicago Bears. My future career in football, and the fear of losing it, consumed me.

I did learn some valuable life lessons on my departure from the Chicago Bears. I would never again voice anything that would put me at odds with the coach or the team's culture... above all - team first! Yet, there was a persistent fear that kept raising its ugly head; not about my football abilities - but about why I was so messed up in my head. I knew it wasn't healthy.

Without realizing it, I was on a rescue mission to find (and fix) the core reason why I responded the way I did when I was released from the Bears. It consumed me because I knew it was just a matter of time, (*either in 10 days, 10 months, or 10 years*) when I would not be playing football in the NFL. And I didn't want a repeat of what happened after being released from the Bears.

With that thought locked in my head and me being unable to shake it off, (even when I was now back playing in the NFL) I retreated to the many self-improvement books and audiotapes I had collected by famous authors on self-esteem, self-improvement, personal growth, dealing with rejection, building a successful life, service to others, etc. I sought comfort and hope in gleaning truth from the books that could make a difference to my messed-up life.

Addicted to Fame, Prestige, & Status

In those many books, I learned that a person could become addicted to many things besides negative things such as drugs, alcohol, cigarettes, or porn. One can be addicted to positive things as well -- fame, prestige, status, looks, worldly objects of success (the car you drive, the neighborhood you live in, the designer clothes, the purse you carry, the schools your kids attend, etc.,). I'm a third or fourth generation (that I'm aware of) of men who had their lives (and families) controlled by addictions to alcohol and/or drugs.

While I did not go down the path of drugs or alcohol, I had all the characteristics of an addict, and it was time I came to terms with it. *When I was out of the NFL, I was consumed with getting back in. When I was in the NFL, I was consumed by fears of losing it. At my deepest level as a human being, my survival was dependent on the power and prestige the NFL afforded me.* I knew deep down that wasn't truth (instead I believed the lies), but it took a great amount of strength and courage to accept that I believed hundreds of lies about my own life, a false sense of 'self-worth' built on a foundation of sand. I was on a mission to solve the riddle of living a good life without the artificial ego satisfaction of needing to be a professional athlete.

My new preferred "addictions" were reading self-help books and listening to motivational cassette tapes. They were a source of energy. I felt like I was on a quest. I was digging for **nuggets of truth** in those books and tapes to replace the many lies. Those expressions of inspiration were spoken by people who had inspired millions of others going through similar trials and tribulations. I felt compelled to absorb their words to find a way to heal my spirit and mind, to ultimately heal the huge hole in my heart.

By the end of the 1976 football season, I had finished reading almost twenty such books and not just once, but some books two and three times. I had listened to hundreds of hours of tapes of people who were motivating me to become a better human being and to give me tools to help turn my life around. When I was reading those books, it was like I was trying to mend something that was broken, but I didn't know what it was or just how deep it went. I wanted all my issues resolved at once. I wanted to evade the garbage brewing within my mind. As I was on my quest, I learned that when I read something that turned my life upside down, it let me see the world in a whole different way.

I recognized that much of my life was built on *an unstable foundation of lies*. I believed a vast variety of false information, hundreds to thousands of lies from mom and dad, from my grandparents, from teachers, for most of my early life. I learned that people I trusted, (parents, relatives, neighbors, teachers, coaches, and even long-time family friends), had either *knowingly OR unknowingly* guided me away from the very path of truth required to be a whole person.

All the while, as I was reading from the many books, and/or listening to the tapes, I was trying to find truth-nuggets that would replace the lies I was brought up with – lies that made me doubt who I was created to be and the abilities I was expected to cultivate. At its core, I was trying to find the underlying truth of **why** I reacted so strongly when released from the Bears.

Why was it so important that I had to play in the NFL?

Why was I not willing to accept my role as a special team's player only?

Why was my self-worth / self-esteem based on needing to be an elite NFL football player?

As I look back, I was really searching to acquire *unconditional love,* and if I could discover it, that would be the catalyst to build a high self-worth and a positive self-image. In my search, I felt constrained to become a better version of me; to be a person who could help guide others facing downtimes in their lives. But I must fix my own messed-up life before I could guide anyone else.

In my extensive search, I stumbled on another piece of the puzzle when reading in one of the older Christian classics. What I uncovered struck my heart like a *mini explosion*. As I began to grasp the significance of what I discovered; I was compelled to find out if that might be the answer to my quest! This quote added even more fuel to my fire:

"I believe that when you search for truth, it will be found. But it often happens when you least expect it." – *Unknown*

Chapter 28
Unshackled Against All Odds

"The thing that scares you the most can often be the start of a path that defines who you are, who you will be in the future, and what you are going to do with your life."   **- Unknown**

In June 1976, prior to being traded to the Chicago Bears, I had been invited to give my "Against All Odds" keynote address to a major corporate event in Charlotte, NC, scheduled for early January 1977. I accepted it, the contract was signed, and the event was officially booked. I didn't think much about it until I saw that the date was fast approaching. In the six months since accepting that speaking engagement, much had transpired in my life.

I...

- was traded from the Cincinnati Bengals to the Chicago Bears / late June 1976

- subleased my apartment, moved to Chicago, reported to the Bears camp in mid-July 1976

- was waived/released from the Chicago Bears in late August 1976, moved back to Cincy

- wrestled with significant personal self-esteem issues due to being cut from an NFL team

- played professional hockey with the Cincinnati Stingers, September / October 1976

- became engaged to Tami in October 1976, with the wedding planned for early April 1977

- moved to New York and played with the NY Giants football team in mid-October 1976

- moved from NY back to Cincinnati in late December 1976

- was scheduled to speak to an audience of over 4,000 business owners on January 8th, 1977.

Yet now I felt "*unworthy*" to tell my story because of my negative reaction from being released from an NFL team and how it affected my self-esteem/self-worth/self-acceptance. I didn't want to be a fraud and pretend that those issues didn't affect my life. I was a different person compared to when I agreed to be a key-note speaker for my Charlotte engagement. Despite now playing in the NFL again with the New York Giants, I needed to find why I reacted to my self-esteem-related problems. I needed to comprehend what was happening, and how I could get to the root cause of my deep insecurities.

I was consumed with two simple, yet complex questions: "Why?" And "Why now?"

When I was originally contacted about speaking to this group of business owners, I was told the projected number of people attending from around the country could be as high as 5,000. I had spoken at similar events before to entrepreneurial-minded groups but in smaller venues – 300 to 1,000 attendees. But as the date got closer, I had mixed feelings about my ability to stand in front of a large audience and be transparent about what I was dealing with mentally and emotionally.

For some unknown reason, I felt compelled to be transparent and share my real-life experiences after being released from the Bears and how it affected me deep in my heart. I wanted to include it in my keynote address, "Against All Odds." Then it occurred to me that I should add another aspect to my talk; "Become the Best Version of Yourself", an uplifting, game-changing speech to inspire people to embrace the concept of becoming unshackled from the many lies that can entangle us if we accept those lies into our lives.

I revamped my story with examples that revolved around the courage and tenacity to never quit, to never coast, to never cheat myself by failing to give my very best, and to never listen to all those who would try to steal my dream, especially when I went through the dry periods of a temporary loss or failure. "Bad" times happen to virtually every person who has a dream or goal, and they only ever reach it after overcoming the obstacles in their path of temporary failures, to become all that they were created to be. I revised my keynote address, which I re-titled:

Unshackled...Against All Odds:

"Become the Best Version of Yourself"

As I mentioned earlier, I was doing research for my revamped speech, when I uncovered a revelation that I had been searching for since I was released from the Chicago Bears. I discovered the ancient Greek word **'SOZO.'** I didn't have a clue what that Greek word SOZO meant.

So, I did some research of the original meaning of SOZO which I found to include **ALL** the following concepts, **to be: *Saved, Transformed, Renewed, Healed, Delivered, Restored, Redeemed, Salvaged, Forgiven, Recreated, Rescued, Loved, Cherished, Chosen, made Whole and Complete.***

In one powerful word, I found that *SOZO* encapsulated all the life-changing concepts I had been diligently searching for. I was so excited about my discovery, even though I didn't know how to state what I was searching for so succinctly. If I could grasp all that *SOZO* means and incorporate that truth in my life, I felt it would fulfill the key solutions to all my deep issues I've been wrestling with -- poor self-esteem, low self-worth, rejection, cold love, lack of forgiveness, self-acceptance, etc. But this represented a new quandary for me. I was absolutely convinced that *SOZO* was what I was searching for, what I needed, but I was clueless on how to achieve it.

****

The time had come to travel the eight hours to Charlotte, NC. Accompanying me on my journey was Tami. We were to be married in less than ninety days. We arrived ahead of schedule, and checked into our hotel rooms, and went downstairs to meet the event's leadership team. They briefed me about my scheduled time to speak on Saturday afternoon. I was going to give my revamped speech for the first time, a raw, unflinching, almost soul-baring in nature - a far more transparent version of my life-story.

I was more excited than normal, and yet very nervous. Something big was on the horizon. I could feel it! I spoke on Saturday afternoon, and *4,500 pair* of eyes were riveted on me. As usual, I was nervous as I was being introduced by the MC, but I just grinned as I grabbed the microphone.

"Hello, friends! How are you all doing today?" I called out.

The audience cheered in response.

"Excellent! My name is Brad Cousino, and we are going on a journey that could positively impact your life, if you'll allow it. My talk is titled: 'Unshackled... Against All Odds: Become the Best Version of Yourself'". This is my true story of the journey to become a far better version of myself. It all starts with..."

It was an amazing atmosphere where I, as the speaker, and they, as the audience, communicated in one accord. It was my best speech up to that time. I was more vulnerable and transparent than any speech I'd given before. I let them peek into my heart and soul and see someone who seemed to have it all together on the outside (as an NFL player) but, deep within, I was really a fractured mess. I was trying to piece myself back together as I wrestled with a sense of shame, low self-esteem, inadequacy, rejection, and false pride that was always lurking just beneath the surface -- that finally surfaced when I was released / waived from an NFL team. Even so, I never quit – but rose from the ashes of the temporary setbacks to continue my quest, which was still in process. The audience loved it!

But it was what happened after my talk that was truly inspiring. It was overwhelming. Over a thousand people seated in that coliseum made their way toward me for autographs, pictures and/or to ask questions. I was shocked at how many different people from all walks of life resonated with my story.

The most common request was *to inquire if I had a book or a video tape about my story and/or cassette tapes they could buy, so they could share with their parents, kids, relatives, brothers-in-law, neighbors, coworkers, etc., I wasn't trying to sell anything – in fact, I didn't have anything to sell or even to give them.* If I had, I think they would have bought them all. Tears moistened my eyes, and my heart was soaring with gratitude.

Later that evening, we enjoyed a celebratory dinner with the leadership of this successful event. We were invited to the morning non-denominational church service for 7:30 am. I politely declined, stating that we would be leaving early the next morning for the eight-hour drive back to Cincinnati. But that was only partially true.

My Deal with God

At this time in my life, I had personal issues about going to any kind of religious service. I hadn't been to a religious church service since high school, and then only because it was required if I was going to play in the game later that day. To be honest, I simply had **no desire** to attend any religious function.

I know I probably shouldn't admit this, but I didn't want to be associated with God or Jesus and anything that looked, sounded, or smelled religious. I couldn't understand it at the time, but I now know why -- I had major trust issues with God. Growing up, I reached out to God many times asking questions that I desperately needed answers to:

1] Why did He allow my parents, especially mom, to reject me and physically abuse me? 2] And if God is the all-powerful, all-knowing, all-loving God that I learned about in my years of grade school religion classes, why didn't He save me from my miserable upbringing?

In a strange way, I had no problems believing in God. But I believed He must be extremely preoccupied with far more critical matters in running the universe, and had little time, inclination, or interest in anyone who had been rejected on planet Earth, such as myself. So, I made a deal with God when I was a junior in high school:

"OK God - if you don't bother me... I promise I won't bother you!"

Unlike many people, I really didn't have a "belief" issue accepting that there was a Supreme Being we call God who may indeed have had a son named Jesus, who came to earth about 2,000 years ago. That was not an issue for me. In fact, I believe it takes far more faith to believe that our universe just popped into existence because of a "Big Bang", and then humanity evolved from a simple single-cell amoeba. Some people believe that somehow, someway, over the eons of time we evolved, without any help or guidance from a higher superior intelligent being, into the *uniqueness that makes up all humanity*! In my opinion, that requires a *massive leap of faith, far more than believing in a Creator.*

But I also remind myself that great people such as Socrates, Plato, Thomas Jefferson, Christopher Columbus, George Washington, and Abraham Lincoln all lived and died hundreds to thousands of years ago as well. Maybe some, or even all, of the great things they did were actual real events, but how and why did those men's actions back centuries ago *somehow make an impact on those of us alive today?*

And in the same vein, how does what the historical Jesus may have done by dying on a cross and then being raised from the dead two thousand (2,000) years ago have an impact on me today; how is that even possible?

As I wrestled with those ideas, a new revelation began percolating in my mind, perhaps I should reconsider and attend the early morning service as it could be another necessary piece to the mystery of figuring out my "self-worth/personal rejection" issues in my unresolved personal puzzle. I was perplexed. Why was I feeling pulled in opposite directions? It was quite strange, for reasons I could not understand-- *I did not want to go to the morning service; yet why did I feel compelled to do so?*

Chapter 29
Rejected & Unwanted... Again ?

"Don't go where it is all fine music and grand talk and beautiful architecture; those things will neither fill anybody's stomach nor feed his soul. Go where the gospel is preached, the gospel that really feeds your soul, and go often."
--Charles Spurgeon

As we arrived back at our hotel later that afternoon, I thought about the events a few hours earlier. I had given what I considered to be the best keynote address of my life. It was significantly better than other speeches I'd given in the past because I shared this from my heart. The reception was beyond anything I could have dreamed. I was far more vulnerable and transparent on stage in ways I had never been before. Those who attended, loved it! Even so, I was confused because of my continuing internal struggles.

This didn't stop me from trying to figure out what was wrong with me. The truth was, and is, as I tried to move along with my life, I hadn't learned how to really 'deal' with the trauma inflicted upon me growing up. I couldn't get rid of the scars that were holding me back, because the wounds I experienced caused me to believe the lies which created them.

I realized I had to choose one of two paths:

1] Either choose to make a stand, face the trauma head-on and begin the process of healing, or

2] Allow those scars to destroy me as I allow the scars from the intense trauma inflicted to define my life and that of my future family.

For me, those seemed to be my only viable options.

***

I mistakenly thought my speech earlier on Saturday afternoon was the end of my Charlotte, NC journey, but it wasn't the end; it turned out to be just the beginning! I was amid a major life struggle to figure out what was the root cause of my lack of self-esteem, self-worth, and rejection issues. In addition, I had all this information and nuggets of truth circulating in my mind from the dozens of books I read and the hundreds of hours of cassette tapes I listened to repeatedly over the last six months. Something was bothering me... over and over in my mind, I was wrestling with a new dilemma, should we (Tami and I) go to the service in the morning or not? I was torn because I really didn't want to go, but there was this tugging on my heart saying that I needed to be there.

A recurring thought echoed through my mind:

What if...whatever I've been searching for was going to be revealed in some way at that service? If I didn't go when I was so close and already here, it would be another foolish, self-inflicted wound. I didn't want to miss out on the possibility of important truths I was searching for because I was too stubborn and proud to attend an early morning religious service. So, later in the evening, Tami and I were reviewing all that had taken place earlier in the afternoon. I then brought up what was really bothering me.

"Tami, something's been on my mind for the past few hours."

"What is it?" she asked.

"Ever since dinner ended, I've been thinking about that invitation to the Sunday service."

"I thought you didn't want to go?"

"I really don't. But maybe we should stay for the church service in the morning, and then leave right after. I feel we need to be there." Her eyes lit up. *"That's a great idea!"*

****

Frankly, I didn't think very many people would attend the service, based on what I know about larger conventions. Saturday nights are typically social events with friends and/or their teams, where people go out for dinner and drinks, stay out late partying, etc. So, my expectation was maybe only a few hundred people out of the 4,500 would get up early to arrive at the Charlotte Coliseum before 7:30am on a cold Sunday morning.

However, this was not what we found. When we arrived at the Coliseum early Sunday morning, there were already long lines to get into the Coliseum at 7:15. By the time the service started, there must have been over 2,000 people attending. I was shocked that there would be this many people early on a cold Sunday morning after many had stayed out late the night before.

The atmosphere wasn't what I expected for a church service either; it was upbeat, with a lot of good-natured teasing, joking, hugging, and laughing. Not anything close to what I expected - a quiet, peaceful sermon, more akin to what a message given at a funeral would be like... somber, quiet, and reflective. I told Tami, "*I think these people are either nuts or they know something that we don't.*"

We were invited to sit with some of the company leaders that we met the day before. Everyone was warm and friendly with no seeming agenda and excited to attend this early morning event. I could tell that some of those attending knew exactly what to expect, and they were going out of their way to help the "newbies" to this kind of church service in such a mammoth convention center. Tami and I were in the "newbie" group.

Upbeat Christian music was playing. It was obvious that this kind of church service was just as important as the business events on Friday and Saturday…you could tell by the crowd's excitement, joy, and passion that this Sunday morning event was almost a culmination to the weekend. I looked around and soaked it in. This was so far removed from how I was brought up in a religious environment.

As I remember our Sunday service growing up, everyone was quiet and somber. I never remember anyone smiling, laughing, or hugging. We either sat, stood, or kneeled in the designated rows, looking to the priest who was behind the altar. I was mesmerized, almost in disbelief, as I looked around and witnessed the sheer happiness and exuberant joy on the faces of many people.

At about 7:35 am, the band started up, and everyone quieted down. There were huge screens with the words to the music, and most everyone was standing and singing loudly and proudly. That didn't happen in my church experience. We had hymnals, the choir director would tell us what hymn number to turn to, and then a few people would join in and sing out loud. Most everyone else moved their lips, mouthing the words with little or no passion - and the music wasn't upbeat at all.

There was about ten minutes of singing some contemporary Christian music. I even joined in and started singing along with Tami. Then it was time for the special guest speaker, Doug Weed, who spoke for about thirty minutes. I can't recall what he said, but I know whatever it was, it was almost as if he was talking directly to my heart and soul. It was strange, but in a good way. I nodded my head in agreement on much of what he was talking about. As he finished his message, he gave a call to action and passionately invited anyone who wanted to come up to the front of the stage, and he would pray for them.

Despite feeling uncomfortable with going forward, I was compelled to get on my feet and walk to the stage. I felt if I didn't go up, I would miss out on something vitally important. So, I took Tami's hand (not realizing she had to make her own decision to want to come forward) and followed the hundreds of others who headed to the front. By the time we got to the front of the stage, there must have been 500 people already there. I didn't know what to expect, but I was amazed at what I witnessed. I saw people who were weeping. Some had huge smiles. Others were laughing and hugging their friends. It seemed that the joy and happiness in the room was authentic.

I was looking all around as the speaker then asked us to bow our heads and repeat out loud the prayer that he would lead us in. Before he led us in prayer, he made it clear that there wasn't anything magic in the words spoken... but it was the attitude of our hearts that God could see – as nothing is hidden from Him.

He then prayed a prayer in short sentences. *I repeated the prayer, word for word, out loud, as sincere as I could possibly be.* **I wanted and needed what he spoke about: a spiritual awakening, transformation, unconditional love, repentance, forgiveness, joy, adoption, sonship, and when I die, I'd go to this perfect place called Heaven.** A spiritual life of no pain or sorrow, just endless peace & contentment that I learned was referred to as "eternal" life – whatever that means!

Unwanted, Unworthy, and now Rejected by God?

For whatever reason, I didn't experience anything close to what the others did. I witnessed others experience a wide range of joy, smiles, laughing, tears, peace, serenity, goosebumps down arms, necks, and backs. I, on the other hand, felt nothing except *emptiness*. I vividly pictured in my mind that *I must have done something so bad, so vile, so horrendous,* that even God couldn't forgive me and wanted nothing to do with me.

Unwanted, Unworthy and REJECTED again! How could I recover from that reality? I was in total despair. I was unwanted and rejected by Almighty God, just as I was unwanted and rejected by my parents! This reality was simply overwhelming. On the outside, I held it together, but on the inside, it was more than I could handle! At least, that's how I felt because I didn't experience the positive, happy emotions that I witnessed all around me. That was not even close to what I hoped for by attending this early morning church service.

After the service, I didn't want to talk with anyone. We quickly departed for the long drive back to Cincinnati. I didn't want to think about what had just happened to me. The voice of my mom was increasing in volume – *as she was already reminding me of being a no-good loser who wouldn't amount to anything good. Yes, even God Almighty has rejected you. You're a S.O.B, a total loser of a person.*

It was like an echo chamber, over and over again. I didn't know how to process that not only was I rejected and unwanted by my parents – but I was such a 'loser' that I was unwanted and rejected by God and Jesus Christ Himself. WHY? Is it possible, God rejected me because mom was right. ***Was I indeed born bad?***

Chapter 30
God Appointments

"You must ask for God's help. Even when you have done so, it may seem to you for a long time that no help, or less help than you need, is being given. Never mind. After each failure, ask forgiveness, pick yourself up, and try again. Very often what God first helps us towards is not the virtue itself but just this power of always trying again.
- C.S. Lewis

We arrived in Cincinnati early in the evening after a long drive. For the next few days, I went over the Charlotte encounter in my head, trying to understand the considerable implication that God had apparently rejected me (or so I thought) and what I should do next. It became apparent at one point that when I die, I will spend the rest of whatever life there is after death in a place horrid beyond comprehension. Without God, I knew I was doomed! I needed some answers, so I put a call into Wendel Deyo. Unfortunately, he wasn't in town.

Out of desperation, I cried out to God, *telling Him how sorry I was for everything I'd done wrong in my life. And that I believed He was the only true God, and that Jesus was His Son who died on the cross to save me and the rest of mankind, and that I knew I was lost without Him. I pleaded with Him to do whatever it took to heal my heart, and to rebuild my spirit and soul, knowing that I couldn't do it without Him!*

While my outward appearance (being a pro NFL player) seemed like all was well compared to the rest of the world, my inner self (my heart, spirit, and soul) was in a horrible mess. I was hoping for a response from God -- anything that would give me "proof" that God heard and answered my prayers, but I got nothing but deafening silence.

Later that week, I walked through Kenwood Towne Center, a popular suburban mall in the Cincinnati area, and passed a Berean Christian bookstore. I felt compelled to turn around and go inside the store. *It's important that you know that I'd never been inside a Christian bookstore before that day -- ever!* I looked around and eventually asked a store employee:

"Excuse me, what would you recommend as a good book to read about God?"

"Come with me," she said, *"I have just the thing."*

She picked out a very thick, leatherbound book, and said this was a popular Bible - <u>The Authorized King James Bible</u>. I purchased it, took it home, and started reading at the beginning of the Bible - Genesis. Reading it was a struggle because it was written in the old English vernacular. After reading about the Creation story and how Adam and Eve got kicked out of the Garden of Eden, I decided to start reading the next book following Genesis --- Exodus. I lasted about an hour before I gave up. I was totally frustrated and lost; it was just too difficult to comprehend for me.

God Appointment #1

Later that week, I was in the same mall and walked by the same Christian bookstore. For whatever reason, I felt a strong inclination to turn back around and go back into that bookstore. I was looking for some books about God to read and ended up in the Bible section again. I struck up a conversation with a friendly shopper who was in the same section.

"Come here often?" I asked.

"Yes," she confirmed. *"I'm trying to find something to help my friends understand God a little more easily."*

I blinked in surprise. *"What a coincidence; I'm in the same boat! I just picked up the King James Bible a few days ago, and honestly, it's quite hard to follow."*

She smiled. *"I can help you out. Perhaps this will help."*

She pulled out a book that was at eye level, The Living Bible. *"This Bible is not a literal translation, but a paraphrase, because it's written in modern, everyday English, but I think it will definitely help you out."*

"Super!" I exclaimed. *"Now I hope I'll understand what Genesis and Exodus were saying."*

Here she held up her index finger. *"Hmmm, you don't start reading the Bible from beginning to end. I'd recommend starting with the Gospel of John, in the New Testament, and going from there."* I thought to myself, *What? You don't start at the beginning of the book? You start reading in the middle of the book? Who would know that?* Then this total stranger opened that Living Bible, pointing me to the New Testament and then where the Gospel of John was located! I had no clue about anything Bible-related.

I believe this lady was the first of many of what I call my "*God Appointments*". These God Appointments were pivotal moments in my life and spiritual journey that greatly impacted me. Think about the odds that a total stranger guided me to a proper Bible for me as a "newbie", then she showed me where the New Testament began, and even showed me where to find the Gospel of John. I'm convinced, *that was not a coincidence, but a specific God Appointment!*

Before I left the store, I bought The Living Bible. As I left the store, I asked myself, *why did I purchase two Bibles in less than a week when I had never read a single word from any Bible until a few days before?* For me, buying two Bibles within a few days was indeed abnormal behavior.

When I got home, I immediately began reading in the Gospel of John, as the lady recommended. I was instantly hooked. I read for hours upon hours, all 21 chapters of the Gospel of John – twice. This Bible was impossible for me to put down. I remembered some of the stories, or parables, from religion classes in elementary school. After the Book of John, I began reading passages from the other gospels in the Bible, such as Matthew, Mark, and Luke.

I consider this my first *God Appointment* because a total stranger opened my eyes to a Bible I could comprehend and couldn't put down once I started reading. I felt this "unknown lady" was on a special assignment from God. While I don't know, I believe this lady probably had no idea she was on such an assignment as an answer to my prayers. This was the beginning of many significant milestones in the transformation process of my SOZO experience.

God Appointment #2

The events described above occurred in mid-January 1977. As it was now in my NFL off-season, I would get up around 8:00 a.m. and read the Bible non-stop for five to six hours at a time, take a break to eat, keep my off-season workouts on schedule for the next football season, and then return to reading. It was as if I had a big void in my heart and soul that I couldn't seem to fill, but when I was reading the Bible or listening to Christian messages or music, I felt a sense of peace, joy, and contentment that I couldn't begin to describe.

This went on for several months. I couldn't seem to get enough of it. The strange thing was, *no one told me I needed to read the Bible, go to church, give money, or do anything religious*. The truth was, no one in the greater Cincinnati area, other than Tami, was even aware of what occurred when I was in Charlotte.

Best of all, my mom's voice in my head repeating the 'lies' I heard over & over was fading from my conscious thoughts. I didn't believe any longer the vicious lies I heard repeatedly, such as...

*"I was a no-good loser, a S.O.B. ba***rd, who wouldn't amount to anything"* any longer.

But instead, new positive, uplifting thoughts emerged from my heart – thoughts like...

"I'm forgiven, I'm accepted, I'm redeemed, I'm loved unconditionally, I'm a favored child of God!" Those words were so foreign to me. Yet now I believed and accepted them as true!

As I continued to read the Bible, my actions became different – far more positive. Tami noticed it right away. *The way I was talking to people around me became different, which was no less a miracle. I used to curse, cuss, swear and blaspheme God, a lot.* I would say curse words that were disparaging to God and/or people I was close to. *My "foul vocabulary" was learned from the many years of hearing my mom and dad cuss & curse, plus all the time I spent in high school, college, and pro locker rooms.* As a result, I had plenty of deeply embedded habits that I never thought were either good or bad issues. It was just the way some people react when they speak, especially when angry or agitated.

Tami noticed just how different I acted; *my entire personality changed for the better. I was more positive towards others and myself. Over a period of about six weeks, I supernaturally stopped cursing, cussing, and blaspheming. It was not me that made the changes, but God.* I can only assume that in my search for truth, *God was transforming me as a person through my words and character. Because of my belief in my heart that Jesus was the son of God, that He died on the cross and was raised from the dead, I was totally forgiven and was now in process of being transformed into a better version of Brad Cousino.*

I can't explain it in detail. But it was God who decided to change some aspects of my character. *He redeemed me, saved me, healed me, and transformed me into a far better version of the old Brad Cousino.* It was not me deciding to become more religious by cleaning up my filthy mouth via my self-effort. I know that I didn't purposely try to change my foul mouth, it could only be GOD transforming me from the inside out!

God Appointment #3

There are other areas that God intervened in my life, namely, my vicious temper. As I grew up, it was natural for me to display my anger on others as my parents did towards me. When I was younger, when I was being hit or screamed at by my parents, I hoped that someone would come to my rescue and protect me. Perhaps that's why I became so enraged when I saw someone bully or hurt my younger brothers or verbally abuse someone younger or weaker. I couldn't bear seeing someone else suffering the same torment I endured. It ignited something in me, a spark that called me to fight for the oppressed. When I lost my temper, I became filled with rage (Beast Mode), and I was unstoppable. It was weird, when provoked, I possessed this supernatural strength and would use it against whoever my foe was. I never lost a fight; in fact, it wasn't even close.

As I reflect on my football career, I played with intense rage. It was a primary reason why I was so successful on the football field. I always played against bigger and stronger players, but I was usually the victor. I am convinced that my playing style was influenced by the intensity of my anger and hostility that I had for the world. I used this intensity of rage and temper to prove that I was a better player than anyone on the field, whether they were my competition – or even members of my team.

****

I remember an incident during my sophomore year in college. It occurred after the 1972 Miami football season (my sophomore year) was over, and I was back in Point Place for the Christmas holiday. On my first night back, I met up with some of my high school buddies at a sports bar near the University of Toledo (UT) campus, a hangout for current and former UT athletes and students. It was good to catch up with some of my football and wrestling buddies: a few of my closest friends in high school were there -- Jerome Addis, Tom Ember, Mike Reilly, Gary Baz, Russ Mobius, Mike Veres, Bernie Hoyt, Jessie Martinez, Willie Sysmanski, Mike Ott, and those crazy Ryzmek twin brothers -- Mickey & Fred to name just a few. I really enjoyed the time we spent laughing and teasing each other over our exploits as former "jocks" getting into all kinds of mischief while students at Central Catholic High School.

It was getting late, about 1:15 am, and I told my group of friends that I was going to head back to Point Place, about a 25-minute drive. As I was leaving, I noticed a huge guy left the bar right after me and headed for his car. At that time, I didn't give it much thought, as I was used to seeing very large guys all the time on my team and/or the players I competed against. I exited the parking lot and turned on to Monroe Street, a major boulevard, when suddenly a car came next to mine, whizzing past me at a very rapid speed. The driver pulled his car directly in front of mine, then reduced his speed on purpose.

I tried to go around him, but he wouldn't let me. As I tried to go to the left and then to the right, he deliberately did the same maneuver. This occurred numerous times. I was getting angrier by the second. After a few minutes, as he continued his purposely slow drive, I decided that I was just going to follow him. After about five minutes, he pulled into a subdivision. Then he drove his car up into a private driveway, which I assumed was where he lived.

I was watching as a very large man got out of the car. I was shocked -- it was the same huge guy from the nightclub. I didn't know or care what this was about. Nothing mattered because I was filled with such rage that I was out of control. He then laughed at me and said, "*What are you going to do, little man?*" *He then declared that he would kick my a**, and there was nothing I could do about that either.*

At that moment, as he tried to attack me, I instinctively made a wrestling move, and within seconds he was lying on his back on the ground. I was all over him, punching him relentlessly, without mercy. I was like a rabid dog. I continued to hit him all over his arms, chest, gut, face, and head. He grabbed my sweater and was choking me, and in doing so, he tore it. Hearing the rip enraged me even more. I punched him with such power, anger, and rage that he became unconscious within 15 seconds.

When he went limp, I purposely searched his back pocket and found his wallet, where I took out a $20 bill to pay to replace my new sweater, then I threw his wallet (with the remaining money) into the next-door neighbor's front yard bushes. He remained unconscious, but I did check, and he was still breathing! It was about 1:50 am when I left him and drove home. ***That kind of intense rage had become a regular part of my life growing up.***

Something Strange was Brewing!

In early March of 1977, about a month before our wedding, I started noticing that I wasn't shouting or yelling at people. I wasn't getting angry or agitated when drivers used to come in front of me or honk their horns or did not use their turn signals. I don't know how else to explain it. Something deep was going on in my spirit and soul. I didn't really understand, but something was changing inside of me. And I was certain that it wasn't me trying to make these changes -- to try to become a better person.

So, I met with Wendel, to get his input as to what I was experiencing. I explained what happened while in Charlotte and all that had transpired once I got back into town. He asked me a few questions which I answered as best I could.

"Wendel, what is going on in my life?" I asked.

Wendel encouraged me, *"Brad, just stay the course... continue reading the Bible and talking to Jesus." And then he said with a knowing smile, "Trust that God is at work – because He is working in your life in a very special way. It is very good!"*

Now, as I look back, I know that my life was being transformed for the better. I used to be an angry beast, but I became a much calmer guy. Over time, I stopped shouting, cussing, or going into episodes of rage. It wasn't because I felt I needed to change. I never felt a need to change my hot temper or foul mouth. I know that it wasn't me trying to make myself into a better human being. It could only be God who brought a miracle into my life. He transformed me in significant ways from the inside out.

By the grace of God, I was in process of what I researched... my own SOZO transformation where I was being *saved, redeemed, forgiven, made whole, restored, salvaged, healed, delivered*, etc. I can't explain it, but God had rescued and liberated me from two serious negative areas in my life - my vicious temper and my corrupt, profane language and as I soon realized that was just the beginning of my transformation.

God Appointment #4

About a week before our wedding, I came out of my apartment to get some items I left in my car's trunk. I noticed my car had been broken into on the driver's side, and glass was shattered all over the seats and floor of the car. I searched the inside of my car to discover the things that were stolen. I found that the culprit stole a carrying case that held my favorite tapes. I would normally have lost my temper, marched to the manager, made a big scene, as I'd be loudly cussing them out to find the person who was responsible and pay back the damage done to my car and for my possessions that were stolen. I would have demanded that they do it...and do it NOW!

But somehow, someway, I was changed on the inside, something that was strange and a relief at the same time. Instead of marching to the manager's office, I leaned against the hood of my car, crossed my arms, and said out loud, "*Lord, whoever stole my tapes, I hope they find the time to listen to them.*"

What? Why would I think or say something like that? Because that case was filled with Christian sermons, teaching tapes, and worship music. I laughed silently to myself as I spoke out loud:

"Brad, what is the matter with you? Your car was broken into, the window was smashed, and valuable stuff was stolen. And your response is, you hope that the thief takes the time to listen to the tapes. Have you lost your mind?" I now know I was not losing my mind, but it was God transforming me from the inside out.

God Appointment #5

Earlier I shared that Tami grew up totally immersed in unconditional love. There were NO raised voices, swearing, or curse words uttered in her home. She knew nothing about being physically abused, deceived, or emotionally abandoned. Howard and Betty Netzly were ideal parents. My hope was to raise my future family the same way.

I know this, *IF* I had exhibited any of my learned behaviors from how I was raised from my family to Tami after we were married, it would have broken her sweet, innocent spirit. God's timing of my internal transformation couldn't have been more perfect. It happened when God wanted it to happen, just weeks before Tami and I were to be married.

Besides my new growing relationship with God, Tami was a primary reason why I wanted to change my life for the better. She was the one woman who had won my heart. I didn't want to lash out at her. I didn't ever want to raise my voice at her. I didn't want to become like my parents to her because I knew she would have gotten wounded.

She would have felt so hurt that there would have been no way she could have recovered from it. If I had done that, it would have devastated her. Ultimately, it would have ruined our marriage. Of course, there have been many times where I get irritated, agitated, or exasperated with people, sometimes even Tami, but the way I handle these frustrations doesn't resemble anything close to the negative patterns of my past, no shouting, cursing, shaming, hitting, etc.**

I believe He protected Tami and my future family from the negative patterns instilled in me. I believe it was another instance of God's miraculous intervention in my life, changing me in profound ways... ways that would impact me and my family for generations into the future.

I am in AWE. Thank You, Lord God for transforming me!

** As a living testimony, since 1977, neither my kids nor Tami have ever heard me cuss, curse, swear or blaspheme. *How is that possible, considering the way I was raised and growing up in locker rooms?* Because only God changing me from within could have intervened to break the generational chain of verbal and physical abuse that had been passed down through generations of my family tree.

Chapter 31
Plan 'B' Exit Strategy

"Show me someone who has done something worthwhile, and I'll show you someone who has overcome adversity."   -Lou Holtz

Did you know that in professional boxing, there are eight traditional weight divisions? They are divided this way to make the sport fair to boxers of all sizes.

In college and pro football, there are no weight classes. I had matured enough to face the reality that the NFL wanted to fill their roster with the heavyweight class. The taller, bigger, stronger, and faster, the better. If they are among the most elite athletes in the world, as most pro football players are, then the tallest, biggest, strongest, and fastest players are going to be given every opportunity to make the starting lineup and experience the longest careers.

After being released / waived from the Chicago Bears in 1976, I had come to accept the realization that my NFL career was going to be far shorter than I wanted. Since my marriage to Tami, I had the new responsibility of providing a secure environment for her, and hopefully, our soon-to-be children. I wanted to be in a position where I could leave the game of football with a seamless transition into my 'Plan B' career, whether it was in the next ten months or ten years. It felt like the off-season of 1977 was the perfect time to return to the real estate investment arena I had briefly explored back in the 1976 off-season. Commercial Real estate ownership and management excited me.

Back in the 1976 off-season, I became friends with two real estate pros who taught me what to look for and how to assess investment properties. Now, in the spring of 1977, I felt I was prepared to begin a real estate business of my own as a manager and owner of rental properties. I intended to become an expert over time and to eventually become a

Certified Property Manager, (CPM), which is the equivalent of a master's degree in commercial property investing and management. So, I started searching for smaller 4-to-8-unit apartment buildings to buy.

One Sunday afternoon, while doing my weekly routine search in the Cincinnati Enquirer Sunday newspaper for available apartment assets, I discovered a brand-new ad for a larger 48-unit apartment complex, with a mix of 20-one-bedroom units and 28-two-bedroom garden-style units. The ad claimed that the owner had to sell due to health issues. This piqued my interest, not that he had health issues, but that the reason for the sale wasn't due to a failing business. The property was located on Cincinnati's far east side, in Amelia, OH, about 25 miles due east of downtown Cincinnati, approximately a 35-minute drive.

I dialed the number listed in the ad and spoke to the owner, Ralph Young. We had a 5-minute conversation and then arranged a time to meet for a tour of the apartment complex. The size and cost of the project were way out of my league. The primary property was about 12 acres in size, with eight four-family apartment units on the front six acres and one sixteen-family building on two acres to total 48 units. There was also a horse barn, a stocked fishing pond, and a beautiful, spacious, secluded 3,500 square foot home on the back four acres where the owner and his wife, Marge, lived.

Young Estates turned out to be a lovely colonial-style apartment community. The buildings were between one to four years old. I met with Ralph, the owner, for quite some time. I didn't want to lead him on, so I informed him that I lacked the financial resources needed for a project of this magnitude, but I might have a real estate investor who might be interested in partnering up. Ralph & I seemed to hit it off and decided to meet again soon.

Despite my lack of funds to purchase Young Estates, I couldn't get it out of my mind. *I envisioned Tami and myself raising our future family in this beautiful colonial home situated on the back four acres, with horses grazing in the adjacent field. I even pictured myself fishing with my children in the stocked fishing pond.* All the while, I'd be managing our apartment investments right outside my front door. As a father, I could be present with my children, a part of their daily lives as they grew up.

Before walking away from what seemed to be an unobtainable dream, I called one of my real estate mentors, Andy.

"Hello?"

"Hey Andy, it's Brad Cousino. How are you?"

"Hey, Brad! What's up?"

"Well, I'd just thought I'd call to see if I could pick your brain for a minute."

I explained the deal, thinking that he would perhaps be interested in partnering with me. At the very least, I hoped he would help me put together a deal with some of my other mentors. Andy specialized in creative financing.

"Would you mind coaching me as I evaluate the offer sheet, the rent roll, vacancies, operating expenses, construction, etc.?"

"Sure, how about tomorrow morning at 8:00?"

"Andy, that's just what I wanted to hear! See you then!"

"Ok, Brad, see you tomorrow."

Andy spent almost 6 hours of his valuable time working with me. However, at the end of the day, he strongly recommended that I shouldn't proceed because of the project's size, and the fact that I would be an absentee owner for almost six months while still playing football.

That advice made sense, except Andy didn't have all the facts. What he didn't know was that I recognized that I'd soon be out of football either by my choice or being released from an NFL team again & again. Closing on an investment like this could become my springboard to leaving the NFL on my own terms. At the very least, I was intrigued by the possibilities.

I remained in close contact with Ralph, and over a period of months, our relationship grew. I learned Ralph and Marge were strong, active Christians. They invited Tami and me to come to their local church for a Sunday service and then to lunch afterward. During lunch, we discussed his properties.

"Brad, I have to sell these properties outright," Ralph said, *"and I need to price it to sell as soon as possible. Marge and I agree that hiring a property management firm wouldn't reduce the stresses of owning a larger rental apartment business."*

"Selling it is the only option." Marge put in. *"I'm not going to lose my husband over this business."*

"Brad, I'm going to make you an offer you can't refuse. I'd be willing to sell these properties on a land contract, meaning I would finance most of the deal."

"Ralph, I appreciate all you're trying to do for me, and believe me, I want to help you out," I said. *"But I don't think you understand. I don't have the funds to put even a 3% down payment ($31,500) on a $1,050,000 real estate investment. There isn't a bank around that would be interested in talking to me about this deal."*

"Hold on, Brad, hear me out. I think we can put together a deal that is a win-win for each of us." Ralph said.

Ralph then unveiled an interesting "package deal" on a land contract of all his rental units totaling 69 apartment units. It included 21 units more than the original deal plus his home, stables, and all the tools, tractors & equipment, as follows:

- A 48-unit apartment complex (Young Estates) plus a 10-unit building, a 7-unit building, and a 4-unit building (total of 69 apartment units). [*]

- The 3,500 square foot home on four acres with a stocked fishing pond and a 10-stall horse stable that would include all the ancillary machinery, tractor, snowplow, power tools, etc., virtually everything needed to operate & maintain the apartments.

- The overall purchase price was $1,050,000.
- I'd assume the current $775,000 first mortgage with Eagle Bank
- Ralph would carry a 2nd mortgage of $260,000 at less than 1% interest annually.
- I'd pay $15,000 cash** down payment at closing.

God Appointment -- #6

I'm sure if Ralph didn't have the health issues, then he wouldn't have been so willing to structure such a favorable deal for me. Even so, it seemed like a win-win situation for all parties at the time. After several meetings with bankers and attorneys, a simple land contract was agreed upon, and executed.

The overall purchase price was $1,050,000. However, Tami & I purchased the 69 units and a beautiful home with all the trimmings for just $5,000 out of our pocket. **

We closed in mid-June 1977 about one month before I needed to report to the New York Giants 1977 training camp.

Thank You, Lord...

Only God can do that!

* See appendix #6 in Photo Gallery to see photos of Colonial Estates

*** Key fact: I didn't have $15,000 to put down. I only put $5,000 of my own funds into the project. I borrowed the additional $10,000 from a well-known Cincinnati business owner and a mentor of mine. As an entrepreneur, he was sympathatic to what I was trying to accomplish. He gave me the funds on a hand shake without any legal paperwork – but I gave him my verbal commitment to pay him back – which I did!*

Chapter 32
Forgiveness in Action

"For this is how God loved the world: He gave his one and only Son, so that everyone who believes in Him will not perish but have eternal life. God sent his Son into the world not to judge the world, but to save the world through Him. There is no judgment against anyone who believes in Him. But anyone who does not believe in him has already been judged for not believing in God's one and only Son."
-- John 3:16-18

I was about to leave for the 1977 summer camp with the New York Giants, and time was of the essence. One of my first goals was to employ a part-time maintenance worker to handle day-to-day tasks such as lawn cutting 12 acres, painting apartments, cleaning hallways, making repairs to the apartments, etc. Ralph recommended a maintenance man (Bernie) to hire who worked on some of his apartment projects over the years. I hired Bernie as our part-time maintenance man.

Also, in my absence during football season, I needed to bring on someone else who would be dependable to oversee the maintenance & help turn over the apartments when vacated and help Tami in the day-to-day operations of the apartments. The first person that came to mind was my dad because he was very talented at working with his hands. Shocked? I was, too. Let me back up for several months.

In my growing journey with God, I realized that I needed to completely forgive my parents for everything that had happened to me from the time I was born until I left for college. I needed to be the one to start the conversation because they wouldn't know where to start. Over the next three to four months, I had many heart-to-heart conversations with both my parents, individually, and as a couple.

I chose not to remind them of all the horrible things they did to me because it would get us nowhere. Instead, I asked questions to learn more about them; to understand how and why they came to abuse me. During these conversations, *I learned and began to understand, for the first time, the ways they were both raised in their own dysfunctional home environments, which become learned behaviors for the ways they abused me. I learned that abused children often grow up to abuse their own children because it's all they know. Hurt people, hurt people.*

More importantly, I wanted to understand and appreciate that my parents may have been innocent children who had suffered abuse themselves at the hands of their own parents. Dad was a simple read; he came from a long generational chain of absent alcoholic fathers who, by choice or temperament, were passive in their own home. My dad abdicated his role as the leader of his home to mom, which allowed her to do what she ended up doing, making me the scapegoat for all their problems. Like the previous generations before him, dad started drinking alcohol at a very early age before he understood the long-term damage it causes. The rest was history.

Mom, on the other hand, the primary author of my misery, was a bit more complex to unravel. Figuring out dad was like solving a six-piece jigsaw puzzle, whereas mom was a Rubik's Cube. Our one-on-one conversations were frustrating for the most part, as I was on a mission to find answers that she was not providing. I asked probing questions to find out what was her childhood like?

Mom didn't like to talk about her upbringing much. In fact, her frequent response was, "That was so long ago, I can't remember." I wondered if she really didn't remember, or if it was too painful to talk about. If I was to understand what mom's upbringing was like, I needed some information about her parents, my grandparents.

I had always looked up to my maternal grandpa, (Cleo Gamble) who was often my lifeline. I didn't get to know my grandmother very well. It seems that my grandma had some major mental health issues, which caused grandpa to commit her to a mental asylum on more than one occasion. She received numerous electroshock treatments. I was too young to remember these events. But according to mom, grandma was a different person (not in a good way) after her electroshock treatments.

When I was about ten years old, my grandpa told me that his parents died in a car accident when he was very young. After that, he was raised in an orphanage. He did not talk much about that phase of his life. Once in the car, grandpa told me he was routinely placed in foster homes, where he performed all kinds of labor, and then he would be returned to the orphanage. Sometimes he would be at the "temporary" foster home for as little as a week, but other times, it would be for a couple of months.

Grandpa shared with me that there was one foster home (Roy) who fostered my grandpa dozens of times over the years. Grandpa liked Roy better than the other foster parents. He shared that Roy had promised him that he would eventually adopt him, but Roy never followed through with a legal adoption.

I still didn't know how mom was raised, so I can only speculate, but I believe that she must have endured some challenging times growing up now knowing how my grandfather was shuttled in and out of foster homes and then being returned repeatedly back to the orphanage.

As part of our research, my co-author, Mitch Neu, found that in the early 1900's, it was widely known, that kids being raised in orphanages often suffered all kinds of physical and/or sexual abuse from the older kids, and/or sometimes even from the staff.

If accurate, that might provide reasonable causes for her behavior passed down from my grandpa. While I have no basis, I do believe that "something" in mom's upbringing caused her to treat me the way she did. ***Hurt people, really do hurt people.***

To Forgive or Not to Forgive

From my understanding of the Bible, because of Jesus' sacrifice on the cross, God forgave me of ALL my sins from my past... to the present... and into the future. And God expects me to do the same for anyone that has "*wronged*" me, and / or who I've "*wronged*". In fact, it is a non-negotiable as far as God is concerned. I really struggled with that concept. I don't want to infer that it was easy – it was not!

How could I forgive my parents for all the physical and emotional pain that was foisted on me at a very young age?

Was it even reasonable to expect that I could forgive them?

Although my parents didn't ask for my forgiveness, I had grown over the last few months to give it to them anyway. In my heart, I knew that I needed to forgive dad and mom, unconditionally and without strings. It didn't happen immediately, but once I committed to doing so, something miraculous occurred over several weeks, I started becoming more compassionate toward dad and especially mom. The callous scars on my heart had begun to soften – to heal.

It was the first time I had ever thought of my mom as an innocent child who had emotional scars of her own. I now believe that both my mom and dad were just children, each in search of someone, anyone, to make them feel loved unconditionally – instead of living out of their own abusive childhoods.

Over a period of two (2) months or so, God led me to ask my parents for their forgiveness for the many years I resented them. *I don't understand how it all works, but I am now FREE of carrying the burden of not forgiving my parents.* God tells us to forgive others for our own best interest. There is something spiritually freeing about giving and/or asking for forgiveness from those who have inflicted pain on us -- or we've sinned against them. *Was this another God Appointment? Absolutely.*

Unconditional Forgiveness

When dad wasn't drinking, he was a dependable, hard worker who could repair almost anything. Dad despised working in the glass factory and wanted to get away from it. I wondered if this opportunity would give him enough motivation to stop drinking because sobriety was a non-negotiable requirement. I reasoned that he'd be in a completely different location, 220 miles away from his drinking buddies and old habits.

Not only did I forgive my parents in my heart, but I wanted to show them unconditional love and forgiveness by offering them a chance to be part-owner in our Colonial Estates project. I made an attractive offer to mom & dad that if they did what was needed – to help manage the apartments -- and to see all the maintenance issues were completed in a timely manner, then they would earn an ownership interest in the 69 apartment units (the offer did not include our home situated on the 4 acres, the fishing pond, & the stables). In addition, I hoped this new environment, opportunity, and responsibility would help my parents save their crumbling marriage.

Even so, I had reservations that my best efforts could backfire, and with good reason. Based on my past upbringing, I was worried about what Tami would experience because she would be left to deal with my parents while I was away. What if dad relapsed, or Tami used the wrong towel or didn't clean the kitchen properly, triggering mom's uncontrollable rage and putting Tami in harm's way? I wasn't certain it would turn out the way I had hoped, but Tami reassured me that she would be just fine.

So, we invited my parents to relocate from Point Place to the Amelia area to assist with maintenance and day-to-day operations. While I was gone playing football with the New York Giants, my parents and Tami would live in our home together. It was agreed that when I returned to Cincinnati, they would move to their own home.

Upon taking over ownership, we immediately changed the name from Young Estates to Colonial Estates for the 48-unit apartment complex. In my view, the property looked like stately colonial-style architecture from the old South with tall pillars, white paint, black shutters, and spacious grounds. Tami and I moved into our 3,500 square foot home about 2 weeks before I reported to the Giant's camp.

As young owners, we cleaned hallways and vacant apartments. We painted and repaired empty units to be rented to new tenants. The new part-time maintenance person (Bernie) was a real find and was able to make most of the more serious repairs.

New Mindset

I demonstrated that I had achieved significant success inside the football realm at both the collegiate level and in the NFL.

At age 24, I negotiated an advantageous business transaction where we secured extensive real estate holdings (69 apartment units and home) for more than one million dollars. I couldn't have done this without God's involvement and blessing. I was in a far better place spiritually, physically, and emotionally. I stopped hearing my mom's voice buzzing around in my head. That nightmare was finally over. Instead, I heard uplifting thoughts in my mind that I believed with my whole being – replacing the years of 'lies' I grew up believing.

I became **UNSHACKLED** from the lies. Instead, new truths replaced the many deceptive lies I had believed for years. New thoughts dominated my mind, I now believed that:

"I am unconditionally loved by our Father God;

I'm saved, spiritually healed, and delivered.

I'm accepted, forgiven, and redeemed;

I am not only chosen, but I am cherished by our great God.

I'm being transformed into a better version of myself."

Jesus Christ, who is my Lord and Savior, Father God, and the Holy Spirit salvaged me from 4 generations of traumatic physical and verbal abuse and broke the generational curse of alcohol & drug abuse.

I now believe with my entire heart, mind, & soul that our lives (Tami's and mine), our future family and grandkids, and their future kids and grandkids lives had been restored, salvaged, and made whole, because I chose to stop believing the lies and accepted this truth:

I was... and am... and continue to be... a SOZO work in progress.

Chapter 33
Life Changes

Guard your <u>HEART</u> above all else, for it determines the course of your life. -- **Proverbs 4:23**

I returned to the New York Giants camp in the middle of July 1977. I left Tami and my parents back in Amelia while I was trying to earn a spot as the special team's captain and to be backup middle linebacker to Harry Carson. I wish I could say that things changed, but it was the same old story. While I was still frustrated, it wasn't because I wasn't getting as much playing time, but instead, my football life became secondary to my new primary career as the owner/manager of Colonial Estates.

There were no cell phones back in that time frame, so I'd have to wait until late every night, where I would talk to Tami or my dad about the events of the day at the apartments. I'd have an ongoing list of things that needed to be done, such as leasing apartments, following up with maintenance requests, rent collections, evictions, capital improvements, etc. I'd often spend over 45 to 60 minutes each night on a payphone going over all the particulars with Tami or my dad. Not surprisingly, my teammates did not appreciate me taking all that time on the public phone.

I had a great summer camp, but as usual, I was on the *bubble*. Once again it was related to my lack of numbers (height and weight) - too small, too short, blah, blah, blah. Ultimately, I was the last defensive player cut from the New York Giants in early September. While I was disappointed, I was anxious to get back to Cincinnati to take care of our apartment investments. This made my transition away from football far easier compared to when I was released from the Chicago Bears.

Because I had proven myself to be a dominant special teams' player in the NFL, I was confident I would eventually be picked up again by another team. I continued to work out to keep myself ready while simultaneously remaining focused on taking care of our real estate investments. Dad had done a good job of overseeing the maintenance on the property. Sadly, I learned that he continued to drink, which was disappointing.

Within about 4 to 5 weeks of my return to Amelia, my parents found and purchased a home that they really liked about two miles from Colonial Estates. Dad continued to do some part-time maintenance on our apartment units. But he wanted his own business, so after doing some research, he bought into a kitchen remodeling concept out of Pittsburgh called Face Lifters.

As I hoped, in late October 1977, I received a call from an NFL team - the reigning Super Bowl Champion Pittsburgh Steelers, who had won the last two Super Bowls! One of their linebackers was injured, and they needed a strong special teams' player and backup linebacker to Jack Lambert, their All-Pro middle linebacker, and future Hall of Fame inductee. As you may remember, Chuck Noll was one of the coaches who called and wanted me to try out as a free agent for the Pittsburgh Steelers after the 1975 draft was completed. He was still interested in having me on the team. I was teetering on ending my career for good, but thoughts of winning a Super Bowl ring won out, so I packed up my belongings and headed to Pittsburgh.

I was now playing with the defending Super Bowl Champions and became teammates and friends with some of the best NFL players of all time. On that one team, there were over a dozen players and/or coaches that would become inducted into the very elite NFL Hall of Fame, NFL Legends such as Mean Joe Green, Terry Bradshaw, Rocky Blier, Lynn Swann, Jack Lambert, Jack Ham, Mel Blount, Franco Harris, Mike Webster, John Stallworth, Donnie Shell, and two Hall of Fame coaches, Chuck Noll, and Tony Dungy.

Unfortunately, the Steelers didn't win a Super Bowl that year. We lost to the Denver Broncos in the conference playoffs. The Broncos made it to Super Bowl XII on January 15, 1978, but were defeated by the Dallas Cowboys, 27-10.

After losing to Denver in the playoffs, I immediately returned home to see my now pregnant wife Tami and to get back to managing our apartment investments. I was seriously evaluating just how much longer I was going to pursue playing professional football. I loved playing football, being a member of a team, the weekly game plan to bring a win, the discipline, the competing...winning each mini battle on any given play excited me.

But now, I had some additional responsibilities to think about. This wasn't just about me anymore. I had a pregnant wife and soon-to-be first child to take care of. Every day, I was dealing with my own personal turmoil...to retire, or not to retire? *I prayed for peace of mind as I pondered what was God's plan for me?*

*****

This Changes Everything ... Cortt Christien Cousino

My prayer was answered on July 7, 1978, with the birth of our first child, Cortt Christien Cousino. Something happened to me on that day that was so beautiful and indescribable that it had to come from God. After Tami and Cortt came home from the hospital, I had my first chance to be totally alone with Cortt as I sat out on our back deck. He was five-days old. *For the first time in my life, holding* <u>MY</u> *son, all wrapped up as newborn babies normally are,* **I experienced unconditional love**. *It was overwhelming!*

With Cortt on my lap, large tears started streaming down my face. I was caught up with such emotion because I realized just how fearful I was that I didn't know how to be a good, loving, caring father that Cortt needed me to be; and that I wanted to be for him. I wanted to lead my family, but deep down, I was so afraid I would become like my parents. I didn't want to inflict any pain, emotional or physical, on Tami or my son.

I was overcome with emotion and gratitude and called out to God:

"Lord, I love you and thank you for Cortt, Tami, and all that you have blessed us with. I ask that you change me in any way that I need to be changed. Please, please, please transform me to be the leader, husband, and to be the good father that Cortt and my future kids will need. May your will be done in my life."

I held Cortt close and tight. I stopped verbally whispering my prayers and felt this sense of unconditional love, contentment, and joy come over me. I went silent, closed my eyes, and was in total peace as I held him even closer to me.

I sensed a still, small voice deep within my heart quietly impressing upon my thoughts:

"My son, I know your heart. I'm so pleased that you asked me to show you how to love and lead the family you have now, and the future children and grandchildren that will be in your family. Trust Me! I'm going to bless you and Tami for your future generations. I'll show you how to be a good, loving father to your son Cortt, (and your future children) and to be a loving, caring husband to Tami."

I sat there stunned for about ten minutes as I tried to grasp what I sensed deep within. With a great sense of humility and gratitude, I held Cortt, who was only a few days old close to my face and whispered with conviction directly into his ear:

"Cortt, I promise that I will <u>learn</u> how to be a good Dad. I will love you and your mom unconditionally. I promise that I will always be there for you and your mom."

I didn't want that moment to end, but now another problem came front and center. In less than a week, I had to leave for the Pittsburgh Steelers' training camp. I was torn because I didn't want to leave Tami and my newborn son. For the first time ever, I was not excited about heading for a training camp. I had mixed emotions and almost decided to forgo camp and retire outright. But Tami and I decided to give it one more shot. I left for the Pittsburgh Steelers' camp in mid-July 1978.

I wouldn't hold Cortt again for six... long... weeks!

From NFL to CFL... to CPM???

I was once again the last player released from an NFL team; this time with the Pittsburgh Steelers in early September 1978. I returned to Cincinnati and Colonial Estates. Less than a week later, I was contacted by the Toronto Argonauts of the CFL (Canadian Football League). They wanted me to play middle linebacker and special teams. Their starting middle linebacker, Rick Razzano, had a serious injury and was out for the remainder of the season. I didn't know much about the CFL but many of the rules are quite different. (* See end of this chapter for CFL info)

I became the starting middle linebacker within days of arriving. I quickly became a top producer for the 'Argos', leading the team with overall tackles, assists, and TFLs (Tackles for Loss) despite playing less than ½ of a season. As the starting MLB, I was in my element. I was fulfilling one of my final desires before I retire... to be a starter as a Middle Linebacker.

At the end of the 1978 season, the Toronto Argonaut coaches encouraged me to return for the 1979 season. They told me that the defensive unit played better when I was on the field. They loved my attitude, and they wanted to incorporate a variety of blitzes that would better utilize my skill sets next season. I told the head coach I would think about it, but I was seriously considering retiring so I could be near my family and our real estate holdings. Surprisingly, I earned more money in the CFL than I ever did in the NFL.

Upon returning to Cincinnati, The Bengals strength coach - Kim Wood and I met over lunch and had some preliminary discussions about me re-joining the Cincinnati Bengals for the 1979 season. If the logistics could work out - that would be an ideal scenario. I'd be playing NFL football again, <u>and</u> I would live at our home in Amelia, where I would be home every night, *and* I'd be able to oversee the management and maintenance of our apartment investments.

But as we researched out the possibility, we found that there was a major complication; I was still under contract with the CFL Toronto Argonauts for 1979. The NFL and CFL honored each leagues' player contracts. So, unless Toronto agreed to release me from my CFL contract, then I could not sign with the Bengals (or any other NFL team) until the 1980 season. I made a formal request, but Forrest Gregg, the new head coach of the Toronto Argonauts wanted me on their team for the 1979 season and would not release me from my contract.

I had three choices, I either play with Toronto in 1979... or sit out 1979 season and join the Bengals in 1980... or officially retire from the CFL and NFL!

* For those football minded people interested in the several notable differences between the CFL and the NFL. Here is a quick overview:
1. the field is longer and wider, the endzones are 20 yards long vs NFL 10 yards
2. they play twelve (12) men instead of the NFL's eleven (11) men rule.
3. the offense is given three (3) downs to gain ten (10) yards for a new set of downs; NFL is given four (4) downs to gain 10 yards for a new set of downs
4. two, three, four or more players can be in motion all at the same time. In the NFL, only one (1) man can be in motion at a time (it is 'chaotic' for a purpose)
5. A maximum of fifteen (15) USA born players out of forty-five are permitted to play on any given CFL team. The balance of the team had to be Canadian born citizens.

Chapter 34
Exit Strategy Implemented

"A soft, easy life is not worth living, if it impairs the fiber of brain and heart and muscle. We must dare to be great; and we must realize that greatness is the fruit of toil and sacrifice and high courage... For us is the life of action, of strenuous performance of duty; let us live in the harness, striving mightily; let us rather run the risk of wearing out than rusting out." **-- Teddy Roosevelt**

I loved playing football! I loved every aspect of the competition, the teamwork, the strategies of coming up with a game-plan, of being a part of a team, the friendships, competing against the 'best of the best', etc. Even so, I was mentally and emotionally prepared to officially retire from professional football during the off-season of 1979. I accepted my reality that I was always going to be on the "bubble" of being one of the last players to make any NFL final roster, not because of my abilities but because of my lack of size. I now was prepared to do the right thing for my family because the timing was right, and I was mentally and emotionally ready to retire from professional football.

The primary reasons were:

As a husband of less than 2½ years, and brand new "dad", I hated to leave my wife and newborn son for 5+ months at a time:

1. I was away from Tami in the fall of the 1977 season while playing with the Giants. It was painful. I really struggled with justifying putting my family (or me) through that "pain" again.

2. Just before the 1978 summer ball with the Steelers, my 1st child was born. I was away from Tami and my newborn son, Cortt, during my time with the Steelers. Unfortunately, Tami and Cortt could not

temporarily "move" to Pittsburgh because I needed her to stay back in Amelia due to our responsibilities as the owners and managers of the 69 apartment units.

3. I believed that my post-Pro football life was going to be in commercial real estate as a manager, developer, and/or owner of investment grade real estate properties.

   a. That became more apparent in the late spring of the 1979 off-season. One of my commercial Real Estate 'mentors' was a good friend of Bob Marcott, a CPM who headed up the OH / KY / IN Regional office of Arthur Rubloff & Co. Rubloff was one of the largest Commercial Real Estate companies in the country, head-quartered in Chicago, IL.

   b. Rubloff was looking to add a key Property Management specialist in the Cincinnati area. I met with Bob over lunch which led to me being considered for that position.

   c. Over a period of 2 weeks, I had a series of intense one-on-one and then two-on-one interviews with several executives that flew in from Chicago.

   d. As I learned more about the company and the position, I was excited and felt it would be a great career opportunity. I would be working with one of the best commercial real estate companies in the country.

   e. I'd be mentored by Bob Marcott himself, a 30+ year pro.

   f. If chosen, I would be Rubloff's Cincinnati senior property manager of a $100+ million portfolio of investment grade suburban office buildings, office / warehouse Parks, two large apartment complexes _and_ work directly with Bob Marcott managing the newest 600,000 sq ft Class 'A' office Tower in downtown Cincinnati – The 580 Building.

It was a wonderful career opportunity for someone my age (26 years old) considering that I had NO commercial property management experience.

Upon leaving the final interview, Bob Marcott told me that I was one of the final two candidates for the position. He'd contact me within 3 days.

Back At Colonial Estates

It was early June 1979; I had just finished cutting the grass at Colonial Estates. Earlier that morning, I received a call from Rubloff's Cincinnati offices. It was Bob Marcott and after exchanging greetings, he let me know that I was the unanimous choice to join their Cincinnati team. He explained the position I'd be filling, the expectations, and gave an overview of a generous compensation package.

He explained that I'd be on a fast-track training program as the senior property manager for a portfolio of investment grade real estate projects comprised of suburban office building complexes, office warehouse properties, a 440-unit apartment community, and two downtown office buildings that included a new 600,000 sq ft class 'A' high rise office building in downtown Cincinnati.

It was an outstanding offer – BUT it came with two strings attached; it required that I...

1) Obtain my CPM (Certified Property Manager) designation by IREM (Institute of Real Estate Management) within the next 12 to 18 months.

    a) The CPM designation is THE professional designation required by virtually all financial institutions that own or manage the billions in Pension fund owned commercial properties. It is those firms that own the many billions in investment grade commercial real estate properties that require professional property management by a CPM.

    b) Earning my 'CPM' was critical to the Cincinnati branch of Rubloff to qualify to get more investment grade property management accounts!

    c) Earning my CPM was a must if I wanted to be considered a top tier Commercial Property Manager. It was already a goal I had set a year earlier; so, I would be recognized as a 'Certified Pro' in the Cincinnati marketplace.

2)   Commit to officially retire from playing professional football.

      a.   the timing was perfect for me to send my resignation to both the NFL and CFL.

      b.   I was excited to embark on the rest of my life journey.

Could it be another God appointment? Absolutely...

How did I know that I KNOW?

I was filled with joy and experienced great peace in my heart!

Overcome with Gratitude

After putting away the tractor, I walked across our front yard, around the pond, and took mental inventory what was before me -- our beautiful home, the horses out for their evening grazing, a dad with his young son fishing in the pond, and the ten (10) apartment buildings meticulously aligned along Estate Drive. Almost on cue, Tami came out the front door, holding our 11-month-old son – Cortt. I called out to Tami to bring our beautiful son, Cortt, over to me.

As I watched my wife with my son walk toward me, I was overcome with a humbling sense of awe, peace, and tranquility. I thank God for the many blessings recognizing that He was there the entire time <u>even</u> when I questioned why He abandoned me...or so I thought.

I'd finally came to recognize that His plan for me was based on **Romans 8:28** from the New Testament:

"We know that all things" (the good, the bad and the ugly – everything) "works together for the best, for those who love God, to those called to His purpose."

Which for me included, (even though I can't begin to explain it or understand it):

- choosing my parents as young teenagers, to my dad working at the

LOF glass factory,

- to my physical and emotional abusive childhood, to my many jobs as a young boy,

- to writing letters begging for a football scholarship, to working in the putrid sewers,

- to being a non-scholarship "walk-on" on Miami University's (OH) Football team,

- to earning a 1/3 scholarship in August 1971 to a full scholarship in May 1972,

- to dating (ultimately marrying) Tami Netzly - the most ideal woman for me.

- to being individually coached by some of the best football coaches on the planet.

- to playing alongside the greatest teammates from the 1973,1974 & 1975 Miami teams.

- to not getting drafted by any NFL team in 1975, being rejected 442 times, but becoming a free agent with Cincinnati Bengals.

- to play in the NFL with the Cincinnati Bengals, Chicago Bears, NY Giants & the reigning Superbowl champion Pittsburgh Steelers.

- to being traded to the Chicago Bears, telling Coach Jack Pardee to either "*Play me or Trade me*" and then being cut/released, which was the catalyst to confront my traumatic past that led me to my SOZO journey.

- to acquire a million-dollar Real Estate investment with only $5,000 of our own money

- to having our first child – Cortt -- and then stand in awe at what a great mom Tami proved to be.

- And NOW -- start a new, exciting career with Rubloff & Co in commercial Real Estate.

Chapter 35
New Beginnings!

"The best and most beautiful things in the world cannot be seen or even touched - they must be felt with the heart."   - Helen Keller

"If you have a dream and you don't give up no matter what obstacles come up, then life's problems will fall away, and you will get what you want. It happens. It works."   -Yanni

Upon accepting the offer with Rubloff & Co, I officially retired from professional football by sending a certified letter to both the NFL and CFL National offices.

It was the wisest and best decision for my family and me!

Epilogue

April 2023

"This is the true joy in life, being used for a purpose recognized as a mighty one... I want to be thoroughly used up when I die, for the harder I work, the more I love. I rejoice in life for its own sake. Life is no 'brief candle' to me. It is sort of a splendid torch which I have a hold of for the moment, and I want to make it burn as brightly as possible before handing it over to future generations."
— George Bernard Shaw

Fast forward 40+ years and you may find me sitting outside on our deck, with my MAC iPad in my hands, scrolling through some photos, with an iced tea sitting by my side. As the sun shines brightly above my head, a certain picture has caught my eye. For me, it is the most beautiful picture I've ever seen. This is the first time we were able to get our entire family including the two youngest grandbabies in our family picture.

I feel my thoughts are taking me to a past where I might feel the darkness surrounding me, but the picture before me makes me see the light even more clearly. Yet as I look at the happy picture in front of me, I can't help but reflect to the time when this felt like an unattainable dream. When I was being disciplined in forced isolation in our basement or garage, I would sit totally alone, often crying, and craving attention and love. I wondered; would I ever find happiness and real love, the kind that provides a sense of peace and contentment in your heart, the kind of love that lasts forever. In my alone moments, I was left to fantasize about it all. I would think about the possibilities of a future I may never get for myself. In that overflowing trail of questions, I always ended up with the same answer: ***"I am never going to get it because it's not in the cards I've been dealt in my life."***

Today however, I am standing in this picture surrounded by my entire family and so much love. The family picture before my eyes causes me to reflect on just where I started from and how far I've come as my former destructive reality fades in comparison to my new *SOZO* reality. Thank you, Lord God, for the many blessings I see every time I look at these and the many other pictures showcased in our home. All smiles, happy and content, my family is looking back at me from the perfectly captured moment inside this very frame.

This picture captures our entire family, consisting of our four kids, their wonderful spouses, with our 11 superstar grandkids. This family photo was taken on Thanksgiving Day last November. I turn 70 in April 2023. I'm the proud husband of 45+ years to Tami, my best friend, who remains beautiful... inside and out. At 70 years of age, we both are active and in good health. [1]

We are more than blessed to be "mom and dad" to our four very special adult kids. Each of our kids have chosen incredible, loving spouses who we love and respect as much as our own kids. In an earlier chapter, I stated that Wendel Deyo, the former chaplain of the Bengals & Reds, would have a continuing major impact on our family. How big? Wendel did the pre-marital counseling and performed the wedding vows for each of our four kids and their spouses. What is miraculous, is that each of our kids only wanted Wendel to be intimately involved in this very special day in each of their lives. From their viewpoint, it was a non-negotiable, even when the wedding venue (Cortt & Jen) would be held 225 miles away from the Cincinnati area where Wendel lives.

Each couple has blessed Tami and me in very tangible ways. At the top of the list is being Gami and Papa to eleven very special grandkids, ranging from ages 14 years old (Connor & Camdyn) down to our youngest grandbaby who is 3 years old (Graycen).

I'm so proud and blessed to be their earthly Dad and Papa. Our...

- oldest, **Cortt,** (married to **Jen Harnett**, with three children Connor, Will, Chloe)

- only daughter, **Shaedyn**, (married to **Alex Bogle** with three children Camdyn, Mcryck, Briggs)

- middle son, **Cole,** (married to **Kelly Johnson**, with three children Kennedy, Caleb, Coco) and

- youngest son, **Case**, (married to **Brooke Boswell**, with two children Hensley & Graycen).

Additionally, each of our kids and their spouses are doing exceptionally well as leaders of their families and in their specific careers.

I believe Tami continues to be the world's best mom to our kids and now "*Gami*" to our 11 grandkids. Tami is the "*secret sauce and super glue*" of our family. She makes every birthday and holiday extra special with the many wonderful traditions that she brings to our home. I am in awe of all that she does on a consistent day in, day out basis.

But Tami learned how to be a great mom and wife, because she was blessed to being *raised by one of the best set of parents of all time,*

Howard & Betty Netzly. "Papa" is now in Heaven with our Lord. "Aukie" (her grandma title) is simply amazing! She is 95, in excellent health, lives in the same house they raised their three kids in Orrville, Ohio. She insists on staying active. She cuts and trims her yard; plants, weeds & harvests her garden, she shovels her walks and driveway, and drives hundreds of miles to see her three kids, twelve (12) grandkids and twenty (20) great grandkids on a regular basis. She is the matriarch of her large family, and we all love her dearly!

Both Tami and I are blessed to witness the loving way that each of our kids are raising their kids, our grandkids. As our kids were growing up, we strived to lavish them with our unconditional love while providing boundaries of Godly discipline when it was needed. And we now see them passing similar important truths down to their own children. We are so blessed to see what great parents they are to our grandkids, teaching them these truths:

1.   Love God first foremost, then love your family, and then love others.

2.   Know who you really are, a beloved child of our great God, who absolutely delights in you.

3.   Always give your very best in everything you undertake – in school, sports, chores, hobbies, jobs, being a friend, etc. *Why knowingly CHEAT yourself by coasting, just because you can get away with it?*

4.   Be a *Difference-Maker* to family, friends, classmates, teammates, neighbors, coworkers, teammates, etc.

5.   *Finish Life WELL*, regardless of your age - whether your 8 or 98. Leave a legacy that benefits your family & friends for generations.

Grateful for My Transformed Life

As I reflect on my childhood dreams, they are dwarfed compared to what became even bigger and better than I dreamed in those long hours of solitary confinement. I am grateful, thankful, and humbled that the many lies I believed growing up are now a distant bad memory.

As I hoped and expected, Tami was the best mom to Cortt, Shaedyn, Cole & Case and created that perfect home-life environment that she had with her parents as she grew up. She brought her great family traditions to our then young family. Without Tami, I wouldn't even know where to begin to create a wonderful family environment based on how I was raised. Tami knew exactly what was needed to be done to create a wonderful family dynamic. She could because she was raised that way. Thank you again Lord God!

I became "**UNSHACKLED**" when I stopped believing the many lies my parents, teachers, relatives, coaches, etc., foisted upon me. I now believe what God said in His word – the Bible.

Instead of the lies forecasting my doom, I now hear and believe these uplifting thoughts in my mind:

- I'm loved unconditionally by the God of the universe.

- I was chosen, and I accepted His invitation and sacrifice.

- I'm saved, healed, and delivered.

- I'm accepted, forgiven, redeemed, and restored.

- I'm salvaged, liberated, and made whole.

- I'm being spiritually transformed into the best version of myself.

- I now know that God delights in me, just because I am His.

- I am so thankful that God intervened in my life when I was released from the Chicago Bears. That was the catalyst that began my SOZO journey of redemption, restoration and transformation of my life.

These things did not happen because I was a wonderful human being; ***I was not and am not!*** There is no way I could have changed the trajectory of my life. I was doomed. I could not have done this without God transforming my heart and spirit as I placed my hope, trust, and faith in all that Jesus Christ did by being God's sacrificial lamb for me, Tami, and our family.

With my whole heart, I want you to know that it was GOD, not me...

- That saved, healed, delivered, transformed & salvaged my life and that of my family.

- That broke the many generations of physical and verbal abuse, drug and alcohol addictions from current and past generations that negatively influenced me, my siblings, parents, grandparents, great grandparents, etc., for multiple generations.

- That changed the trajectory of the future lives of Tami and me, our kids, our grandkids, and their kids and grandkids for generations into the future.

The Good News

I close <u>Unwanted, Unworthy, UNSHACKLED</u> with these thoughts:

- I'm in total awe of my life journey. I realize there's more gratitude in my heart for how my life has turned out more now than ever before.

- Thank you, thank you, thank you, Lord God for all the many ways you've blessed Tami and me, our four kids & their spouses, and our very special grandkids.

- Lord Jesus, may you use <u>Unwanted, Unworthy, UNSHACKLED</u> to encourage, and bless all those searching for ultimate truth!

Jesus then goes on to tell His disciples just what the ultimate truth is. For context, in less than 18 hours Jesus would be savagely beaten, crucified on a cross, die & be buried. But Jesus wanted to make sure that His disciples knew that he would rise from the dead in 3 days and that the disciples would know the way. But Thomas, one of the twelve apostles, then asked this key question to Jesus.

"Lord, we do not know where you are going – how can we know the way? Jesus answered Thomas (but His response was directed to all future Christ-followers) with this emphatic statement:

"I am the <u>ONLY</u> way to God (the Father); and I'm the real <u>Truth</u>; and I'm the real <u>Life</u>; NO ONE can come to the Father <u>but</u> through Me. John 14:5 & 6

In closing, allow me to share a few final nuggets of TRUTH. My view of God was negatively skewed based on my relationship to my parents. I found out that is not who God is... not even close. I didn't know what a good, loving, positive father / son (or daughter) relationship was as I never saw it in action - until I met Tami's parents and then spent time with Wendel Deyo and his family.

Please know that our great God is a good, good Father who just happens to OWN the Universe that He created out of nothing – with just His word. He is all powerful, all knowing, and possesses unlimited resources! Every aspect of my view of God was inaccurate and based on false information. I had bought the LIE and believed it as being the TRUTH. I had been scammed! I had to reject the lies I was told over and over for decades: Subtle Lies that needed to be challenged, such as:

- God isn't too busy for me.

- I am not a nuisance to God.

- God does not have a "grudge" against me nor is He keeping score of how many times I've blown it – (which is quite often)

I replaced the above lies and many more, with these amazing nuggets of truth that I purposefully choose to believe:

- HE encourages me to come to Him just to talk *'heart to heart'* about anything (prayer)

- I'm His child and He is *especially fond* of me (as He is of you).

- The one true God of the Universe not only loves me; but He *DELIGHTS in me* as a precious member of his family!

- He proved it by sending Jesus to rescue, redeem, and transform me... and all those I love and care about!

The above bullet points radically changed how I viewed God as who He really IS and not what I formerly believed. As such, I decided the wisest thing I could do was to become *UNSHACKLED* from the many false deceptions & lies that I believed for decades! My life & family was rescued, salvaged, redeemed, and transformed. ***And so can YOURS!***

In my research, I also learned that the ancient biblical word translated *Gospel* means – **Good News.** It is indeed good news that *this SOZO journey is available for anyone who wants to be redeemed, transformed, saved, healed, forgiven, made whole, etc.*

What reasonable person wouldn't want those FREE GIFTS?

In closing dear reader, have you perhaps believed some lies in exchange for the TRUTH somewhere in your past. If so, you don't have to accept those lies any longer. God is for you! He wants you to be in HIS family. [2] God gives us humans the ultimate power of free will to choose our future. We each have the sole responsibility to decide if we want to become UNSHACKLED from the lies. *He does not, and will not, force us.* When we do choose to become UNSHACKLED, we get the awesome honor of being welcomed into HIS FAMILY. Where we may experience for the 1st time ever of being *Totally* **Wanted, Worthy, UNSHACKLED.**

If all the above is true; and God's Word says that it is indeed TRUE:

This Changes Everything!

[1] *A question I'm often asked – "Brad, what do you do to stay active at 70?" In 2021, I started playing Pickleball (PB)! I now play 5 to 7 days per week for about 2 hours / day. It provides excellent intermittent cardio exercise, great mental stimulation that satisfies my competitive nature PLUS it enhances meaningful social interactions with new friends I would never have met without PB. If you really desire to remain physically, mentally & socially active while having FUN, FUN, FUN; I believe Pickleball is the ideal "LIFETIME" sport that can be played at a competitive level even though our bodies continue to grow older. I know my spirit is young, but my physical body... not so much! However, my blood pressure, cholesterol, resting heart rate, blood glucose, etc., have all improved significantly since I lost 35+ lbs. just playing PB. I'm convinced that keeping physically & mentally active is more critical than we can imagine.*

[2] See Appendices #1A, #1B, & #1C

I Dedicate...

Unwanted, Unworthy, UNSHACKLED to:

My Lord & Savior:

You rescued and salvaged my life. I was a broken mess, going down a very dark & dangerous path. Even though I thought you abandoned me, YOU intervened and salvaged my life. YOU transformed me to a far better version of Brad Cousino. I'm so thankful and grateful!

Tami:

I'm in AWE that God choose you to be my wife of 45+ years, you are my best friend, my true love and in my opinion the world's best mom and now 'Gami' to our eleven (11) grandkids. I love you *'gumpfuls'* and am so grateful that we are mom & dad to our 4 wonderful adult kids. You are indeed the 'super-glue' in our family, our family dynamic would be vastly different without you!

Our Four Children and their Families:

I'm so honored that God allowed me to be your earthly dad and to be Papa to your kids. Each of you have made me a better man, husband, dad, and Papa. I love, respect, admire and am so proud of each of you! I wrote this book as a legacy for you, your children, and their children, and for our combined future generations.

Tami's Parents: Betty & Howard Netzly:

<u>Aukie</u>**: You are the very best wife, mom, grandma and now great grandma. Tami is the best wife, mom, & "Gami" because of your influence as her mom. I see <u>you</u> in everything she does.

<u>Papa</u>: Even though Papa is now in heaven, he remains a hero to me. His influence is legendary in the Netzly / Cousino families. I purposely chose to go by the name "Papa" because I want to be like him as an earthly dad and Papa.

*** Aukie' is her "grandma" name that Cortt called her when he was about a year old – it stuck; and now all 12 of her grandkids and her 20+ great grandkids call her "AUKIE".*

Contents & Page Numbers
For the Appendices

Appendix #1A
Five Immutable Spiritual Truths

1] There is a vastly superior Being (God) who is the Life Force of the Universe. He created the Universe by His will, intelligence, and His Words. He owns everything, created all that is good, has always existed and will never stop existing. It is HIS Universe, and as the creator & owner, He gets to make ALL the rules. ***

2] We are Spiritual Beings having a Human experience; we're not Humans trying to have a spiritual experience.

3] We are eternal beings. God created us with a body, soul, & spirit. Our body is temporary. But our spirit & soul are eternal... together they will never stop existing – somewhere! If you've ever seen a corpse (a dead body) – you know that something is missing – the source of life is in the spirit & soul.

4] God has put into place the *"Law of Cause & Effect"* ('Sowing & Reaping') that always manifests itself in both the physical (seen) realm and the Spiritual (unseen) realm.

5] God allows every human being absolute Free Will. We have total responsibility to choose our course in this life which leads to the next most important phase of our spiritual journey – we literally choose our future.

**** It doesn't matter if we like His rules or not. It doesn't even matter if we know and / or believe in His rules. God's laws always work regardless e.g., the Law of Gravity works whether you like it - OR even believe in the law or not - case in point, if you jump off the roof of a 3-story building, whether you know the law or not; or believe in the law or not - regardless of your belief or mindset when you jump -- you're going to fall **fast and hard** to the ground every single time! (This truth nugget is vital that we understand all the long-term repercussions that will directly affect each of our lives AND all those we care about.)*

The hard truth for some people to accept is that He (our Triune God = the Father, Son & Holy Spirit) is the Creator and sole Owner of HIS Universe. As such, HE alone has the authority and responsibility to make the RULES of HIS Universe, a few of which was shared in the Five Immutable Spiritual Truths above.

Appendix #1B
The basis of the prayer of salvation

Many have asked me... "what did you pray"? Based on my understanding of scripture, a salvation prayer, is a heartfelt prayer one would say to:

1] admit that they have sinned and want to repent, (have a change of heart)

2] ask God for His forgiveness and confess your belief that Jesus Christ paid the price for our sins by dying on the cross,

3] Confess and accept Jesus as your Lord and Savior.

A	**Admit that you are a sinner.** Romans 3:23 "For all have sinned and fall short of the glory of God." Romans 6:23 "For the wages of sin is death."
B	**Believe that Jesus paid for your sin at the cross.** Romans 5:8 "But God demonstrates His own love for us: while we were still sinners, Christ died for us. Romans 6:23 "but the free gift of God is eternal life in Christ Jesus."
C	**Confess that Jesus is the Son of God, and commit your life to Him.** Romans 10:9 "That if you confess with your mouth that Jesus is Lord and believe in your heart that God raised Him from the dead, you will be saved."

God knows each of us intimately.

We can't fool or deceive God...EVER!

He always knows if we are being authentic... or not!

Appendix #1C:
Example of a 'Salvation' Prayer

Heavenly Father, I come to you in prayer,
asking for the forgiveness of my Sins.
I right now confess with my mouth and believe with my heart that
Jesus is your Son, and that He willingly died on the Cross at
Calvary as my substitute so all my sins would be forgiven
and have Eternal Life in the Kingdom of Heaven.

Father, I believe that you raised Jesus from the dead,
as proof that His sacrifice was accepted by You.

Lord Jesus, I ask You to be my personal Lord and Savior!
I repent (a change of heart) of my Sins!
Because your word is truth, I confess with my mouth
that I am now a beloved (son or daughter)
and cleansed by the precious Blood of Jesus!

I surrender my life to you; the good, the bad, and the ugly.
I acknowledge You as my God, my Lord, & my Savior.

Thank you for beginning to transform me to be the person
you created me to be. I pray all this under the authority of the
precious name of Jesus my Lord & Savior.

** There is NO MAGIC in the words written above. What is most important to God is... do the words & private thoughts expressed truly represent the attitude of our hearts. God can't be tricked nor deceived. Based on scripture, praying a simple prayer like the one above, is a great foundational first step in growing a SOZO relationship with the one true GOD of the Universe.

If you sincerely prayed the above prayer and believed in your heart the words you stated, then you are now a member of God's family. You are in the beginning process of all that I shared about SOZO. Its real! This is EXTREMELY critical since it deals with your **eternal** spirit, that will always exist and will never stop existing – somewhere! It is the most important decision that you will ever make. (See Appendix # 1A)

I encourage you to begin reading in the New Testament, starting with the Gospel of John. Our God will lead you from that point on; just be honest and transparent with God

Appendix #1D.1:
Original front side content (side 1of 2) of the free autographed handout

Appendix #1D.2:
Original back side content (side 2 of 2) of the free autographed handout

Once Upon a Time...(a true story)

I wanted to go to college but my family had NO money. I wrote letters begging for a football scholarship...but was turned down from every college. I secured a job cleaning out crap, garbage, mud & sludge from storm sewers...and earned enough to pay for one quarter at Miami University. I then "walked-on" as a non-scholarship football player. (ala the classic movie –RUDY)

Unlike 'Rudy', I was able to earn a full scholarship by the end of my 1st year. I became the starting middle guard (nose-tackle) @ 5' 11" & 195 lbs and never missed a game in 4 years. Even though I weighed 50+ lbs less than I should have for my position, I played with such passion and so dominated the teams we played, that I was voted defensive M.V.P. in the Mid-American Conference 2 years in a row and named to many All American teams in my junior & senior years.

In spite of a stellar college career -- I did not get drafted. At that time, the NFL drafted 17 rounds (442 players) and I was totally ignored due to my size.

I got the chance to try out as a non-drafted free agent with the Cincinnati Bengals. I received a $500 signing bonus...and the minimum NFL salary of $21,000. Despite huge odds, I played in the NFL for 4+ years by being the BEST on special teams – I was fearless! But I knew my Pro career would be very short. The reality was I was an average athlete...but had great DESIRE. I used every ounce of my potential. I played with all-out PASSION on the field... and off... still do!

Like most people, my journey has been filled with many ups & downs. I struggled with being told that I was not good enough to even play at a D-3 college...to becoming a D-1 All American...to being rejected in the NFL draft.. to playing under legendary

Hall of Fame (HOF) Coaches Paul Brown & Chuck Noll... to being cut twice... to becoming teammates of HOF superstars Terry Bradshaw, Jack, Lambert, Franco Harris, Rocky Blier, Jack Ham, Mean Joe Green, Lynn Swann, Mike Webster, Mel Blount, etc.

In closing, do I believe in miracles... absolutely! God has been so GOOD... in so many ways. I married my college sweetheart and we've raised 4 great kids. I now have the awesome privilege (and responsibility) of speaking / sharing my life story of being raised in an alcoholic (dad), rage-a-holic (mom), dysfunctional home... to becoming a college football "star"... to making it in the NFL... to dealing with the many wounds & scars inflicted in my childhood...that so affected me after the NFL. I was on a quest to find the REAL meaning of life on this planet. If this resonates with you... then turn this page over and see the TRUTH I discovered on my life journey...

Appendix #1E – The Greek Word 'SOZO'
Examples of how SOZO is translated based on context

Imagine experiencing what few have...to play in the NFL in front of millions of adoring fans, to be on legendary teams that won 4 Super Bowls, and to become friends & teammates with future Hall of Fame legends. That was me. I was there. I've been fortunate to be at the very top – AND also witnessed life in the valleys.

I'm convinced that as life marches forward we ALL must face real questions that life throws at us. Such as *'after the crowds have left, and the fame & money is gone and the rings have tarnished...and the body ages...and the dreams of our youth are forgotten... and cherished loved ones begin to die... is this all there is to life? what happens next?* I've been on a quest for 30+ years – searching for real TRUTH. It has been a life journey that has affected me in every way...my past, my family, my friends, and my future.

In the journey I found that my belief or non-belief does not affect ultimate TRUTH. As an example, it doesn't matter if you do believe (or don't) in the Law of Gravity...because this immutable law works regardless -- Jump from any tower and you ALWAYS go down...regardless of your belief.

So what is the Ultimate TRUTH? There is a vastly Superior Being who is the creator & sustainer of the Universe and everything in it. I refer to Him as GOD and He transcends space & time. It is impossible to fully understand God with our human minds. By His very nature, God is all-powerful, all-knowing, all-present, all GOOD, and He is the essence of LOVE. Being God, He alone makes ALL the Rules of His Universe. It doesn't matter if we humans like His 'house' rules or can understand them. Every discovery of truth (Law of Gravity) is just us humans uncovering something He created...period. He is the Sovereign God. It's His Universe!

Here are 3 of God's Rules that affect each of us directly.

1. God created human beings to live forever! We are Spiritual Beings having a human experience. We begin this human journey at our conception and we will never cease being "ALIVE" somewhere. Our very short time on this earth is but a 1st Act, a fleeting mist – a vapor - as compared to ETERNITY. Our spirit & soul (i.e. mind, will, emotions, personality, etc) is very much alive. We will never, ever NOT be "alive". Physical death occurs when our spirit & soul separates or 'ejects' from our temporary 'earth suits' or body. When this 'exit' occurs all that remains is a cold, lifeless shell we refer to as a corpse).

2. God also mandated an immutable Law of "Cause & Effect" (also referred to as "sowing & reaping") that must manifest itself in the spiritual and / or physical realms. It always works... whether you know it or not.

3. God GRANTS every human being absolute "FREE WILL". Even though all His "rules" are in place, He allows each of us the "Power to Choose" whatever way we want to go.

When we break any of God's Rules – it is called SIN and God takes it seriously...even if we don't. Since I compared myself to others I thought I was not a sinner because I never robbed a bank...or killed someone. As I found out more about the Ultimate Truth that God is supreme and I've got to to play by the 'house' rules. As such, I realized I was a "messed up" individual. I recognized how often I was breaking His rules. I continually lied, cheated, stole, gossiped, had sex outside of marriage, cursed God, hated people, etc. Even more painful was that I discovered much worse issues buried deep in my soul...lack of character and integrity...a despicable secret thought life that revolved around idols of pride, ego, status, prestige, reputation, lusting, coveting, judging others, etc.

My friend, I found that my SIN was a major problem for me and God. Why? The pinnacle of God's creation is us human beings. We are created in God's own image. God wants a close personal relationship with us BUT He absolutely can't tolerate SIN of any kind... SIN is a very BIG deal to God. I know this is difficult to comprehend (at least it was for me) – but God not only LIKES us...He is crazy IN LOVE with us. God is by nature totally GOOD. It is impossible for Him to lie, cheat, deceive or 'wink' at our SIN– He couldn't resolve the "Sin" issue without ignoring His own rules... the penalty for sin was eternal 'separation'.

But that is also where the "rub" is. And then God did what only He could do. In His amazing grace and mercy He implemented a plan so mind-boggling...so bold...so incredible... so "over-the-top" that only His Son Jesus would be able to pull it off. In essence, the Creator of the Universe agreed to become one of His creatures to experience every phase a human being goes through starting as an embryo, fetus, birth, nursing baby, infant, child, teenager, adult male..., to eventually become the perfect GOD sacrifice. Jesus came to this earth and lived a perfect life with no sin so that He would be the perfect acceptable sacrifice for the SIN of mankind. Jesus came for ONE reason...to Die for us... to REDEEM man by becoming a one-time sacrificial lamb in our place. That is what the

CROSS is all about. Jesus, God's Son, choose to do the impossible... to give up His life as a sacrifice so we can chose to be restored to HIM – fully forgiven, accepted, pleasing, and yes - He even adopted us into HIS family.

Remember what I shared earlier. God makes ALL the rules... it is His Universe. Why did He choose this specific plan to redeem mankind? I don't know, but I now know that God has given us the only "approved" escape plan to restore our relationship with the Master, Ruler and Creator of the Universe. My friend, please don't think you can beat the system... or try to earn your way by living a 'good' life... or that you can make it on your own... or you have a viable plan B. You either choose His way (Plan A)...or you must deal with the Law of Cause & Effect. You get to decide!

It is our GOD who actually provided the only certified solution to redeem you and me. Jesus said *"For God so loved the world (mankind) that He gave His only begotten Son, that whoever (that means you) believes in Him should not perish but have everlasting life. For God did not send His Son into the world to condemn the world, but that the world through Him might be saved. He who believes in Him is not condemned; but he who does not believe is condemned already, because he has not believed in the name of the only begotten Son of God".* (John 3:16-18) Remember this is Jesus talking, and you can trust this fact: Jesus can't lie or deceive – it is impossible for Him to do so. *HE is the Way, the Truth and the LIFE! No one gets to God the Father without trusting that Jesus is God's Son and that He is the "lamb of God who takes away the sins of the world".*

You get the freedom and awesome responsibility to choose what you will do about your future. It is the most important choice you will ever make – period! FACT: how you choose will have far reaching impact on the people you love the most...your spouse, kids, parents, grandkids, friends, coworkers, etc. It is my hope and prayer that you start and / or complete your own life journey searching for the ULTIMATE TRUTH. If you do than you will find that God always answers... often in amazing ways!

Brad G. Cousino

Former Cincinnati Bengal, Pittsburgh Steeler, New York Giant
Current Husband, Father, Papa, friend and Christ follower

If you desire to begin your own quest for the ultimate TRUTH, then the best place to start is to get God's wisdom found in His instruction manual... the bible. I recommend to start by reading the Gospel of John. Be Thirsty!

The ancient Greek Word SOZO is found over 110 times in the New Testament alone. The words in BLUE are the original Greek word SOZO. The words in RED are those attributed to Jesus in the bible. The scriptures listed below represent less than 12% of the times SOZO is found in the New Testament and is but a brief sampling.

1. Matthew 18:11 For the Son of man is come to save (SOZO) that which was lost.

2. Mark 5:34 And he said unto her, Daughter, thy faith hath made you whole (SOZO); go in peace and be whole of thy plague.

3. John 11:12 Then said his disciples, Lord, if he sleeps, he shall do well (SOZO).

4. Acts 14:9 The same heard Paul speak: who steadfastly beholding him, and perceiving that he had faith to be healed (SOZO),

5. Luke 8:36 They also which saw it told them by what means he that was possessed of the devils was healed (SOZO).

6. II Timothy 4:18 And the Lord shall deliver me from every evil work and will preserve (SOZO) me unto his heavenly kingdom: to whom be glory for ever and ever. Amen.

7. Luke 19:10 For the Son of man is come to seek and to save (SOZO) that which was lost.

8. Matthew 9:22 But Jesus turned him about, and when he saw her, he said, Daughter, be of good comfort; thy faith hath made thee whole (SOZO). And the woman was made whole (SOZO) from that hour.

9. John 3:17 For God sent not his Son into the world to condemn the world; but that the world through him might be saved (SOZO).

10. Acts 4:12 Neither is there salvation in any other: for there is none other name under heaven given among men, whereby we must be saved (SOZO).

11. Romans 10:9 That if thou shalt confess with thy mouth the Lord Jesus, and shalt believe in thine heart that God hath raised him from the dead, thou shalt be saved (SOZO).

12. Romans 10:13 For whosoever shall call upon the name of the Lord shall be saved (SOZO).

13. I Corinthians 1:18 For the preaching of the cross is to them that perish foolishness; but unto us which are saved (SOZO) it is the power of God.

14. Ephesians 2:8 For by grace are ye saved (SOZO) through faith; and that not of yourselves: it is the gift of God.

Appendix #2A: Our Family

Unless the Lord Builds the House... Psalm 127:1

Tami / Mom / Gami *** Brad / Dad / Papa

*Grandkids Photo (L to R) Will, Chloe, Connor, Kennedy, Coco,
Meryck, Graycen, Camdyn, Hensley, Briggs & Caleb*

Our adult kids with Tami and me; Case, Cortt, Shaedyn, & Cole

Shaedyn (Cousino) & Alex Bogle, Meryck, Briggs & Camdyn

Cole & Kelly (Johnson) Cousino: Kennedy, Caleb & Coco

Cortt & Jen (Harnett) Cousino: Connor, Chloe & Will

Case & Brooke (Boswell) Cousino: Graycen & Hensley

Appendix #2B: Results of Our '*Miami Merger*'

What is a "Miami Merger"? It's a popular "Miami" phrase when a young man & woman meet at Miami as students who then go on to get married. That was Tami and me. As you may remember, I stated that Miami University was one of the great public colleges in the country. I meant it then... and even more now. Like most parents... we always wanted the very best for our four kids. I believe that the truest, most authentic endorsement a parent could give about any college is based on "where did you send your kids to college?" *Tami and all our kids graduated with degrees from Miami! ***

When all factors were considered, Miami University was the best college choice on so many different levels...quality of academics, wide range of competitive sports, Miami's infrastructure, quality professors, size of school, downtown Oxford, college atmosphere, reputation, national recognition, etc.

In addition, Miami's main campus was less than an hour drive from our home in Cincinnati. It was a special time for each of our kids. And we wanted to be a part of their college life. As such, we were able to attend most of their many college games and drive up on occasion to treat them to dinner or Sunday brunch. All four of our kids LOVED every aspect of Miami, as did Tami and me.

♦ Cortt, at Cincinnati Indian Hill High School was All Ohio in football and baseball. He was recruited by West Point and attended their Prep School (Military Academy's solution for a "red-shirt" year) for one year, playing football & baseball. He decided he didn't want the military life and transferred to Miami after his "prep school" year. He walked-on and earned a full Football scholarship and played Linebacker and special teams and graduated with honors.

- Shaedyn, at Cincinnati Indian Hill High School was All Ohio in Soccer, and was recruited by Miami, Auburn, Kentucky, etc. Shaedyn and her freshmen teammates were a major catalyst to thoroughly dominate women's soccer for four years in the MAC. Shaedyn was an All-MAC player for four years and an All-American in soccer. She was inducted into Miami's prestigious Athletic Hall of Fame in 2016.

- Cole, at Cincinnati Indian Hill High School was All Ohio in football and Lacrosse. He attended an east coast prep school (The Hotchkiss School) but after one year decided he wanted to attend Miami and then chose to walk-on on the football team as a slot-receiver. After one fall football season, he decided to play Club Lacrosse with his brother Case, where they were dominate players.

- Case, at Cincinnati Indian Hill High School was All Ohio in football and Lacrosse. He was recruited by Butler University and was a starter on the Football team his freshmen year, but decided he wanted the full college experience that Miami offered compared to what he experienced at Butler. Case joined Cole playing Lacrosse and together they were both dominate players for Miami's young club team.

** To be fully transparent, Tami and all our kids graduated with degrees from Miami University. I DID NOT. As I mentioned in Chapter 19, I attended four years at Miami, but I was 16 credit hours short of graduating (I originally started out as a Pre-Med major, and I foolishly kept putting off taking those organic and inorganic chemistry classes.)

I intended to go back to Oxford and finish up the classes needed. I should have done it before getting married. But playing in the NFL, owning & managing Colonial Estates, and working with Nautilus, plus being a new dad afforded me no extra blocks of time to drive to Oxford to attend 16 credit hours of chemistry classes (especially considering I was no longer interested in pursuing a career in the medical field). In hindsight, I wish I would have changed to a business major. (Miami has a national reputation as having a great business undergrad program – Farmer's School of Business) That would have given me far more incentive to complete my degree because I could use that information in my commercial real estate career.

Not following up and taking the necessary courses to graduate was another of my many "self-inflicted" wounds that would come back to "haunt" me decades later. How?

It prevented me from being voted into Miami's prestigious Athletic Hall of Fame (HOF). Even though it is an "ATHLETIC HOF" (not based on scholastics), per Miami's criteria, one must be a Miami graduate to be eligible for Miami's Athletic HOF. It would have been extra special because my only daughter, Shaedyn, was inducted into Miami's HOF in 2016. We would have been the first Father / Daughter duo in the history of Miami's HOF. Considering my positive football career at Miami, if I'd graduated, I would have been inducted into the HOF four decades ago. It would have been very special to share that great honor with my only daughter.

Not graduating from Miami is near the top of my life-time regret list!

Appendix #3A Miami Football - I

1973 & 1974 Miami All MAC 1st Team players
Longest Winning Streak in the Country - 23-0-1

It is rare to have a team be so in sync that they can go the whole season with no losses. It is exceptionally rare to have two back-to-back seasons without a single loss. I learned how important a REAL GOOD TEAM must operate as a player with Miami, and again when I played with the Pittsburgh Steelers & Cincinnati Bengals. All football teams are comprised of offensive & defensive football players of all shapes & sizes, offensive & defensive coaches, medical trainers & doctors, equipment managers, student managers, athletic director & staff, Sports information Director, and front office administration & staff, etc., Each person must perform their jobs to perfection – to be the 'best of the best'. For space constraints, I was only able to mention the players that achieved 1st team all MAC at their positions.

Miami 1st Team all M.A.C. 1973 (11-0)

Dan Cunningham, Center

Dan Rebsch, Safety

Bill Blind, Defensive End

Mike Monos**, Linebacker

Mike Biehle*, Offensive Tackle

Tim Williams, Tight End

Herman Jackson, Defensive End

Brad Cousino*, Middle Guard / Defensive MVP of Mid-American Conf (M.A.C)

Coach Bill Mallory**, 1973 M.A.C. Coach of the year.

Miami defeated all M.A.C. teams played + Cincinnati, Purdue, South Carolina and Florida Gators

Miami finished **#15 in the country; #1 Defense** nationally in Division 1 football

Miami 1st Team all MAC 1974 (10-0-1)

Jay Fry, Defensive End

Dave Draught, Place Kicker

John McVay, Safety

Mike Biehle*, Offensive Tackle

Chuck Varner* Linebacker

Joe Spicer, Cornerback

Jeff Rolands, Punter

Pat Kief, Guard

Brad Cousino*, Middle Guard / Defensive MVP of Mid-American Conf (MAC)

Coach Dick Crum**, 1974 MAC Coach of the year

Miami defeated all MAC teams played + Cincinnati, Kentucky, Georgia & Purdue (7-7 tie) Miami finished **#10 in the country; #3 Defense** nationally in Division 1 football.

Appendix #3B Miami Football - II
Miami's Major Contributors of the '73 & '74 teams

Besides the 1st team ALL MAC players, I wish I could single out everyone who makes up a team, which means they contributed to a total team effort... whether it is a scout team player, backup players, starters, roll players, injured players, etc., every single member of a team has an important and necessary function. The teammates mentioned on this page achieved outstanding success; as collegiate players & coaches, NFL Players & coaches, future leaders of 1975 & 1976 Miami teams, captains, and future captains, etc., I know someone will be missed – it was not intentional!

Sherman Smith* **, Rob Carpenter*, Randy Walker,** Randy Gunlock, Steve Sana, Ricky Taylor, Jack Schulte, Earl Harbin, Dave Draudt, & Larry Harper were major contributors to our offense.

Petey Rome, Bill Driscoll, Jeff Kelly, Brad Miller, Jim Feucht, Steve Kramer, John Roudabush, Bill Wiggins, Mel Edwards, **Jack Glowick**, & Ron Zook**,** were major contributors to the nationally ranked defenses from 1973, 1974, & 1975.

Special thanks & kudos to the four primary Centers I practiced against during my Miami career from 1971 thru 1974 – Mike Poff, Dan Cunningham, Steve Kramer, and Randy Gunlock – Every practice was a session of "Iron sharpening Iron". Each of you made a huge difference in my football life. I trust you benefited from our spirited sessions as much as I did!

*** Those with one bold * asterisks played or tried out at the NFL or CFL level.**

**** Those with two bold asterisks coached or were scouts at the college or Professional level**

Appendix #3C Miami Football - III
Coaches, Trainers, Administrators that were VIPs to Me

In college football, there are national honors designated to the best players in the nation from each position. The winners are awarded the title, "All-American". I was awarded this title in both my junior and senior years, but while I might have gotten the votes, there were significant members of Miami University Administration team and extended staff who were vital to my and our football teams' overall success:

- President of Miami University: Dr Phil Shriver (a great president & leader),
- Athletic Director: Dick Shrider & staff,
- Sports Information Director: Dave Young & staff,
- Athletic Trainers: Head Trainer: Ken Wolfert & staff, Rocky, Tom
- Strength & Conditioning: Kim Wood, various Miami position coaches
- Equipment managers & Student managers: Tom Gunlock, Terry Martin; Donnie

I would be negligent if I didn't acknowledge that I was blessed with some of the best position coaches in all of football. These coaches were like mentors to me, some showing me how to be a "man" in the game of life as well as the responsibilities of being an excellent teammate, for the good of the entire program. And other coaches who taught me the intricacies of playing middle guard, special teams and linebacker and then developing into becoming a consistent "difference maker" for my team.

Please note the men mentioned below impacted my life in a very positive way and I acknowledge they helped me become a better football player and even more important a better person:

- Head Coaches: Bill Mallory, Dick Crum, ***Paul Brown, Chuck Noll, & John McVay Sr***.
- Defensive Line Coaches: ***Jerry Angelo***, Ron Corradini, Jim Tresler, & ***Jay Fry Sr,***
- Defensive Coordinators: Dick Crum & Joe Novak
- Offensive Line Coaches: Bob Reublin and Denny Marcin
- Strength Coaches***: Kim Wood***
- Scout Team Coordinators & Coaches: ***Jerry Angelo*** & John Roush

Coaches' names in bold italics represent NFL coaches, pro scouts, or admin staff.

Appendix #4A
What Happened to Mom?
A frequent question asked during Q&A from audiences.
Annette 'Toni' M. Cousino (64) 11/17/35 – 1/9/2000

I totally forgave mom in 1977. I believe our mom / son relationship was as good as it could possibly be considering all the trauma inflicted on me in my early years. Dad and mom separated in 1982 and officially divorced in late 1983. Mom and my baby sister, Kristie (18 years younger than me), continued to live in the house mom & dad bought in Amelia.

Fortunately, Kristie never experienced the "mom" I grew up under. Mom had "mellowed" significantly. Kristie was literally 6 days old, on the night of my high school graduation. Mom & Kristie seemed to have a good "mother / daughter" relationship. Mom met Joe Popp, a widower, and they eventually got married.

Mom was diagnosed with an advanced case of Multiple Myeloma in early November 1999. Right after Thanksgiving 1999, mom was admitted to Jewish Hospital in Cincinnati. She went through all kinds of tests, procedures, and then directly proceeded into aggressive chemotherapy, blood transfusions, radiation, etc.

In my opinion, the fall-out of the treatments was far worse than the cancer. It weakened her to where she was a shell of the person I knew. She lost her hair, taste, smell, and had trouble swallowing. I barely recognized her. Right before the new year, mom dropped into a coma where she remained for about 10 days.

I knew mom did not want to be kept artificially alive, as we had talked about it before she went into the coma. Then all us kids, (Rick, Mike, Kristie and me), held mom's hands as we prayed for a miracle of healing AND for her to believe in her heart that Jesus died for her and He is her Lord & Savior. Hoping for a miracle. Then the required paperwork was signed, and the machines were disconnected. The nurses had prepared us of what to expect and when...

Mom passed away 55 minutes later (1/9/2000) – she was 64 years old.

Appendix #4B
What Happened to Dad?
A frequent question asked during Q&A from audiences.
Eugene 'Gene' J. Cousino (56) 9/29/1934 – 7/16/1990

Dad and I had reconciled years earlier in 1977, just prior to taking over the ownership & management of the Colonial Estates rental properties. Dad and mom separated in 1982 and officially divorced in late 1983. Dad moved to Ft Lauderdale and then married Patty, a divorcee, about a year later.

Dad continued to drink to excess and smoked heavily. He was diagnosed with Lung Cancer in 1989. He did not have health insurance, nor did he have the funds for the mounting medical costs. Dad was able to participate in a special "clinical trial" program for a new lung cancer treatment at The Cleveland Clinic (TCC).

Tami and I paid for his travel back and forth from Florida and for his medical costs. Dad would go to TCC every 6 to 8 weeks for more "special trial cancer treatments". In July 1990, he was back at TCC for another round of trial cancer treatments.

I received a call mid-morning on July 16, 1990. The person who called stated that my dad was found dead in his room about 30 minutes earlier. He failed to show up for one of his early morning tests. They checked his room and found dad had passed away earlier that morning... alone in the room with a partially smoked cigarette.

Dad had promised me that he gave up smoking when his oncologist told him *"If you want to live longer, you must quit smoking immediately".* I'm sure he tried, but I learned that nicotine addiction is exceptionally difficult to beat.

It was sad knowing that dad died totally alone, in a far-away city, in a strange room on the main campus of the world-renowned Cleveland Clinic.

Dad passed away on July 16, 1990 – he was 56 years old.

Appendix #5A – Ellie Mallory
Widow of Head Coach Bill Mallory *

My husband, Bill Mallory, was Brad Cousino's Head Coach at Miami University from 1971 thru 1973. Like most coaches, he cared about all his players…but Brad turned out to be one special person and a pivotal, important player on a very successful Miami University Football team.

First of all, Brad was very intense and a non-scholarship walk-on…not a star recruit. But he had goals…boy did he have goals! He was driven…and Bill really liked him, and he also worried about him. One day Bill came home, and something was on his mind.

Now you must know that I know nothing about coaching football, but I'm a pretty good listener. He started talking about this walk-on player from the Toledo area who wants to play middle guard. He's undersized for that position…but he's smart, quick, intense, he makes things happen, he's a team player and has a "fire in his belly". I said, sounds like your kind of player! Oh boy, was he ever!

Opposing coaches would congratulate Bill after we had won that game, "wow that Cousino kid is really good; he totally disrupted our plays. …and he's not that big". Bill would just smile! Brad was now a full scholarship player, a key player who earned the respect of our Miami team…players and coaches…and even the opponents!

Now I would be remiss if I didn't mention Brad's grandfather…one of my favorites. After games I'd wait for Bill outside the locker room and mingle with the other coaches' wives and families of the players. His Grandfather really loved Brad…but until I read Brad's manuscript, I really didn't understand what his grandfather was trying to tell me about Brad and his family…now I do!

Now I know how strong Brad was... and is. Brad and his wife have won a huge battle: overcoming that terrible generational path of family abuse. Bless them both.

Ellie Mallory - September 2022

** Coach Mallory passed away suddenly, due to a tragic fall while on his daily walk. He dropped into a coma and passed away a few days later -- May 25, 2018 -- he was 82. He was an awesome coach and leader. I learned so much about being a "total man" from him.*

Appendix #5B – Coach Ron Corradini
Miami Assistant Football Coach 1969 - 1973
Head Wrestling Coach 1969 -1972

Dear Brad,

Great job of sharing your story of coming of age (as an 18- to 22-year-old). I vividly remember your Miami years as I was a part of them. ** My memories of you are some of the most pleasant of my coaching career.

I really enjoyed reading your story (<u>Unwanted, Unworthy & UNSHACKLED</u>) because I *thought* I knew how it was going to turnout. I felt your success lay in being so much quicker than the interior offensive lineman. But I never suspected the inner turmoil that you were going through.

I admire your toughness and strength. I wish that I could have been more aware of all that you had to deal with.

You did a magnificent job of defeating the inner beast. May God continue to bless you and your family.

Ron Corradini August 2022

Varsity Defensive Line Coach 1969 - 1973
Head Freshmen Football Coach 1971
Head Wrestling Coach 1969 - 1973

PS: Brad, something you didn't know... is how many times at the University of Colorado we (as a coaching staff) openly wished we could find another "<u>Cousino</u>".

** *For context from my perspective: Coach Ron Corradini was my freshmen 'head coach' in 1971. In my Sophomore & Junior years (1972 & 1973) he was my defensive line coach for the interior line (defensive tackles and middle guards). When Coach Mallory got the head coaching job at the University of Colorado Buffaloes (Big Eight Conference) in 1974, Coach Corradini was selected to go to Colorado with the rest of the Miami football staff.*

Coach Corradini was also the Head Wrestling Coach for Miami University in 1969 thru 1973. He was a phenomenal football & wrestling coach, and he helped me learn to be a difference maker on and off the football field. Coach Corradini was a great role model for me to learn how to become a better 'man'.

Appendix #5C – Miami Coach Dick Crum
Miami Defensive Coordinator 1969 - 1973
Miami Head Coach 1974 - 1977

Re: Brad Cousino as a player for Miami's 1973 & 1974 undefeated seasons **

Brad's story is one of pure determination; and what that character trait can do for a person -- and for a team. He NEVER GAVE UP, no matter the odds! The men who played at Miami University with Brad can attest to this fact. His leadership, attitude, and example were never more evident than Miami's 1974 football season. The entire 1973 Miami football coaching staff moved to University of Colorado with Coach Mallory after Miami's stellar 1973 undefeated season. Even more challenging was that seven of the 1973 top defensive starters from the number #1 defense in the country graduated.

Brad was the returning All MAC 1st team middle guard and the 1973 defensive MVP of the Mid-American Conference. As a key returning defensive player, it fell on Brad's shoulders to take the responsibility for helping lead Miami's 1974 defensive unit. Brad rose to the challenge and did an outstanding job. He repeated as the defensive MVP of the Mid-American Conference for 1974 and was named to most every All-American team. But I later learned that Brad was most humbled yet proud to be chosen by the Miami coaching staff and his teammates as Miami's 1974 Most Valuable Player. He considers it his highest achievement.

All his great plays, recognition, and success at Miami had been a direct result of Brad's determination to be a '*Difference-Maker*' for his team... and to keep the unbeaten winning streak intact throughout his senior year.

Dick Crum, October *2022*

*** For context from my perspective: the Miami's 1973 team was undefeated at 11-0. They had the #1 ranked defense and 15th ranked team in the country. In 1973 Miami beat Purdue University (Big 10), South Carolina (SEC), University of Cincinnati, and the University of Florida Gators (SEC) in 1973 Tangerine Bowl, (now it's the Citrus Bowl).*

But the 1974 schedule was even more intimidating which included a rematch with Purdue University (Big 10), University of Kentucky (SEC), Cincinnati Bearcats, University of Georgia Bulldogs (SEC) in the 1974 Tangerine bowl. Despite the daunting schedule, I was ecstatic that Coach Crum was named Miami's new head coach for my Senior Year. Coach Bill Mallory won MAC coach of the year in 1973 and Coach Crum won MAC coach of the year in 1974; both coaches were the Best of the Best!

Appendix #6 : Photo Gallery

Tami and me with Cortt when he was about 18 months old.

Aukie (Betty) and Papa (Howard) Tami's Parents -- the BEST Parents!

Mom & I weeks before she was diagnosed with Multiple Myeloma

Tami's parents (Howard & Betty Netzly)
My parents (Toni & Gene Cousino) April 2, 1977

Speaking at H.O.F. Banquet as President of NFL Alumni Chapter

Anthony Munoz, Brad Cousino & Boomer Esiason at Munoz H.O.F Banquet

Colonial Estates: 16-unit Apt Building / Stocked Fishing Pond
Our home is hidden by trees in upper left.

Colonial Estates: 50 Estate Dr - our home for 17 years (1977 thru 1994)

Colonial Estates: typical four (4) family unit

Colonial Estates: Eight (8) Four-Family units aligning Estate Drive

1975 Official Cincinnati Bengal Team Picture (I'm in 3rd Row)

A small sampling of Miami University and NFL **"Cousino"** Headlines

2934 123rd Street: My childhood house in Point Place, OH

Brad Cousino featured in the 7/11/1977 Sports Illustrated

My Friends…

I'm amazed at how life has worked out! You should know…

I was turned down from over 25 colleges for a football scholarship – I wrote letters and made phone calls - but every school said NO scholarships were available for me. They said I was too slow and too small. I eventually tried out as a "Walk-on" (ala the movie RUDY) at Miami University in Oxford, OH.

As you can see by the pictures - I made it in a BIG way! I started at Middle Guard as a Sophomore @ 195 lbs and never missed a game. I led the nation in tackles, sacks, fumbles caused, and blocked kicks in my senior year.   And I was voted MVP in the Mid American Conference 2 years in a row and earned 1st Team All American. Honors.

In spite of an outstanding college career -- I was not drafted in the NFL. Once again they said I was too small and too slow. In fact, that year they drafted 442 players… (even two basketball players that never played a down of college football) and I was not drafted.

So it really is a miracle when you see my picture s with the Cincinnati Bengals and Pittsburgh Steelers … I played in the NFL from 1975 – 1979. Imagine being told I could never even play college ball… and then make it to the NFL…it really was pretty amazing. Fact is I was not a great athlete… I just had great DESIRE. It was an awesome experience to play under the legendary Paul Brown as a rookie in 1975… and then I was traded and ended up with the Pittsburgh Steelers during their great run of the late 70's and early 80's.

In closing, do I believe in miracles… absolutely! I've been blessed with a great wife of 34 years… 4 wonderful grown kids… and now 4 grand kids. God has been so GOOD… in so many ways. I wish for you that you have an awesome life – Love God with your whole heart and your friends and family the same.

Brad Cousino
Cincinnati Bengals, NY Giants, & Pittsburgh Steelers

Example of an earlier version of my popular FREE handout

If you see my Ohio "SOZO" License; I'm either driving or nearby

Brad Cousino...

... was unwanted, rejected and raised in a mean-spirited, dysfunctional, alcoholic home where physical, verbal, and emotional abuse were the norm.

There was no money for college, so Brad cleaned sewers to pay for his 1st quarter at Miami University. He needed a scholarship, so he tried out as a non-scholarship "*walk-on*" for Miami's division one football program. Despite overwhelming odds, he became a two-time All-American and was voted the best defensive player in the Mid-American Conference two years in a row. Despite his success, he did not get drafted in the NFL because the scouts said he was too short, too small & too slow. Against all odds, he made it in to the NFL as an undrafted "free-agent" with the Cincinnati Bengals, the Pittsburgh Steelers, and the New York Giants.

On a personal level Brad has been married to Tami for 45+ years, is Dad to four amazing adult children and Papa to eleven superstar grandkids.

As a keynote speaker, Brad has captivated hundreds of audiences with his true life-story as depicted in his published memoir...

"Unwanted, Unworthy, UNSHACKLED"

Robert "Mitch" Neu...

... is a surviving triplet, being born twenty-five weeks premature at one pound, seven ounces. Mitch overcame many challenges associated with his severe prematurity.

Overcoming huge odds, Mitch graduated with honors, leading his class in the graduation ceremony as a Student Marshal from the University of Cincinnati in 2019. Mitch received his degree from UC's Digital Media Collaborative, specializing in screenwriting. His long-term goal is to write screenplays.

Brad, impressed by Mitch's skill set and work ethic, asked Mitch if he would like to be a co-author on his memoir. Mitch accepted and together they spent countless hours researching and tweaking the many editions of the evolving manuscript that is now their published memoir...

"Unwanted, Unworthy, UNSHACKLED"